ONE BIG BEAUTIFUL BOOK OF CHRISTIAN DISCIPLESHIP LESSONS

Guy Calandra

Calandra Publications

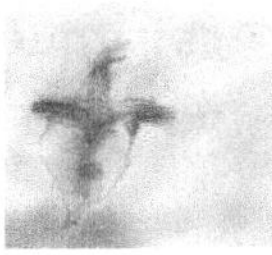

Cover design by: Denise Calandra
Denise Calandra Photography
Websites
https://denisecalandraphotography.picfair.com
https://denise-calandra.pixels.com

Guy Peter Calandra @ spiritquestletter@yahoo.com

Dedicated to the command, Matthew 28:18-20.
"And Jesus came and spoke to them, saying, "All authority has been given to Me in heaven and on earth. Go therefore and make disciples of all the nations, baptizing them in the name of the Father and of the Son and of the Holy Spirit, teaching them to observe all things that I have commanded you; and lo, I am with you always, even to the end of the age." Amen.

CONTENTS

INTRODUCTION

This One Big Beautiful Book of Christian Discipleship Lessons is a compilation from my twelve individual lessons on discipleship. It also, is my attempt to obey Matthew 28:18-20, ***"And Jesus came and spoke to them, saying, 'All authority has been given to Me in heaven and on earth. Go therefore and make disciples of all the nations, baptizing them in the name of the Father and of the Son and of the Holy Spirit, teaching them to observe all things that I have commanded you; and lo, I am with you always, even to the end of the age.' Amen."*** My attempt to go into the nations to make disciples of Jesus is through written material gleaned from years of study.

As in days of old, so it is so today,

***"My people are destroyed for lack of knowledge.
Because you have rejected knowledge,
I also will reject you from being priest for Me;
Because you have forgotten the law of your
God, I also will forget your children."
Hosea 4:6 NKJV***

How horrible are those words spoken by Hosea? Bible students and followers of Christ should know the bitter destruction the Israelites faced in their history. The horror of the Babylonian captivity to the destruction of Israel by Rome and the holocaust are evidence of the folly of lacking the knowledge of God. The sad truth, this is happening in Christendom today. The lampstand of many denominations and churches are being removed from the body of Christ, and western Christian civilization is collapsing. This is all due to a lack of knowledge and a "new" gospel, which is not.

"Remember therefore from where you have fallen; repent and do the first works, or else I will come to you quickly and remove your lampstand from its place—unless you repent," Revelation 2:5 NKJV.

"I marvel that you are turning away so soon from Him who called you in the grace of Christ, to a different gospel, which is not another; but there are some who trouble you and want to pervert the gospel of Christ . . . O foolish Galatians! Who has bewitched you that you should not obey the truth, before whose eyes Jesus Christ was clearly portrayed among you as crucified?" (Galatians 1:6-7,3:1 NKJV)

Unfortunately, there is a plague of sin upon so-called Christian leaders and the sheep who follow them. Why is this so? The reason is, the Bible is no longer regarded as the Inspired Word of God. It has been replaced with the wisdom of men and women. Therefore, ***"Behold, the days are coming, says the Lord God, That I will send a famine on the land, Not a famine of bread, Nor a thirst for water, But of hearing the words of the Lord. They shall wander from sea to sea, And from north to east; They shall run to and fro, seeking the word of the Lord, But shall not find it,"*** Amos 8:11-12 NKJV. The only answer is for us to follow Peter's advice. **"Therefore, laying aside all malice, all deceit, hypocrisy, envy, and all evil speaking, as newborn babes, desire the pure milk of the word, that you may grow thereby, if indeed you have tasted that the Lord is gracious,"** 1 Peter 2:1-3 NKJV.

There are twelve lessons in the One Big Beautiful Book of Christian Discipleship Lessons which can be read and studied in any order, although they are written in an order to build a great Biblical foundation. The lessons are formatted to be used in personal study, Sunday School classes, or cell group meetings. The Apostle Peter said we must, ***"As newborn babes, desire the pure milk of the word, that you may grow thereby, if indeed you have tasted that the Lord is gracious,"*** 1 Peter 2:1-3. Christian Discipleship Lessons are based by letting Scripture be its own teacher under the guidance of its writer, the Holy Spirit. If you are wanting to strengthen your faith and knowledge of the Bible, these lessons are for you. The first lesson concerns the danger of being deceived. Lesson Two teaches about faith. Lesson Three teaches why the world is in an evil mess. Lesson four is about responsibility. Lesson five a preparation to face death. Lesson Six proclaims the infallibility of Scripture. Lesson Seven puts forth the teaching of the Lord concerning a proper foundation. Lesson Eight is a warning against pride of all types. Lesson Nine takes us into a deeper understanding of Jesus our Lord. Lesson Ten is a clarifying understanding concerning obedience to the will of God. Lesson Eleven teaches the way of the Spirit in our life. Lesson twelve is a warning to remain faithful to Christ and not to be part of the *"great falling away."* The saving grace of God is given to us by faith in the death, burial, and resurrection of Jesus Christ, the Son of God. In Christ we find forgiveness, restoration, reconciliation, liberation, and renewed fellowship with God. Unfortunately, these graces are replaced by legalism in many lives of believers. Christian Discipleship Lessons seek to return all to the simplicity found in Christ who came to proclaim, ***"Liberty to the captives, and to those who are oppressed,"*** Luke 4:18-19. Therefore, if you are hungry for God may Christian Discipleship Lessons be the spoon which feeds you the nourishing milk of the Word.

As one who loves God and His word, I write these lessons to help bring Christians back to the pure milk of the word! Furthermore, to grow in the grace and knowledge of our Lord and Savior, Jesus Christ and to join me in a lifelong quest to be

His disciple.

These studies are made to be simple and to the point. Start by reading them non-stop. Then read a second time prayerfully and meditatively. Finally, answer the reflections and make what you learn part of your life. In all of this, trust the Holy Spirit to teach you and the Lord to enable you.

ONE BIG BEAUTIFUL BOOK OF CHRISTIAN DISCIPLESHIP LESSONS

LESSON ONE: DECIEVED

CAN CHRISTIANS BE DECEIVED?

Do not be deceived, my beloved brethren!

James 1:16 NKJV

Let us start this investigation off with a question, when God asked Eve if she ate the forbidden fruit, what did she say? (Before you read on, answer the question, for it is important we know the answer.) The answer given by Eve to God was, "The serpent deceived me!" ***"And the Lord God said to the woman, 'What is this you have done?' The woman said, 'The serpent deceived me, and I ate,'"*** Genesis 3:13 NKJV. Strong's Concordance, number H5377, tells us Eve spoke the word, "nasha," pronounced "naw-shaw," to describe what happened to her. This is translated as deceived. Strong's defines this as, *"a primitive root; to lead astray, i.e. (mentally) to delude, or (morally) to seduce: --beguile, deceive."* (Take some time and look each word up in a dictionary to get the full understanding of how Eve was "deceived.") The devil-serpent was a huckster (and still is), putting on the big swindling speech to defraud Eve into buying a lie and eating the fruit. He was successful, *"she ate!"* The sinless pure intelligent mind of Eve could be deceived, led astray, deluded, seduced, and beguiled by a lying huckster. How much more can we be deceived, who struggle between the flesh and the Spirit?

The funny or not so humorous problems with being deceived are:

1. You do not realize you have been deceived until you find yourself in the precarious situation,

2. While being deceived you do not care because it is satisfying some deep-down longing or lust,
3. The deception makes you feel intelligent, as if you know better than anyone else, God included.

Revelation 12:9 teaches us an important lesson on the author of deception. ***"So the great dragon was cast out, that serpent of old, called the Devil and Satan, who deceives the whole world; he was cast to the earth, and his angels were cast out with him."*** Look at what this verse teaches.

- The great dragon, Lucifer who deceived himself thinking he was greater than God, (see Isaiah 14:12-17) was cast out to earth.
- He is the serpent of old who deceived Eve at the tree of the knowledge of good and evil.
- He is now called the devil and Satan and has an army of demonic angels with him.
- Their one purpose is to deceive the whole world.

What type of a moral character does the devil have? He has no virtuous character. Jesus describes his amoral traits to the religious leaders of His day who were deceived by the devil. ***"You are of your father the devil, and the desires of your father you want to do. He was a murderer from the beginning, and does not stand in the truth, because there is no truth in him. When he speaks a lie, he speaks from his own resources, for he is a liar and the father of it,"*** John 8:44 -NKJV.

How is Jesus describing the devil?

- He is a murderer.
- There is no truth in him.
- When he talks, he speaks only lies.
- The devil's inward resources are evil.

What does Jesus say about people who are deceived by Satan's lies, rejecting Him and His word?

- Their father is the devil.
- They want to do the desires (same things) as the devil. These desires plague human beings such as murdering, lying, and so on.

Many people are happy being within the kingdom of darkness. They gain much power through intimidation and lies. Jude said, ***"These are grumblers, complainers, walking according to their own lusts; and they mouth great swelling words, flattering people to gain advantage,"*** Jude 1:16 -NKJV. Jude the brother of Jesus understood the Lord's teaching about deceivers. Jesus warns us about them in the Sermon on the Mount. ***"Beware of false prophets, who come to you in sheep's clothing, but inwardly they are ravenous wolves. You will know them by their fruits."*** Matthew 7:15-16 NKJV.

This is the same warning the apostle Paul gave to the Ephesian elders. ***"Therefore take heed to yourselves and to all the flock, among which the Holy Spirit has made you overseers, to shepherd the church of God which He purchased with His own blood. For I know this, that after my departure savage wolves will come in among you, not sparing the flock. Also from among yourselves men will rise up, speaking perverse things, to draw away the disciples after themselves. Therefore watch, and remember that for three years I did not cease to warn everyone night and day with tears."*** Acts 20:28-31 NKJV.

Jesus and His apostles are deeply concerned over the reality of evil deceivers coming into the church. It is unfortunate how today's church is overwhelmed with deceivers, and they do not even know it. In fact, many in the church defend the ravenous savage wolves! Let us look at what these two verses say.

- Jesus said to beware of *false prophets.* Who can these prophets of falseness be? In the church, they can be bishops, deacons, priests, ministers, pastors, teachers, university professors, popes, so-called apostles of this day, and men and women in the pews, to name a few. In the world, they can be politicians, professors, teachers, and all those who oppose the grace of our Savior Jesus Christ!

- Their appearance or outward behavior is very alluring. They know how to talk the talk. Their demeanors are charming and disarming. They have a smile to their face, which pulls you in unwittingly. Paul told Timothy about them. ***"Having a form of godliness but denying its power. And from such people turn away!"*** 2 Timothy 3:5 NKJV
- Their aim is *not to spare the flock!* Which means to destroy the church of our Lord Jesus Christ.
- How do they destroy the church? *They speak perverse things!* These ravenous wolves speak perversely against the truths and sound doctrines of the Holy Bible. They question everything sacred with the supposition, *has God said?* Or *Is this the word of God?* These speak and question God like their father the devil who destroyed Eve with his deceiving rhetoric. ***"Now the serpent was more cunning than any beast of the field which the Lord God had made. And he said to the woman, "Has God indeed said, 'You shall not eat of every tree of the garden'?"*** (Genesis 3:1 NKJV)
- What is the aim or purpose of the wolves which are false prophets? The false prophet has one purpose only, which the devil wants and tempted Eve with, to be like God. Listen to the head wolf, the serpent as he mouths perverse statements to Eve. ***"For God knows that in the day you eat of it your eyes will be opened, and you will be like God, knowing good and evil,"*** Genesis 3:5 NKJV. How tempting is it to be like God? If I am like God, everyone must listen and worship me. This is what is meant by, *"to draw away the disciples after themselves."* Instead of God has said, their mantra is, *"I have said!"* (With a heavy emphasis on "I").
- The warning against deceivers must be a continual alarm. This example was set by Paul. ***"Therefore watch,***

and remember that for three years I did not cease to warn everyone night and day with tears," Acts 20:31 NKJV.

The apostle John, the beloved disciple had a great concern about deceivers and the church falling to their perverse teachings. ***"For many deceivers have gone out into the world who do not confess Jesus Christ as coming in the flesh. This is a deceiver and an antichrist,"*** 2 John 1:7 NKJV. Did you notice how he labeled those ravenous wolves? He called them antichrists! This is strong language for a feminized snowflake church to hear. The apostle John had a fight with a false prophet, himself.

"I wrote to the church, but Diotrephes, who loves to have the preeminence among them, does not receive us. Therefore, if I come, I will call to mind his deeds which he does, prating against us with malicious words. And not content with that, he himself does not receive the brethren, and forbids those who wish to, putting them out of the church," 3 John 1:9-10 NKJV.

Let us examine the false prophet, Diotrephes. It is important to understand; God knows, by name, all the false prophets. It is no small matter Diotrephes has his name written in Scripture, in infamy. This is to teach us about false prophets.

- What did Diotrephes desire? He desired the preeminent position in the congregation. He spoke, as Paul warned the Ephesians, perverse things to draw the congregation to him. How do we know this? John said, his deeds were perverse against him (as Jesus said concerning fruit) and his speech was malicious.
- Once Diotrephes gained authority, what did he do? Did he serve as the Lord taught? ***"And whoever desires to be first among you, let him be your slave,"*** Matthew 20:27 NKJV. No, he did not. Whoever tried to walk godly, he excommunicated. Diotrephes was self-serving. He would not let those brethren, who understood the truth, any entrance to oppose him. He would not receive them. He was

a tyrant! I wonder if he coined the word racist, using it to destroy his opposition?

We must use some imagination to see how Diotrephes gained the congregation, removing an apostle and even Christ, Himself. Diotrephes followed the pattern of deception as described by Jude. He was a flatterer. He had a silver tongue. He could mouth great swelling words of flattery to gain advantage. Wow, we would say, "What a convincing liar, what a smoothie Diotrephes was! He had a smile which could disarm you of your defenses. With his cunning and craftiness, he became the leader of the church. Probably, a majority were taken in by him. It did not take long before his evil theology was replacing the sound doctrine. The church was deceived! Many who followed him did not even receive John. Did you notice what John wrote? ***"But Diotrephes, who loves to have the preeminence among them, does not receive us!"*** Jesus said to beware of false prophets. Through deceptive practices, they will destroy the church and gain advantage, especially with the tithes.

Are men the only people who are false prophets? The answer is, no they are not. There are the dangerous false prophets of women. They are immensely powerful due to their alluring sexuality. The Lord specifically opened the apostle John's eyes to this fact. This problem was raging against the church of Thyatira.

"Nevertheless I have a few things against you, because you allow that woman Jezebel, who calls herself a prophetess, to teach and seduce My servants to commit sexual immorality and eat things sacrificed to idols," Revelation 2:20 NKJV.

What was happening in Thyatira?

- The congregation was in support of a false prophetess.
- The congregation accepted her teachings.
- Jezebel was a self-proclaimed prophetess.

- Her doctrine was anti-biblical concerning the meaning of, how God made them male and female, marriage, and sex. With her teachings, anything and every sexual practice were approved.
- She also was an antichrist, promoting idolatry.
- She was a true picture of a wolf in sheep's clothing.

The Jerusalem Council gave a specific command for Paul and Barnabas to give to the gentile church. It was remarkably simple and precise concerning Christian behaviors.

"For it seemed good to the Holy Spirit, and to us, to lay upon you no greater burden than these necessary things: that you abstain from things offered to idols, from blood, from things strangled, and from sexual immorality. If you keep yourselves from these, you will do well. Farewell," Acts 15:28-29 NKJV.

The church at Thyatira was deceived by Jezebel and broke all the Jerusalem Councils edicts. They were deceived! James said, *"Do not be deceived!"* It only took one false prophet to deceive them.

How did she get exalted in the congregation? Like her idol, Jezebel the wife of the Israel King Ahab, she used her beauty to get what she wanted. The only time Ahab's wife's beauty failed her was when Jehu came and brought judgement on her. ***"Now when Jehu had come to Jezreel, Jezebel heard of it; and she put paint on her eyes and adorned her head, and looked through a window,"*** 2 Kings 9:30 NKJV. He did not fall prey to her. She died that day! Solomon wrote proverbs about such a woman. ***"For the commandment is a lamp, And the law a light; Reproofs of instruction are the way of life, To keep you from the evil woman, From the flattering tongue of a seductress. Do not lust after her beauty in your heart, Nor let her allure you with her eyelids. For by means of a harlot A man is reduced to a crust of bread; And an adulteress will prey upon his precious life,"*** Proverbs 6:23-26 NKJV.

The church in Thyatira, was not like Jehu, nor did they heed Solomon's warnings. They fell for their Jezebel's beauty. The problem is death is now a judgement they face together. God is not mocked by us being deceived.

"Indeed I will cast her into a sickbed, and those who commit adultery with her into great tribulation, unless they repent of their deeds. I will kill her children with death, and all the churches shall know that I am He who searches the minds and hearts. And I will give to each one of you according to your works," Revelation 2:22-23 NKJV.

Jesus does not like false prophets of any sex, nor His church submitting to them. What does He say here? The deceived behavior in Thyatira could only be fixed by Him! He did not want this deception spreading throughout His body!

What were His judgements on the false prophet and the deceived followers?

- Jezebel will become extremely sick and bedridden.
- The deceived Christians, who committed adultery with her, will be punished with great tribulation.
- Her children will be killed.
- All will be judged according to their works.
- All their hearts and minds will be examined.
- The purpose of the judgement is to produce the fear of the Lord in the churches.

Jesus is serious about His warning to not be deceived by false prophets. The Bible has two types of children examples for us to learn from. The first is a good example set forth by Jesus. This child is the trusting and faithful one. ***"Assuredly, I say to you, unless you are converted and become as little children, you will by no means enter the kingdom of heaven. Therefore whoever humbles himself as this little child is the greatest in the kingdom***

of heaven. Whoever receives one little child like this in My name receives Me," Matthew 18:3-5 NKJV. This child has faith and cannot be deceived by false prophets. Christians, like this child, are always searching the Scriptures and keeping their eyes on Jesus. They stand on solid rock.

The second example from Paul is not one a Christian should be like! They are the head in the cloud child whose nature cannot be satisfied by anything. It always needs something else. They are crybabies, constantly wanting more! They also think they know it all. These Christians who are like this can be deceived and usually are. They stand on shifting sand. ***"That we should no longer be children, tossed to and fro and carried about with every wind of doctrine, by the trickery of men, in the cunning craftiness of deceitful plotting,"*** Ephesians 4:14 NKJV.

What is a foolish child-Christian subject too?

- They are easily deceived and fall prey to false prophets.
- They are prone to every wind of doctrine, which blows their way.
- The child Christian cannot discern the tricks of false prophets. They can fool the child into questioning their faith.
- They are subject to the cunning craftiness of the false prophet who works like their father the devil.

The childish Christian is never at rest or peace within themselves. One minute they believe one thing the next they believe another. They become theologically unsound, scripturally ignorant, and hardened to the guidance of the Holy Spirit. Jesus spoke about this problem to the church in Pergamos. ***"But I have a few things against you, because you have there those who hold the doctrine of Balaam, who taught Balak to put a stumbling block before the children of Israel, to eat things sacrificed to idols, and to commit sexual immorality. Thus you also have those who hold the doctrine of the Nicolaitans, which***

thing I hate," Revelation 2:14-15 NKJV. This type of deception is even happening today in many of the churches.

Paul's warning must be taken seriously to stop being a child easy to be deceived. James said we should be careful and not be deceived. The Lord said to beware of false prophets. Unfortunately for us, if we are not rooted and grounded in the faith, we can be deceived. I write as one who went through a trial of this in the 1980s, when I was new to the faith, walking in pride. Thankfully, there were mature Christian men and women around us. They helped to keep us from falling into deception. Furthermore, the hand of the Lord was heavy upon us to turn us around. We are not immune from being deceived today. This problem was predicted to happen by a true prophet, the apostle Paul.

"Now the Spirit expressly says that in latter times some will depart from the faith, giving heed to deceiving spirits and doctrines of demons, speaking lies in hypocrisy, having their own conscience seared with a hot iron," 1 Timothy 4:1-2 NKJV.

What is the Spirit saying?

- In the latter times (those days which are near the end) there will be believers who will depart from the faith. (Reader beware!)
- They will listen to false prophets or prophetesses.
- These will be ***deceiving*** spirits. They will speak as spiritual the doctrines of demons.
- They will behave saintly but speak and spew lies of deception about God and His Christ. They will be the biggest hypocrites ever.
- They will have no conscience. Their hearts will be as hard as a hardened criminal.

With a silver tongue, they will question the Bible. The false prophet will declare it is not the infallible, inerrant Word of

God. Their aim is to destroy the Bible. They will speak the lie God did not create all! Genesis 1:1 is unscientific and foolish. The false prophets and prophetesses will promote sexual immorality only a demon could conceive. They will bless Molech worship by promoting abortion rights. The deceivers will nullify the words of Christ, ***"I am the way, the truth, and the life. No one comes to the Father except through Me,"*** John 14:6 NKJV. The new claim is all roads lead to God. The cross will be held by their hardened hearts in derision. The Scripture tells us about them plainly. ***"But know this, that in the last days perilous times will come: For men will be lovers of themselves, lovers of money, boasters, proud, blasphemers, disobedient to parents, unthankful, unholy, unloving, unforgiving, slanderers, without self-control, brutal, despisers of good, traitors, headstrong, haughty, lovers of pleasure rather than lovers of God, having a form of godliness but denying its power. And from such people turn away!"*** (2 Timothy 3:1-5 NKJV) (Reader beware!) ***"For those who are such do not serve our Lord Jesus Christ, but their own belly, and by smooth words and flattering speech deceive the hearts of the simple,"*** Romans 16:18 NKJV.

The Lord gives us more warnings concerning deceiving false prophets in the Olivet discourse, Matthew 24.

- ***"Take heed that no one deceives you. For many will come in My name, saying, 'I am the Christ,' and will deceive many,"*** verses 4-5.
- ***"Then many false prophets will rise up and deceive many,"*** verse 11.
- ***"Then if anyone says to you, 'Look, here is the Christ!' or 'There!' do not believe it. For false christs and false prophets will rise and show great signs and wonders to deceive, if possible, even the elect. <u>See, I have told you beforehand,</u>"*** verses 23-25.

We have been forewarned of this problem of being deceived but are overlooking the reality of it; ***"We can be deceived!"***

The strangest and the most dangerous aspects of false prophets and deceivers are their ability to turn societies and congregations, upside down. They preach life, but they bring death. They subvert and pervert all which is true and right by reversing the good and magnifying it as evil. These then make evil the good. They are masters of the doctrines of demons. Well, was Isaiah's condemnation of these false prophets.

"Woe to those who call evil good, and good evil;

Who put darkness for light, and light for darkness;

Who put bitter for sweet, and sweet for bitter!"

Isaiah 5:20 NKJV

The questions we need to answer, as the church today, concerning how we have fared with false prophets and deceivers in the church, and society are numerous. The Scripture has warned us voluminously about the dangers of deceivers and false prophets and prophetesses. We are without excuse if we have accepted the doctrines of demons as the "gospel." Those who do so are downright disgusting and a stench to the name of Christ! The evidence of the acceptance is all around us. The discerning eye can see it. Those who accept false prophets cannot discern between good and evil. In fact, they will adamantly defend the deception! I challenge you to search the Scripture to see if this is true. We should let the example of the Jews in Berea be our guide. When Paul preached the gospel to them, they took out the sacred scrolls to validate what Paul taught. ***"Then the brethren immediately sent Paul and Silas away by night to Berea. When they arrived, they went into the synagogue of the Jews. These were more fair-minded than those in Thessalonica, in that they received the word with all readiness, and searched the Scriptures daily to find out whether these things were so. Therefore many of them believed, and also not a few of the Greeks, prominent women as well as men,"*** Acts 17:10-12 NKJV. How wise it is to hold the Scripture in high authority! The Berea Jews were said to be fair-minded. They looked to the sacred word. The Thessalonica Jews were not fair-minded. They were set in false information and interpretations. They persecuted Paul mercilessly. ***"But when the Jews from Thessalonica learned that the word of God was preached by Paul at Berea, they came there also and stirred up the crowds,"*** Acts 17:13 NKJV. How important are the correct understanding and knowledge of Scripture and the ability to search it out for a proper interpretation? This is very needful to happen. It will keep us from false prophets and deceivers. In fact, the first letter of John was written because of deceivers coming into the church. ***"These things I have written to you concerning those who try to deceive you,"*** 1 John 2:26 NKJV.

May we follow the example of those at Berea and always search the Scriptures, because we can be deceived! May we get back to Apostolic Christianity.

"Do not be deceived, my beloved brethren!" James 1:16 NKJV

Reflections

1. What is the command of James 1:16?
2. What does the word deceive mean?
3. What was the question God asked Eve?
4. How did Eve answer Him?
5. How was Eve deceived or beguiled?
6. Where did this deception take place?
7. How does deception aid a temptation in causing a person to yield to it?
8. How serious should we take deception?
9. What are the three, not so funny, problems occurring with being deceived?
10. Can you name more problems from being deceived, which enables us to sin?
11. What is the lesson of Revelation 12:9 concerning the devil?
12. What type of moral character does the devil have?
13. How did the Lord Jesus describe the devil in John 8:44?
14. Who are the devil's children?
15. Many people are happy being in darkness. Why is this so?
16. What does Jude 1:16 say about people in darkness and their

behaviors?

17. What is Jesus' warning about the people of Jude 1:16 in Matthew 7:15-16?
18. What is the warning of Paul concerning people who deceive in Acts 20:28-31?
19. How concerned are Jesus and His apostles concerning false prophets and deceivers?
20. Who can be a sheep in wolf's clothing?
21. What type of outward demeanors does false prophets exude?
22. What facial expressions do deceivers show? How disarming is "the smile" they show you?
23. What did Paul tell Timothy about the smiler in 2 Timothy 3:5?
24. What is their aim?
25. How do they destroy the church?
26. How did the serpent twist the words of God to deceive or beguile Eve in Genesis 3:1?
27. Has he done this to you? Have you bitten the fruit of his lies?
28. What is the aim or purpose of false prophets?
29. How tempting is it to "be like God?" How stupid and sinful are thoughts like that?
30. How many years did Paul warn the church at Ephesus about false prophets in Acts 20:31?
31. If you are a Christian, have you ever been taught about deceivers?
32. How does the apostle John, warn us about deceivers in 2 John 1:7?
33. Describe Johns fight with Diotrephes, 3 John 1:9-10.
34. What did Diotrephes desire?
35. How did Diotrephes behave in authority?
36. How do you think Diotrephes deceived the church to gain power?
37. Are men the only false prophets we need to be concerned with?
38. Who is the deceiver of Revelation 2:20?
39. Describe what happened In Thyatira, Revelation 2:18-29?
40. How did the false deceiving prophetess Jezebel break the Jerusalem Council Edict, Acts 15:28-29?
41. How was Jehu able to resist Jezebel, while the Thyatira

Church was not able to resist Jezebel?

42. What is the warning for both men and women concerning Jezebel?
43. What did Jesus promise to do to Thyatira Christians and Jezebel, Revelation 2:22-23?
44. List the Lord's judgements on Thyatira.
45. How should we understand them in our life and congregation?
46. Describe the two types of child behavior set before Christians. See Matthew 18:3-5 and Ephesians 4:14.
47. What is a foolish child-Christian subject to?
48. Describe the restless foolish child-Christian, how they are never satisfied but always seeking something new. Use the Pergamos Church in Revelation 2;14-15 to answer.
49. Take a moment and apply James 1:16 to all we have thought about.
50. Are we immune from being deceived today?
51. What is the warning of 1 Timothy 4:1-2?
52. List the warnings of Paul to Timothy. It may be good to memorize them or be aware of them.
53. What is the aim of the deceiver?
54. What is a silver tongue and how should we be weary of one who has such?
55. What will happen in the last days according to 2 Timothy 3:1-5?
56. What are we told to do in this verse?
57. What does Romans 16:18 teach about deceivers?
58. List the warnings about deceivers and false prophets, Jesus gave in Matthew 24.
59. How serious is Jesus concerning false prophets?
60. How serious should you be?
61. According to Acts 17:11, what is the best way to keep oneself from the deceiving false prophet or prophetesses?

LESSON TWO: FAITH

FAITH WILL JESUS FIND FAITH AT HIS SECOND COMING? A HAUNTING QUESTION

"Nevertheless, when the Son of Man comes, will He really find faith on the earth?" Luke 18:8 NKJV

What a perplexing and fearful question each generation of Christians must answer, *"Will Jesus really find faith on the earth?"* Since no one knows the hour of His return, Christians of all generations have been and are being challenged, by Luke 18:8, to examine themselves and the faith they exhibit. Someone may say, *"Yes, Jesus will find faith on the earth, when He returns!"* We may agree with this person. However, an honest inspection of our behavior and lack of answered prayer will quickly prove us wrong. Our salvation faith may be strong, but our salvation walk might be littered with faithless failure after failure. How hardened and disenfranchised our hearts become when the reality of living and dealing with people come crashing down on us. Seemingly, through the temptations and travails, the promises of God feel mute. God also, seems far away. How hauntingly sad our cry is with Jesus, ***"My God, My God, why have You forsaken Me?"*** (Matthew 27:46 NKJV) With this agony, our faith seems to be buried in the tomb of Joseph of Arimathea, hoping for a resurrection. Amid this, we know the probing of Jesus, examining our faith. Secretly, we wonder about ourselves, if Jesus sees, "Me" as one exhibiting the faith

He is looking for!

As I examine this perplexing problem of Jesus looking forward to finding if there is faith on the earth, I must study it from my own perspective. We have a human problem of not seeing all the positives we have in life, but we look at and gravitate to the negative. We also fail to view the promises of God from His perspective. Paul said to a confused and carnal church at Corinth, their lives and faith must be in, by, through, and for the person of Christ. ***"For the Son of God, Jesus Christ, who was preached among you by us—by me, Silvanus, and Timothy—was not Yes and No, but in Him was Yes. For all the promises of God in Him are Yes, and in Him Amen, to the glory of God through us. Now He who establishes us with you in Christ and has anointed us is God, who also has sealed us and given us the Spirit in our hearts as a guarantee,"*** 2 Corinthians 1:19-22 NKJV.

The problem in "modern" Christianity is we are always on the outside looking in and not on the inside looking out. It is remarkably interesting to notice the three vantage points of 2 Corinthians 1:19-22.

1. View one, concerning salvation, ***"But in Him was Yes."***
2. View two, concerning promises, ***"In Him are Yes and in Him Amen."***
3. View three, concerning the building of the church, ***"Establishes us with you in Christ."***

One further point of this section concerning proof of being in Christ, is the guarantee of the Holy Spirit ***"In our hearts."***

There is one word we need to pay intense interest to in 2 Corinthians 1: 19-22. The word is the preposition, in. This word in the original Greek is Strong's Concordance G1722, en. Strong's, definition is:

"a primary preposition denoting (fixed) position (in place, time or state), and (by implication) instrumentality (medially or constructively), i.e., a relation of rest."

If we remember our English, a preposition comes before a noun to show its relation to other words. (A check with the New Oxford American Dictionary will confirm this.) Therefore, in, is pointing to or telling of the instrument by which God does things. When Paul, Timothy and Silvanus preached the Gospel of Jesus Christ to the Corinthians, they did not preach it according to their own power or wisdom. They had the Holy Spirit in their heart and through Him; they preached the Gospel. The response of the Corinthians was a resounding, Yes, in Christ, and they were saved. How many times have you tried to witness and the answer from those hearing the Gospel from you was, No! I would dare to say, after many attempts and failures you have stopped witnessing for Christ.

How are you at obtaining the promises of God and moving mountains? Are you only receiving mercy drop answers to prayers and not the showers of blessings? Honesty is the best policy here. Once again, we notice the preposition, in. The prepositional phrase, in Christ, is the relation or instrument where the promises of God are obtained. They become a resounding, ***"Yes and Amen"*** (where) in Christ. Therefore, who has the promises as yes? Do we have them or does Christ have them? Are we claiming promises or are we appropriating Christ, who has the promises already fulfilled in Him? What does Paul think about this? He thinks, in Christ everything is hidden for us to find, ***"In whom are hidden all the treasures of wisdom and knowledge,"*** Colossians 2:3 NKJV.
It is with little wonder Jesus said, ***"Will He really find faith on the earth,"*** when He returns.

Furthermore, where is the church established by God? Is the church established, and interpersonal Christian relations acquired, through our own interpretations and ability to love? Once again, we notice the preposition, in. Paul was teaching about where this happens, when he said, "He who establishes us with you." Let us pause here. Paul is talking of the "establishment" of the one body of Christ, especially where it is accomplished. Therefore, we have the prepositional phrase, *"in Christ"* to modify where God establishes Christian relationships. Do the various interpretations of the rapture and second coming of Christ establish Christian unity? How about the umpteen reasons and procedures of baptism, do they make for brotherly love? What do you think, does transubstantiation, consubstantiation, or a memorial view of the Eucharist, producing Christians in harmony? How about the battle between once saved and always saved with those who fear you can walk away from God, do these exhibit God's grace to each other? According to Paul, how many bodies of Christ are there? Is there more than one Spirit? How many different salvations are there? Is the Lord divided among many bodies? Is God in us all or not in us at all?

The Answer

"There is one body and one Spirit, just as you were called in one hope of your calling; one Lord, one faith, one baptism; one God and Father of all, who is above all, and through all, and in you all," Ephesians 4:4-6 NKJV. It is with little wonder Jesus said, ***"Will He really find faith on the earth,"*** when He returns.

The last *"in"* of 2 Corinthians 1:19-22, describes where God has placed Himself with us. Paul said, ***"God had given us the Spirit."*** Now where does the Spirit dwell? The prepositional phrase, *"in our hearts"* provides the answer. Paul gives us the two-test understanding of this. ***"Therefore I make known to you that no one speaking by the Spirit of God calls Jesus accursed, and no one can say that Jesus is Lord except by the Holy Spirit,"*** 1 Corinthians 12:3 NKJV. Therefore, if a Protestant exclaims to a Catholic, *"Jesus is Lord,"* does the Catholic hear it? Does the Protestant hear the Catholic, who professes *"Jesus is Lord?"* Does the Charismatic hear the Evangelical or the Evangelical hear the Charismatic when they both say, *"Jesus is Lord?"* Do any of us hear each other when we confess, *"Jesus is Lord?"* Christian superiority is a great sin! It is with little wonder Jesus said, ***"Will He really find faith on the earth,"*** when He returns.

When Jesus asked the question of finding faith when He came back, He was not asking about finding people who are saved. He was asking about the saved living an inside life of faith which leads to victorious living in Him! Two truths written by Paul explain this.

- ***"Therefore we do not lose heart. Even though our outward man is perishing, yet the inward man is being renewed day by day,"*** 2 Corinthians 4:16 NKJV.
- ***"For this reason I bow my knees to the Father of our Lord Jesus Christ, from whom the whole family in heaven and earth is named, that He would grant you, according to the riches of His glory, to be strengthened with might through His Spirit in the inner man,"*** Ephesians 3:14-16 NKJV.

The Christian life is a life of relationship with the Father, Son, and Holy Spirit in our inner man. This relationship is a oneness initiated by our Savior who ever lives to make intercession for us. The Son of God brings us to the Father and gives to us of His Spirit. This happens in the heart of the inner man, the new heart which God has promised to give us. ***"Then I will give them one heart, and I will put a new spirit within them, and take the stony heart out of their flesh, and give them a heart of flesh, that they may walk in My statutes and keep My judgments and do them; and they shall be My people, and I will be their God,"*** Ezekiel 11:19-20 NKJV. Most of us lose heart because we stumble through our salvation walk in the outer man, the old heart, the man of sin, and have no deep relationship with God in us. Jesus said we are to know this reality of His life and presence. He exclaimed it to the apostles during the last supper. ***"At that day you will know that I am in My Father, and you in Me, and I in you,"*** John 14:20 NKJV. Do you notice the three occurrences of the preposition, *in*? How many times did Jesus' use "*in*" here? What two places does Jesus say He is? Where does He tell the apostles (and us) where they (and we) will be? Are the apostles (and us) going to know? By deduction, if we are in Christ and Christ is in the Father, where are we? Furthermore, if Christ is in the Father and Christ is in us, where is the Father?

Let us repeat the verse again, ***"At that day you will know that I am in My Father, and you in Me, and I in you."*** Therefore, describe Jesus' constant fixed position. After we accept Him as our Lord and Savior, describe His established position. Explain the fixed position of a Christian. I believe one of Jesus' names describes this concept exceptionally. ***"Behold, the virgin shall be with child, and bear a Son, and they shall call His name Immanuel," which is translated, "God with us."*** (Matthew 1:23 NKJV)

Therefore, how can we summarize God's Scriptural point of view of "in" with us? Take a moment and look around you. Are you in a room or outside of a room? If you are in a room, what are you surrounded by? It would be fair to say you are surrounded by four walls, a ceiling, and a floor. You stand on the floor, under the ceiling, and are surrounded by walls. With this truth, would it be correct to say you are in the room? The answer is yes; you are in the room. This is how you are in Christ. Furthermore, this is how He is in you. He is a real person surrounding us, and we are saved people each surrounding Him. In a Trinity point of view, Christ in the Father, and us in Christ, which brings us into the Father, who can only accept us in Christ! It is a strange problem with modern Christians, concerning their faith in the living Christ in us and us in Him. This is a problem which Jesus addressed when He wondered if He would find faith when He returns, the faith, not only in salvation, but of His ever-present presence for a life which overcomes in a fallen world. Furthermore, for the appropriation of all His completed work for a Godly life. There is a modern saying when we "dig" something; we say, "I'm into it!" I hope you, and I get into the "*in*" of God; we have with Christ. Do you "dig" it, Christ in you and you in Christ?

It is without a doubt; the Apostle Paul had an incredible Christian life filled with great adventures, miraculous witnessing, along with many hardships and sufferings. If Jesus came back in Paul's time, He would find faith flourishing. Paul was told by Jesus through Ananias, ***"For I will show him how many things he must suffer for My name's sake"*** Acts 9:16 NKJV. Nevertheless, Paul was more than a conqueror because he understood the preposition, in. Paul's position in Christ and Christ in Paul enabled Paul to establish churches, suffer hardship, endure temptations, handle imprisonment, have long-suffering through beatings, stoning, and persecutions. (Read his autobiographical account in 2 Corinthians 11-12.) How deeply did Paul understand the new reality of what God has done for us in Christ? The answer to this is found in his writings in Ephesians 1:3-7.

"Blessed be the God and Father of our Lord Jesus Christ, who has blessed us with every spiritual blessing in the heavenly places in Christ, just as He chose us in Him before the foundation of the world, that we should be holy and without blame before Him in love, having predestined us to adoption as sons by Jesus Christ to Himself, according to the good pleasure of His will, to the praise of the glory of His grace, by which He made us accepted in the Beloved. In Him we have redemption through His blood, the forgiveness of sins, according to the riches of His grace."

Paul's Understanding

- Every spiritual blessing God has; He has given them to Paul (and us), in Christ.
- He (and we) was (were) chosen by God in Christ before the foundation of the world.
- In God's love for him (and us) through Christ, he (and we) is

(are) holy and without blame!

- He found his destiny and his true Father, God, and in Christ, he became a child of God (as we have also).
- Even though Paul considered himself to be, "a Hebrew of the Hebrews," Philippians 3:5, a keeper of the law, "Blamelessly," Philippians 3:6, and one of God's chosen people, he finally felt accepted with God in Christ (as we should too).
- In the blood of Jesus, Paul experienced, redemption and (even though he considered himself the chief of sinners, 1Timothy 1:15) the forgiveness of sins.

These six, *"in,"* facts were the foundation of Paul's faith, understanding, and comprehension of his existence in the world. In plain language, Paul stopped looking at his reality as himself or self-centered, and by faith and trust started looking at himself through God's reality or God-centric existence. God's reality in Christ became real to him and enabled him to develop into the Apostle Paul! Simply stated, Paul did not have an evil heart of unbelief but a good heart of trusting faith. He was fearful of the Lord's words, concerning, if Jesus would find faith on the earth when He returned. He also penned these words concerning faith in what God has declared in Christ, ***"Beware, brethren, lest there be in any of you an evil heart of unbelief in departing from the living God,"*** Hebrews 3:12 NKJV.

A question we, Christians today, need to ask is, "How important is it for us to believe the *"ins"* of our relationship with Christ? The answer should be an obvious one. Nevertheless, most of us are blind to these truths of us in Christ and Christ in us. We read it, but it makes no difference to our lives. We have the problem of repetitious history on us. We are as dull as the Israelites who were delivered out of Egypt. They were saved from bondage but died in the wilderness. We, also, are saved from our bondage to sin but are slowly dying in our dry wilderness, we call Christianity. What is the reason for both of our failures? ***"For indeed the gospel was preached to us***

as well as to them; but the word which they heard did not profit them, not being mixed with faith in those who heard it," Hebrews 4:2 NKJV. They saw God's work miraculously visible and did not believe. We experienced the born again wonder and after this, we do not believe. I must add here, this is the problem the Lord addresses concerning faith. I do not know what happens or why it happens; we can fully believe in Jesus as Savior, then not believe every word, which proceeds out of the mouth of God written in the Bible. We have selective faith.

This brings us to the whole meaning of trusting, abiding faith in the ins of God. Jesus was and still is very adamant about this, in Christ and Christ in you, reality. He told the Apostles on the night He was betrayed, ***"Abide in Me, and I in you. As the branch cannot bear fruit of itself, unless it abides in the vine, neither can you, unless you abide in Me,"*** John 15:4 NKJV. What is Jesus saying and what are we to pay attention to, since we are closer to His return by each passing day?

- I believe we should notice the *"in"* again. The faith Jesus will be looking for is the abiding faith in Him.
- Jesus has the abiding faith of Himself in us. This is what is meant by, *"I in you."* He is there whether you believe it or not.
- Jesus compares our life in Him and Him in us to the natural life of vine plants. The vine has shoots or branches, the branches flower and gives forth fruit. This is an earthly picture of a God-human relationship.
- The branch cannot bear fruit of itself unless it is attached to the vine. Nor can we, Christians, bear fruit for Christ, unless we are attached to Him!

Furthermore, on this subject, Jesus said, ***"I am the vine, you are the branches. He who abides in Me, and I in him, bears much fruit; for without Me you can do nothing,"*** John 15:5 NKJV. Jesus clarified the whole point of us in Him and He in us. He is the vine. In other words, He is God the source of life, power, and nourishment. We are the branches, created, redeemed people, who need Jesus for everything, only branches (the saved) in union with the vine (Christ) produce fruit. The grape vine brings forth grapes on its branches. The Jesus vine produces the fruit of the Spirit and a Christ-filled life. The point of this is emphatic, Jesus said, we can do nothing (concerning all the will of God) without Him. You heard Him correctly. We may argue and say, "Why, I do many things for Him!" Well, that is the point, you are doing it for Him, not with Him. Jesus speaks concerning this argument, ***"Many will say to Me in that day, 'Lord, Lord, have we not prophesied in Your name, cast out demons in Your name, and done many wonders in Your name?' And then I will declare to them, 'I never knew you; depart from Me, you who practice lawlessness!'"*** (Matthew 7:22-23 NKJV) When we look at a grapevine, we see the whole vine as one grapevine. The branches are attached to the vine, and the vine is attached to the branch. The vine cannot have grapes unless it has the branch, nor the branch its fruit unless it has the vine. They are part of one another, with the vine being the main source of life and the branches being the fruit-bearing source. Thus, is a Christian in Christ and Christ in the Christian.

Whether we accept this statement or not, the truth is, in Christ and Christ in us has made us part of God and God part of us. Jesus' point of, will He find faith on earth, concerning this is valid. I fear the understanding and faith in the mystery of, *"in,"* is lost today, even though the mystery has been revealed. Paul said, ***"To them God willed to make known what are the riches of the glory of this mystery among the Gentiles: which is Christ in you, the hope of glory,"*** Colossians 1:27 NKJV. What a glorious reality we have, Christ (God) in us, and most of us have no belief in this truth. Why is this? It is so because we do not feel Him. This only becomes a reality if we exhibit trusting faith in what God has said in Christ, Christ in us and us in Christ. Unless we grasp this truth, a dying church will remain the reality, because without Him we can do nothing and are nothing.

"Nevertheless, when the Son of Man comes, will He really find faith on the earth?" (Luke 18:8 NKJV)

REFLECTIONS

1. How do or did you interpret and answer the question of Jesus, "Will He really find faith on the earth?
2. Does anyone know when Jesus will return to earth? (See Mark 13:32-37)
3. What is the warning concerning faith and the second coming for us?
4. How does behavior give us an answer to the church, or individual's faith?
5. Have you examined your own faith? If yes, where are you at?
6. What type of a salvation walk are you having? Is it littered with failures, sprinkled with a few victories, or more than a conqueror?
7. When we deal in the reality of interacting with people, what can happen to our hearts?
8. Does God seem mute to you? How did Jesus feel when He cried out "My God, My God, why have You forsaken Me? Did Jesus lose His faith over the quietness of God? Have you?
9. Does Jesus examine us and our faith?
10. How tainted can our view become towards God, when we fail to see the positives but only acknowledge the negatives? What disciplines can we do to stop being negative?
11. What did Paul say to a confused and carnal church in Corinth concerning where they need to place their faith?
12. Write your own commentary on 2 Corinthians 1:19-22.
13. What is the problem of modern Christianity considering our vantage point?
14. What are the three vantage points of 2 Corinthians

1:19-22?
15. What is the Christian guarantee?
16. What is the preposition, we need to pay close attention two concerning 2 Corinthians 1:19-22?
17. What does Strong's concordance teach about the preposition in?
18. Where does a preposition get positioned in a sentence?
19. Concerning 2 Corinthians 1:19-22, how did Paul, Timothy and Silvanus preach the Gospel to the Corinthians?
20. Where are all the promises of God yes?
21. How is your witnessing going? Is it fruitful or unfruitful? How was Paul able to be productive?
22. After salvation, are you able to obtain the promises of God?
23. What is the instrument of God, which he uses to dispense the answers to promises made?
24. Who has the guarantee of the promises? Are we claiming promises or appropriating them? What are the differences between the two methods? Exactly, where are the promises of God already fulfilled? How is this an earth-shattering revelation?
25. Where is the church and interpersonal Christian relation established?
26. What are the Biblical interpretations which cause division of the body of Christ?
27. According to Ephesians 4:4-6, how many bodies of Christ are there? Is there more than one Spirit? How many different salvations are there? Is the Lord divided among many bodies? Is God in us all or not in us all? Considering these answers, will Jesus find faith when He returns?
28. Do Christians of various persuasions hear each other when they talk?
29. Who can call Jesus Lord?
30. If someone truly calls Jesus Lord by the Holy Spirit, what type of faith should you have towards them?
31. Where is the life of faith found, in the inner man or outer man?

32. What is the teaching of Paul in 2 Corinthians 4:16 about the inner man?
33. Describe Paul's prayer for the Ephesians in Ephesians 3:14-16.
34. Is this something you pray for yourself and others, if not, why not?
35. Where does the fellowship with God happen in our lives, the outer man, or the inner man?
36. What is the promise of Ezekiel 11:19-20? Does this happen in the outer man, or the inner man? Will Jesus find faith in this promise by His followers when He returns?
37. According to John 14:20, what are we to know?
38. Where is Jesus constant fixed position?
39. After a person accepts Him as Savior, where is His established position?
40. What are the three "ins" of John 14:20? What positions are they pointing to?
41. Summarize God's Scriptural point of view concerning, in, with us.
42. How does this point to Jesus asking a question about finding faith on the earth?
43. What enabled the Apostle Paul to be a great witness? What enabled Paul to suffer greatly for the name of Jesus?
44. Write a point-by-point summary of Ephesians 1:3-7. Do we have faith to live and believe this?
45. From Ephesians 1:3-7, how did Paul view reality?
46. What is the dire warning of Hebrews 3:12? How serious is unbelief to be taken? Will Jesus find you in belief or unbelief if He returned today?
47. How important is it for us to believe the "ins" of our relationship with Christ?
48. Why did Israel fail? What does Hebrews 4:2 teach about them? Is this a possibility for us today?
49. What are the commands and teachings Jesus instructed in John 14:4 concerning trusting, abiding faith?
50. Will Jesus find this type of faith on the earth when He

comes again?
51. How did Jesus teach the abiding faith when He walked on the earth? Read John 14:9-11 and describe the life of Jesus.
52. Can we do anything for God without Jesus? In John 15:5, what does nothing mean?
53. Do a study on grapevines and apply what you learn about them spiritually with faith.
54. What is the frightening warning of Matthew 7:22-23?
55. With this warning before you, how can the "ins" of God keep us safe, enabling Jesus to find faith on the earth when He returns?

Meditation

"But without faith it is impossible to please Him, for he who comes to God must believe that He is, and that He is a rewarder of those who diligently seek Him!"

Hebrews 11:6 NKJV

God Bless You Richly!

LESSON THREE: THREE WORDS THAT CHANGED THE WORLD WHY IS THE WORLD THE WAY IT IS? A WARNING OF FAITH

EXAMINATION ONE

Three Words That Changed Our World "God Has Said!" or "Has God Said?"

Our world is full of ideas, dogmatic statements, falsehoods, and truth. Our world has many schools of thoughts and beliefs. On the one hand, one school may say, they are liberal and on the other hand, one school may say they are conservative. Again, on the one hand, one school may say, "We believe there is a God," on the other hand, the other school may say, "We don't believe there is a God." In the case of thoughts and ideas, on the one hand, one may see things this way and on the other hand; one may see things the opposite way.

This phrase, on the one hand, is an indicator of one's opinion or point of view, while, on the other hand, is an expression of an opposing opinion or point of view[1]. These two phrases together usually teach us, there are two sides to every story. To illustrate this, let us look at many everyday situations. For those who are married, on the one hand, there is the husband's point of view and on the other hand, there is the wife's point of view. For those who are parents and children, on the one hand, there is the parent's point of view and on the other hand, there is the child's point of view. For employers and employees, on the one hand, there is the employer's point of view, and on the other hand, there is the employee's point of view. In the context of nations, on the one hand, one nation has their world view, and on the other hand; another nation has their world view. Even, at this moment, you and I may be playing the game of, on the one hand, and on the other hand. This may be so because, I see this lesson a certain way, and on the other hand, you may see this lesson another way.

As we consider, on the one hand, and on the other hand, scenarios, I think we should consider three basic points. Firstly, the, on the one hand, side, and the, on the other hand, side, may both be correct, even though it is seen in opposite understanding. Secondly, one of the sides could be right, and the other side could be wrong. Thirdly, both sides could be wrong in their views. Let us now consider four basic outcomes concerning, on the one hand, and on the other hand, scenarios. Firstly, the two camps could have a civil discussion. This discussion could lead to earnest investigation by both camps to learn the truth. This type of behavior leads to a happy and agreeable end. Secondly, the two camps would not have a real discussion but have an amicable, agree to disagree attitude. This leads to no resolution, but no great disruption in friendship. Thirdly, the two camps could have a vehement disagreement. This disagreement could lead to a destructive resolution. In history, we have seen countries torn apart by this, marriages and families split, and friendships destroyed. Fourthly, the two sides could agree on the false assumption. This agreement, will lead the behavior of people or businesses or governments, into actions, policies, or laws built on false assumptions. The outcome of this is not good for anybody.

Let us now consider where the first, on the one hand, and on the other hand, argument began. For the Biblically minded, we understand this argument began in the Garden of Eden. The first camp, on the one hand, was God, Himself. The other camp was the rebellious angel, known as the devil. On the one hand, God's point was, is, and unfailingly will be, "I have said," or for us, "God has said!" The demonic camps' point of view was, is, and constantly will be, "Has God said?" The persons caught in the middle of this argument were the first humans, Adam and Eve. Their choice of sides would be of the utmost importance to them and their offspring. Their choice of sides has eternal consequences for all.

When we read the book of Genesis, we learn about the beginning of human history and creation. The person of faith learns in Genesis 1:1,

"In the beginning God created the heavens and the earth."

The subsequent verses in chapter one through chapter three instruct us about creation. These chapters also bring us to the monumental history changing first, on the one hand, and on the other hand, crisis. On the one hand, we see God's point of view in Genesis 2:15-17,

"And the LORD God took the man, and put him into the Garden of Eden to dress it and keep it. And the Lord God commanded the man, saying, 'of every tree of the garden thou may freely eat: but of the tree of the knowledge of good and evil, thou shalt not eat of it: for in the day that you eat thereof thou shalt surely die.'"

Here we read about God's plan for His creation, especially for man. Adam, was created at this time, Eve was not. God, gave Adam his purpose and the rule he must follow in the purpose. Adam was to be the gardener and conservator of Eden. His provision for this labor from God, were all the trees of the garden, except one. Adam was prohibited from using, as food, the tree of the knowledge of good and evil. A penalty for breaking the rule and eating of the prohibited food was a death sentence. On the one hand, we now see God's side of the story, He said emphatically,

"For in the day that you eat of it you shall surely die."

Let us now move forward in the story. After God placed Adam in the garden, He said,

"It is not good that man should be alone; I will make him a helper comparable to him." Genesis 2:18

God created a woman for Adam, and Adam named her Eve. It is assumed Eve was created with equal intelligence as Adam had been, we also assume, Adam taught her all God had said and commanded.

Let us now continue on to chapter three of Genesis and investigate the "On the other hand," side. This side will be the antithesis of what God had said. In this chapter, we experience the entrance of the devil, known as the serpent, a being who in himself did not believe, "God has said," but believed in his heart, "Has God said?" The serpent accepted, in his heart, this false assertion, "Has God said," and believed in his side of the story, "That he was greater than God," see Isaiah 14:12-15. Therefore, he now brings this assertion to Adam and Eve in the Garden. We read in Genesis 3:1-7,

> *"Now the serpent was more cunning than any beast of the field which the Lord God had made. And he said to the woman, "Has God indeed said, 'You shall not eat of every tree in the garden'?" And the woman said to the serpent, "We may eat the fruit of the trees of the garden; but of the fruit of the tree which is in the midst of the garden, God has said, 'You shall not eat it, nor shall you touch it, least you die.'" And the serpent said to the woman, 'You will not surely die. For God knows that in the day you eat of it your eyes will be opened, and you will be like God, knowing good and evil.' So when the woman saw that the tree was good for food, that it was pleasant to the eyes, and a tree desirable to make one wise, she took of its fruit and ate. She also gave to her husband with her, and he ate."*

Let us now examine, from this chapter, the demonic psychology of deception, which produced doubt against the "God has said," side. How did the serpent deceive Eve into distrusting what God said, thus destroying her faith in God and her relationship with Him? How did the serpent bring her to his side of the story and ultimately her husband with her?

1) First, he questioned Eve, in order to find out what she believed by misinterpreting, what God said. He knew what God's side of the story was, now he wanted to see what Eve thought about it? He said to her,

> *"Has God indeed said, 'You shall not eat of **every** tree of the garden'?"*

Do you see the misrepresentation of God's side of the story? The serpent reversed what God had said. Let me explain it in today's language, "So, Eve, you are not allowed to eat of any of the trees in the garden? Is all this food forbidden to you? What exactly has God said to you? I would really like to know what has God indeed said here. The serpent put the bait on the hook and cast it out to Eve. Eve swallowed the bait and was hooked into the discussion. She said to the serpent,

> *"We may eat the fruit of the trees of the garden; but of the fruit of the tree which is in the midst of the garden, God has said, 'You shall not eat it, nor shall you touch it, lest you die.'"*

From the above quote, we clearly can see the serpent now knows what Eve believed. He also understands how Eve expanded the prohibition of what God said, to include, "Thou shall not touch." The serpent understands the humans have some misunderstandings and conceptions concerning, "God has said." Therefore, the serpent moves to part two in his psychology of deception in producing doubt to the "God has said," side.

2) He made an emphatic lying misrepresentation towards the assertion of the consequences of what the other side said. He questions the motives of the "God has said," side, by proclaiming there is an underside of evil, selfishness and jealousy on God's part. He appealed to Eve's pride and

vanity, her emotions and sensual perception, to invoke a response for her to accept his side of the story. Thus, with great urgency and false authority, the serpent said to the woman,

"You will not surely die. For God knows that in the day you eat of it your eyes will be opened, and you will be like God, knowing good and evil."

In today's language, "Come on Eve, how stupid is that statement, 'You shall die?' I tell you the truth, 'You shall not die!' God is really a selfish person and is fearful of you. He knows this fruit is wonderful and has miraculous powers to make you God's equal. Take a look at it, it is beautiful. How could anyone, but a selfish evil person, deny something like this from you? Therefore, making his misrepresentative case to Eve, the serpent moves to part three, in his psychology of deception, in producing doubt to the "God has said," side.

3) He becomes very silent, to allow his deceptive words of doubt to take hold in Eve's mind. He lets her consider all he said and feel all the emotions he has invoked in her. He now allows Eve to make the decision to believe his side of the story over God's side of the story. We now see Eve, in a very confused state of mind and misunderstanding of what, "God has said," begins to choose sides. On the one hand, she knows God has said, "Do not eat, because death will be the penalty." On the other hand, the serpent told her, "God is a liar; you will not surely die!" Therefore, looking at the tree,

"She saw that the tree was good for food, that it was pleasant to the eyes, and a tree desirable to make one wise,"

Eve makes a decision to believe the serpents side and agrees, "Has God said?" Therefore,

"She reaches out and took of its fruit and ate. She

also gave to her husband with her, and he ate!"

What were the results of this act? The results were, death of innocence, Genesis 3:7, the death of intimate relationship with God, Genesis 3:22-24, the death of God's provision of sustenance, Genesis 3:17-18, the death of the man and woman relationship, Genesis 3:16, the death of life, Genesis 5:5, and the death of peace, Genesis 4:8 and Genesis 6:5. The culmination of this act resulted in the judgement and condemnation of all, Romans 5:18.

The lesson of this account is not hard to understand. It is very evident and a serious affair for a created being to play, the, on the one hand, and on the other hand, game with God. One should unfailingly side with, "God has said." If we side, with the other side of the story, trouble will certainly be our lot.

However, in the midst of calamity, God has said one more important point. He promised to send the Savior to save Adam and Eve and their seed, who is Christ for us, from the penalty of this sin. In Genesis 3:15, God said and promised to the serpent,

"And I will put enmity between you and the woman, and between your seed and her Seed, He shall bruise your head, and you shall bruise His heel."

This Seed is Christ, God's own Son. What side are you on concerning this, the side which believes, "God has said," or the side which questions and asks, "Has God said?" The Bible is full of God has said points. God has said many things, yet many are always questioning Him and saying to themselves, "Has God said?" Let us heed the warning of Moses in all of what God has said, and not say has God said anymore. Moses said,

"See, I have set before you today life and good, death and evil, in that I command you today to love the Lord your God, to walk in His ways, and to keep His

commandments, His statutes, and His judgments, that you may live and multiply; and the Lord your God will bless you in the land which you go to possess. But if your heart turns away so that you do not hear, and are drawn away, and worship other gods and serve them, I announce to you today that you shall surely perish." Deuteronomy 30:15-18

Therefore, I now ask, "What side of the story do you believe, God's side or the serpent's side?" Consider this important fact, the choice is always yours to choose what to believe. As we have seen, Adam and Eve chose the serpent's side. The consequence of not believing, "God has said," and choosing to believe, "Has God said," was a world-changing event. The world changed from being a Paradise, into a world of nightmares, misery, agony, sadness, pandemonium, torment, despair, illnesses, diseases, poverty, disparity, death, and filled with humans who are evil, selfish, vile, godless, and self-centered. What a very depressing place to live. The only good in this world is the good God has reentered into it through His salvation plan. Without the promises of His grace, from the Garden of Eden to the fulfilling of them through the nation of Israel and the giving of the Ten Commandments through Moses and the sending of His Son to die for the sin of the world, in order to reestablish the Kingdom of God on earth, the self-destruction of mankind would have been totally accomplished long ago! The penalty of death would have completely been accomplished, and no one would be living today, see Genesis 6 to 9.

Finally, I would like to say to whoever is reading these words today, you also face the same choice as your grandparents, Adam and Eve. You have the same choice as them to believe, "God has said," or to believe, "Has God said," concerning, what God has said about getting right with Him through Jesus Christ,

"Nor is there salvation in any other, for there is NO OTHER NAME under heaven given among men by which we must be saved." Acts 4:12

Jesus confirms this with His own testimony,

"I am the way, the truth, and the life. NO ONE COMES TO THE FATHER EXCEPT THROUGH ME." John 14:6

How you respond to this is more than world-changing, it has eternal consequences for you; heaven and hell are in the balance of your response. I hope you choose, God has said!

Moreover, for Christians, do not say in your heart, Has God said. You and I are not exempt from this; "God has said," or "Has God said," argument in our hearts. For God has said to us, love one another as I have loved you, do not lie, love your wife, respect your husband, be the servant to all, do not steal, let all bitterness, wrath, anger, clamor, and evil speaking be put away from you, with all malice, be kind to one another, be tenderhearted, be forgiving, pray without ceasing, do not be immoral, argumentative, and spiritually prideful, be filled with the Spirit, and more. Please read your Bible, God has said this. Therefore, not to practice, "What God has said," is to agree with the serpent, "Has God said to me, I must really do what He said, after all I am saved!" Unfortunately, the serpents' voice is heard in the church more than the voice of God. If you are listening to the serpent, then you are causing all sorts of problems in Christianity. The state of the church is littered with splits, dissensions, false doctrines, and unloving hurtful people, because many do not believe what God has said. To those who follow what God has said, keep up the good work for you are a blessing and to those who follow what the serpent said about God, stop it because you are a curse!

In conclusion, to all, make sure you are not following the serpent and always being, "On the other hand," against God. Please take God at His word, for He has said what He has said. He speaks clearly for Himself with no ifs, ands, or buts! Remember, what happened to all because of Adam and Eve. This historical account is a warning to all.

Chapter One Self-Analysis

1) What does the phrase, "On the one hand," mean?

2) What does the phrase, "On the other hand," mean?

3) What do these two phrases teach us when used together?

4) Do you have any, "On the one hand and again on the other hand," moments?

5) What are the three basic points of, "On the one hand and on the other hand," scenarios?

6) In your life, in the home, on the street, at work, and at church, have your own, on the one hand and on the other hand, scenarios, lined up with the three basic points?

7) What are the four basic outcomes of the, on the one hand and on the other hand, scenarios?

6) In your life can you relate to any of these outcomes?

8) Where did this type of argument make its first appearance?

9) Who were the participants in this argument?

10) What was God's side of the story?

11) How did the first humans understand this?

12) What did the serpent say on the other hand about what God has said?

13) Describe the demonic psychology of deception, which produced doubt and disobedience to God.

14) How did Eve perceive what God said in response to the serpent's, on the other hand comment, "Has God indeed said?"

15) How evil do you think the misrepresentation of the truth is?

16) What was the ultimate result of Adam and Eve listening to the, "Other side of the story," "Has God indeed said?"

17) Have you gone through the demonic psychology of deception, which produced doubt against, God, or parents, or friends, or spouse, or your church?

18) How did you fair?

19) What is the ultimate lesson of this lesson?

20) What is the, God has said promise, to the serpent in Genesis 3:15?

21) Who is this Seed?

22) Where do you stand concerning Christ, the Savior?

23) What was the consequence for Adam and Eve, and us because of their choosing the wrong side of the story?

24) Would the world exist with people today if a gracious God did not give us another, God has said promise to the serpent?

25) Are you a Christian who sides with God has said, or do you side with, has God side, "I really need to obey Him"?

26) Finally, self-examine, yourself, are you a blessing or a curse?

1) McGraw-Hills Dictionary of American Slang and Colloquial Expression. Copyright 2006 by McGraw-Hill Companies, Inc. On-line version.

EXAMINATION TWO

The Deeper Problem of Listening to "Has God said?" The *Doubting* of Indecision

In chapter one, we learned the serpent's side of the story is to bring doubt to God's side of the story. His purpose is always to keep people doubting the Word of God. Therefore, further study of doubt or doubting and its consequence is needed. We all must learn how harmful and foolish doubting God is. In the New Testament, there is one specific word for doubting we need to explore. This word, from the original Biblical Greek text, is distazw, pronounced, "dis-tad'-zo." The Bible shows the Lord Jesus used it in Matthew 14:31. He used dis-tad'-zo (doubt) in a question, He asked the Apostle Peter,

*"O you of little faith, why did you **doubt?**"*

A literal translation of this verse would be as such,

"And He(Jesus) says to him(Peter), 'Little faith, why did you doubt?'"

When Jesus questioned Peter, He used the past tense of the verb dis-tad'-zo.

The past tense of this verb is edistasas, pronounced, e-dis-tas-us. Jesus, spoke this word in the aorist active second person singular. The aorist tense is the tense of past action. This action is to state the time for the action, with or without regards to its continuance or results. The use of the past action is to make a statement to show something happened. The active voice states the subject of the verb who was doing the action. In Matthew 14:31, the subject of this verb was the person called, you, who was the Apostle Peter. The doubting action of Peter invoked a response from Christ. The response from Christ was a stinging rebuke concerning Peter's faith.

Let us study Matthew 14:22-33, to find out why Jesus was upset with Peter. A summary for this section teaches; Jesus was walking upon the water. He was heading out to his disciples, whom He had sent away earlier. The disciples were in their boat struggling against wavy seas because of a heavy wind storm. This storm was affecting the Sea of Galilee, making boat travel extremely difficult. The time for this event was late in the night. As Jesus was approaching the boat, the disciples saw Him walking toward them. This sight caused His disciples to become afraid. They thought it was a ghost approaching. Why would they not be afraid? Who has ever seen anyone walk on water before? Jesus seeing their fear, calls out to them, saying, "Do not be afraid, it is I." Peter, realizing who it was, shouted out for permission to walk on water to Him. Jesus answered and said to him, "Come!" Hence, Peter, feeling full of faith, jumps out of the boat and begins to walk on water to Jesus. However, what happens to Peter? Instead of listening to the Lord, who said, "Come," Peter began to listen to the other side of the story. He took his eyes off of Christ, listened to the boisterous winds, became afraid, and thought to himself, "Has Christ really given me the ability to walk on water?" With these thoughts in his heart, the feeling of porous water beneath him and winds blowing him down into the sea, Peter stopped walking. At this moment, he lost faith in what Christ had said and began to sink! With all this happening a terrible paralyzing fear came over Peter. Peter, being filled with fear and panicking because he was starting to drown, cried out to Christ, saying, "Lord, save me!" Peter began to doubt and this doubt produced great loss of faith in him. This is the doubt which upset the Lord and caused Him to rebuke Peter, Matthew 14:31,

"And immediately Jesus stretched out His hand and caught him, and said to Him, 'Oh you

of little faith, why did YOU DOUBT?'"

What a haunting question of rebuke from Jesus to Peter. I wonder if we can really feel the sadness Jesus had in His heart, the sadness of heart caused by a doubting disciple. If we extrapolate this event to ourselves, how many times have we grieved Jesus with our own doubt?

An interesting note on the word, dis-tad'-zo (doubt); it is only used one more time in the New Testament. The Apostle Matthew, also used the word in chapter 28 verse 17. The event centers around Jesus Christ' last appearance to His disciples before His ascension.

"And when they saw Him, they worshiped Him; but some DOUBTED."

From these two instances, doubt apparently means, to be skeptical or uncertain about something. However, there is a deeper meaning to the Biblical Greek word dis-tad'-zo (doubt). A study of this word in Strong's Concordance, teaches it is from a combination of two different words. The first is dis, which means twice. The second is stasis, which means standing. In putting the two words together, dis-tad'-zo, would literally mean twice-standing or to stand in two ways. This literal meaning implies uncertainty in the mind deciding which way to go. The mind, of this type of doubting person, sees two choices and does not know which choice to make. The mind is between two points of view and cannot choose a side. The indecision of choice causes one to doubt. In other words, there is a struggle with, "God has said" or "Has God said." The problem of not choosing a side becomes a doubt as doubtful as choosing the "Has God said," side!

Peter's, walk upon water disaster, showed how he was in a place of two standings. In the midst of his leap of faith, Peter was confronted with two decisions. He had to choose to keep on walking or stop and sink. Peter started out well, but soon fell into a state of panicked confusion. At the start, he saw Jesus and heard His command to come. In the midst of the walk, he saw and heard the boisterous winds and waves commanding him to sink. Peter is now caught in the middle with Jesus beckoning to him and the storm crashing on him. Peter wants to hear Jesus and not listen to the wind. However, with the voice of Jesus in one ear and the noisy storm in the other, Peter freezes and becomes indecisive. In the standing of two ways, Peter does not know who to believe or what to do. Therefore, a non-decision produced doubt and Peter began to sink like a rock. At least, amid his panic, Peter had enough sense to cry to Jesus for help.

Graciously, the Lord Jesus grabs Peter and rescues him. However, did you notice the name he called Peter? He called him, "Little faith!" Additionally, He questions Peter, on why he was a doubter, a person who stands in the middle of two ways. Perhaps, the Lord was saying to Peter, "Why is your faith not filled with conviction and certainty?" We need to learn from Peter's behavior and check ourselves for this type of doubt. We must examine ourselves asking, "Am I like Peter always in doubt between what, 'God has said,' and 'Has God said?'"

Unfortunately, this problem of doubt followed Peter for most of his life. This doubtful problem caused Peter to deny the Lord three times. Before his denials, Peter told Jesus, he would die for Him. Peter tried to prove this by cutting off the ear of the servant of the high priest to save Jesus at His arrest. However, a few hours later, when his faith in Christ should have shown like a beacon of light, he denied Christ three times. This denial caused considerable grief to Christ; Luke records what happened,

"The Lord turned and looked at Peter!"

(Luke 22:60-61)

Oh, the pain caused by doubts, indecisions and being caught between two standings. Finally, Peter also was rebuked by the Apostle Paul for his, dis-tad'-zo (doubtful), behavior at Antioch. In reading Galatians chapter 2, we see Peter originally accepts Gentiles as fellow believers. However, when Jewish Christians came down to Antioch,

> *"He withdrew and separated himself, fearing those who were of the circumcision." Verse 11*

What did his behavior cause?

> *"And the rest of the Jews also played the hypocrite with him, so that even Barnabas was carried away with their hypocrisy." Verse 13*

This behavior of Peter caused Paul to rebuke him, because,

> *"Peter was to be blamed." Verse 11*

Therefore, he said,

> *"But when I saw that they were not straightforward about the truth of the gospel, I said to Peter before them all, 'If you, being a Jew, live in the manner of Gentiles and not as Jews, why do you compel Gentiles to live as Jews?'" Verse 14*

What a nightmare, to be standing in the middle of two ways and not knowing which way to go. It is quite evident, Peter's life of doubt, caused many hurts and problems for himself and others. The deep darkness of doubt is a great danger for spiritual life.

I believe, this word, dis-tad'-zo, is directed toward believers in Christ. In the two instances of use, it was used in regard to the disciples of Christ. The first use to the Apostle Peter and the second time to some of the other apostles. The scripture is clear, Peter doubted when he walked on water, and some of the other apostles doubted before the ascension. How about you, a believer in Jesus, where are you standing in your walk with Christ? Are you standing in the doubtful way of two positions? Is your life a mirror image of Peter; a life of continuous indecisive doubt?

Perhaps this problem of dis-tad'-zo, is best understood at Elijah's victory over the prophets of Baal. Elijah was defending true faith in the God of Israel. Israel turned away from the Lord to worship idols such as Baal. Elijah was on a mission to prove to Israel their doubt in God was wrong. Elijah was accused, by King Ahab, of being a trouble- making prophet. The Israel king blamed Elijah for Israel's troubles, not their idolatry. Elijah, being accused, had to respond to Ahab's allegations. This response is in 1Kings 18:18-21,

"And he answered Ahab, 'I have not troubled Israel, but you and your father's house have, in that they have forsaken the commandments of the LORD, and have followed the Baals. Now therefore, send and gather all Israel to me on Mount Carmel, and the four hundred prophets of Asherah, who eat at Jezebel's table.' So Ahab sent for all the children of Israel and gathered the prophets together on Mount Carmel. And Elijah came to all the people and said, 'How long will you falter between two opinions? If the LORD is God, follow Him, but if Baal, then follow him.' But they answered him, not a word."

Did you understand the question Elijah asked the people of God? He asked them,

"How long will you falter between two opinions?"

This question of Elijah, is the exact meaning for the word dis-tad'-zo, standing between two ways. The children of Israel were standing in two ways, on the one hand, serve God, on the other hand, serve Baal. What was Israel's response to Elijah's question? There was no response to Elijah,

"But the people answered him not a word."

The people of Israel, were in a confused state of indecision, between two points of view. This indecision caused their doubt. They were uncertain and skeptical; concerning God and

Baal, they lacked conviction or certainty. However, in their indecision, they were guilty of Baal worship. No wonder they kept silent to Elijah's question.

Let us now go back to the Apostle Peter and his history of doubt. In all his indecisive doubting instances, the Bible is silent concerning Peter's response to all the questions put before him. Concerning the Lord's and the Apostle Paul's questions on why Peter doubted; it is clear, Peter, like Israel, answered not a word. Peter and Israel were in the standing of two ways; they could not choose a side. This indecision caused their mouths to stay closed. How could they respond, they were doubters having evil hearts of unbelief? It is one thing to be an unbeliever living in doubt; it is another for a believer to be living in doubt. It is very evident; life brings many hurts and problems to us. However, an unbelieving doubtful life causes many pains and consequences a believing heart would never experience.

This deeper look into doubting is a hard lesson for us to learn. Likewise, listening to the Lord's question of, "Little faith, why do you doubt," can cause a painful self-examination of our relationship to Him. Remember, it is a serious affair for a created being to play, the, on the one hand, and on the other hand, game with God. Therefore, let us all heed the warning of Hebrews 3:12,

> *"Beware, brethren, lest there be in any of you an evil heart of unbelief in departing from the living God."*

> *"And to the angel of the church of the Laodiceans write, 'These things says the Amen, the Faithful and True Witness, the Beginning of the creation of God: I know your works, that you are neither cold nor hot. I could wish you were cold or hot. So then, because you are lukewarm, and neither cold nor hot, I will spew you out of My mouth.'"*
>
> *Words of Jesus, Revelation 3:14-16*

Chapter Two Self-Analysis

1) How foolish is it for us to doubt God?

2) What does the Greek word distazw pronounced dis-tad'-zo mean?

3) To whom did Jesus use this word?

4) According to Matthew 14:22-33, what did Peter do to cause Jesus to say this to him?

5) What caused Peter to have paralyzing fear?

6) Define what it means to be standing in two ways?

7) How does indecision cause doubt?

8) Has the Lord Jesus ever said, "Come," to you?

9) How did you make out? Did you do it to completion? Did you start out well, but got caught between two standings, and did not complete the task? Did you just doubt from the beginning and ignored the task?

10) How did any of these decisions you made make you feel?

11) What happens when we take our eyes and ears off Christ and begin to listen to the has God said side?

12) Did you ever hear Jesus say to you, "Oh you of little faith, why did you doubt?

13) Where else was the word, dis-tad'-zo, used?

14) Why do you think some of these apostles were caught in the standing of two ways?

15) What does the mind of this type of doubting person see?

16) What lesson did Peter teach us, as he was beginning to drown?

17) How smart is it to cry out in our doubt, "Lord save me?"

18) Why did the Apostle Paul rebuke Peter?

19) Do you think Peter was walking around with a load of guilt?

20) What does the account of Elijah and the prophets of Baal teach about indecision?

21) Why did Israel not answer a word to his penetrating question?

22) Summarize this lesson and how it will give you better understanding to stop indecisive doubt.

important to note; doubt has no place when walking with God nor does misunderstanding of, "God has said," give us an excuse not to agree with God. Adam and Eve, failed to understand this. When they were tempted by the devil, they agreed with the devil and severed their walk with God. The Lord Jesus understood the importance of unfailingly agreeing with God when He was tempted by the serpent. Perhaps, you are familiar with the fourth chapter of the book of Matthew, the devils' three attempts to tempt Christ from his acceptance of God has said, to a doubting mind of, has God said?

Temptation One: Matthew 4: 3-4, The tempter said to a fasting Jesus,

"If you are the Son of God, command that these stones become Bread."

In other words,

"Come now, has God said you are His Son, prove it, prove you are God make a miracle!"

Christ' response: Firstly, He does not take the bait to eat from the tree of good and evil as Adam and Eve did. Secondly, He agrees with God has said. Jesus answered the tempter,

"It is written, 'Man shall not live by bread alone, but by every word that proceeds from the mouth of God.'"

Simply put,

"I agree with everything that God has said; I am the Son of God."

Temptation two: Matthew 4: 5-7, has God said,

"He shall give His angels charge concerning you, and in their hands they shall bear you up, lest you dash your foot against a stone."

The tempter took Jesus to the pinnacle of the temple in Jerusalem and wanted Jesus to prove God has said, "You are my Son I will protect you!" In other words, has God really said this, prove it!

Christ' response: Once again, He does not take the bait to doubt what God has said, "He is His Son." Jesus agrees with what God has said, He answered the tempter,

"It is written again, 'You shall not
tempt the Lord your God.'"

Simply put,

"There is no need to prove what God
has said, I agree with it!"

Temptation three: The devil understanding, Jesus knows who He is, tempts Jesus into switching allegiance. He now wants the Son of God to worship him and not His Father, Matthew 4:8-10. The devil offers Jesus the world and all its glory,

"If Jesus would fall down and worship him."

Christ' response: Jesus was not like the Apostle Peter, nor the Israelites of Elijah's time. He was not caught in the middle of two opinions, worship God or worship Baal. He said, very emphatically, to the devil,

"Away with you, Satan! For it is written,
'You shall worship the Lord your God,
and Him only you shall serve.'"

The Result: Matthew 4:11,

"Then the devil left Him, and behold, angels
came and ministered to Him."

Jesus experienced the victorious life by agreeing with God. He withstood the Satanic onslaught, by faith in God's word. The results of Christ' action were tremendous; the devil left Him and He went on to become the Savior of the world. Jesus was not like Adam. Adam sold the world to Satan. Adam did not have faith in God's word but disagreed with God. Nor was Jesus like Peter, when the boisterous waves broke in on Peter, he doubted and sank. Jesus did not doubt and sink when the boisterous words of Satan broke in on Him. Each of these events happened in a moment of time. In the moment of Adam's temptation, Adam failed. In the moment of Peter's temptation, Peter failed. In the many moments of Israel's temptations, Israel failed. In the moment of Jesus' temptation, He succeeded.

In the moments of our life, with all its ups and downs and temptations, we must follow Jesus' example, not the examples of Adam, Peter, or Israel. We must learn how to agree with God. We cannot walk together with God, unless we agree with Him. If we try to make God agree with us, or if we always agree with the devil, we will not have a victorious, fruitful Christian life. To agree with God, we must actually hear what He is saying. What God says is written in His word, the Bible. All spiritual words given to us must agree with the written word. Remember, Jesus said to Satan,

"It is written!"

Like our Lord, we must have faith in,

"What God has said."

After faith in the Word of God, we must appropriate the word into our life as Jesus did. Jesus accepted, received and agreed with the Word of God, concerning Him,

"He is the Son of God."

Likewise, we must believe and agree with God, concerning all He proclaims about salvation in Christ. Moreover, we must constantly defend and keep the Word of God in our heart moment by moment, by fighting the forces which proclaim,

"Has God said?"

This is not a magical formula; it is what God desires. God wants us to agree with Him. If we agree with Him, you have the victory. How this all works out in your life, only God knows.

History teaches many outcomes for people who agree with God totally. However, one thing I can say, "Believe on the Lord Jesus Christ and you will be saved!" If you agree with God on this point, you have victory. This is our first step in walking with God and our most important need.

In conclusion, the syntax concerning the use of the three words, *"Has, God, and Said,"* is of the utmost importance. We need to think of the power in the way these words are phrased. The biblical narrative teaches these three words were phrased in two ways. The first way these three words were used was, *"God has said."* The second way these three words were used was, *"Has God said."* The choice of accepting the one phrase or the other is ours. Which syntax of these three words do you choose?

Chapter Three Self-Analysis

1) How have you tried to have a victorious life? Were you successful or not, or up and down with it?

2) Have you experienced Peter's battle of being caught between two ways?

3) In some of these two way experiences, which way did you turn?

4) Did you enter into the Broad Way or the Narrow Way, Matthew 7:13-14?

5) What happens to you when the storms of life beat on you, are you standing strong or swept away, Matthew 8:24-25?

6) How do you handle the stinging words of the serpent, "Has God said?"

7) According to Amos 3:3, what is the instruction for a victorious life with God?

8) Can you remember any outcomes when you chose to agree with something or someone? Were the outcomes good or bad?

9) Can you remember any outcomes when you chose to disagree with something or someone? Were the outcomes good or bad? Who should you disagree with one-hundred percent?

10) List some God has said scriptures you should agree with. For example, 1John1:9, *"If we confess our sins, He is faithful and just to forgive us our sins and to cleanse us from all unrighteousness."*

11) How will the serpent try to cause you to disagree with this scriptural promise?

12) What type of power is there in being in agreement with God?

13) How much power does evil have when people agree with evil?

14) What do you think the end results are when we agree with good or evil?

15) Where does the responsibility of agreement belong with God or with you?

16) Do doubt or misunderstanding of what God has said act as an excuse for what we choose?

17) Describe how Jesus agreed with God to victory in temptation one.

18) Describe how Jesus agreed with God to victory in temptation number two.

19) Describe how Jesus agreed with God to victory in temptation number three.

20) What was the final result at the end of Jesus' three temptations?

21) In your life's moments and temptations, whose example

should you imitate, Adam and Eve, Israel, the Apostle Peter or Jesus Christ?

22) Walking with God is not a magical formula, how are we to do this?

LESSON FOUR: RESPONSIBILITY GOD TAKES RESPONSIBILITY AND SO CHRISTIANS SHOULD! A COMMAND!

TAKING RESPONSIBILITY

Humans Did Not Take Personal Responsibility

"Then the man said, 'The woman whom You gave to be with me, she gave me of the tree, and I ate.' And the Lord God said to the woman, 'What is this you have done?' The woman said, 'The serpent deceived me, and I ate.'"
Genesis 3:12-13 NKJV

God Shows How He Takes Responsibility for His Creation

"But God demonstrates His own love toward us, in that while we were still sinners, Christ died for us."
Romans 5:8 NKJV

How misunderstanding we are of the death of Christ. We do not comprehend His death was planned before the creation of the world. ***"He indeed was foreordained before the foundation of the world, but was manifest in these last times for you who through Him believe in God, who raised Him from the dead and gave Him glory, so that your faith and hope are in God,"*** 1 Peter 1:20-21 NKJV. Sin did not catch God off guard, nor surprise Him. Rebellious activity by angels and disobedience of human beings created in His image, was a very understood problem, He could or would face, when He began creating intelligent free-thinking beings. The words, ***He (Christ) was foreordained before the foundation of the world,*** confirms the preparedness of God for the responsibility of His creation. For us, God's responsibility is a redeeming preparation and for the fallen angels, it is perdition.

If we remember our history lessons concerning President Harry S. Truman, he said one thing concerning responsibility, *"The buck stops here."* The meaning is, he will take responsibility for whatever comes his way as President. God is the originator of personal responsibility. In His perfection of character, He cannot be irresponsible nor passing of blame onto others (although, He never does anything wrong, because there is no sin in Him, 1 John 3:5). God will take responsibility for whatever comes before His throne.

We as humans, men and women, adults and children suffer a lack of integrity in responsibility of accepting the consequences of our behavior gone bad. To put it bluntly, we do not hold ourselves accountable for our sins against God and one another. The popular responses we use when we are caught in sin are, *"The devil made me do it" or "It was not my fault, but he or she caused it!"* We like to pass the buck and not accept the fact of the buck stopping at our desk. Adam and Eve were the originators of the passing the buck syndrome of irresponsibility of their own personal actions in sinning. Adam and Eve had only one prohibition given to them. They were given total freedom to enjoy all of creation in the goodness of the image of God; they were created in. They could eat, be merry and intimate with each other. The two could enjoy all the wonders of the Garden of Eden and a personal relationship with God. Let us peek into Scripture to learn.

Paradise Created

"And out of the ground the Lord God made every tree grow that is pleasant to the sight and good for food. The tree of life was also in the midst of the garden, and the tree of the knowledge of good and evil," Genesis 2:9 NKJV.

Paradise Given to Humans with One Prohibition

"Then the Lord God took the man and put him in the garden of Eden to tend and keep it. And the Lord God commanded the man, saying, 'Of every tree of the garden you may freely eat; but of the tree of the knowledge of good and evil you shall not eat, for in the day that you eat of it you shall surely die,'" Genesis 2:15-17 NKJV.

Fellowship with God a Delight

"Out of the ground the Lord God formed every beast of the field and every bird of the air, and brought them to Adam to see what he would call them. And whatever Adam called each living creature, that was its name," Genesis 2:19 NKJV.

HUSBAND AND WIFE INTIMACY ENJOYED

"And they were both naked, the man and his wife, and were not ashamed," Genesis 2:25 NKJV.

The Garden of Eden was a paradise for Adam and Eve, and all the created birds and animals and fish of the sea. Everything was in perfect harmony. One-day Eve decided to take a walk. Adam follows along. What a pleasant walk the two were experiencing. The fragrance of the flowers, the lullabies of the birds, the singing of the animals, filled their senses with joy. The presence of the Lord was felt everywhere. As Eve wanders around the Garden, she walks by the incredible tree of the knowledge of good and evil. She looks at Adam, knowing it is not correct for them to eat from this tree, when she hears a voice calling to her from the tree. Eve, it cries. Eve come here. Eve, not knowing fear, lets her curiosity overtake her common sense and goes over to the tree to see who is calling her. Adam follows Eve to the tree. Before the two understand what is happening, the beast in the tree, a serpent which allowed himself to be controlled by the devil, cleverly through questioning, confuses Eve, and disparages God and His prohibition on eating the fruit, which should not be ate. The serpent dangles the incredible fruit before Eves' eyes, and Eve makes a willful decision to eat it. Upon eating she turns toward her husband, who listened to the discussion and did nothing about it, to give him the fruit, and he willfully takes and eats it too. ***"So when the woman saw that the tree was good for food, that it was pleasant to the eyes, and a tree desirable to make one wise, she took of its fruit and ate. She also gave to her husband with her, and he ate,"*** Genesis 3:6 NKJV.

Much can be said concerning this action and its results. However, it is the responsibility we are studying. Adam and Eve clearly did not take the responsibility of obeying God and not eating from the tree of the knowledge of good and evil. They also, did not consider their responsibility towards one another. They did wrong. This is an act of sin against God. The first lesson we learn here, is a responsible person takes seriously the charges given to them. They knew the word of God and His commands. Adam received them personally from God. ***"And the Lord God commanded the man, saying, "Of every tree of the garden you may freely eat; but of the tree of the knowledge of good and evil you shall not eat, for in the day that you eat of it you shall surely die,"*** Genesis 2:16-17 NKJV. Adam was highly intelligent, probably an intellectual. This is shown through his naming of all the animals, Genesis 2:19. Considering the volume of animals and birds created the naming of them is no small matter. This proves Adam and Eve could reason, think, examine, and make decisions based on their conclusions. This, naming of the animals, enables us to understand Adam took the responsibility of this seriously, ***"And whatever Adam called each living creature, that was its name."***

The question we wish we could have answered is, *Why, did a sinless mind succumb to disobedience into sin?* If Adam could handle the responsibility of naming the animals and birds, why was he and Eve so irresponsible about the command of God, do not eat? God, by placing his commands on Adam expected Adam to be responsible to them. Adam and Eve had three commands given to them. Two commands were positive, and one was negative.

THE THREE COMMANDS OF PARADISE

1. *The Command of Purpose,* ***"Then God blessed them, and God said to them, "Be fruitful and multiply; fill the earth and subdue it; have dominion over the fish of the sea, over the birds of the air, and over every living thing that moves on the earth,"*** *Genesis 1:28 NKJV.*
2. *The Command for Nourishment,* ***"And God said, 'See, I have given you every herb that yields seed which is on the face of all the earth, and every tree whose fruit yields seed; to you it shall be for food,'"*** *Genesis 1:29 NKJV.*
3. *The Command of Prohibition,* ***"And the Lord God commanded the man, saying, 'Of every tree of the garden you may freely eat; but of the tree of the knowledge of good and evil you shall not eat, for in the day that you eat of it you shall surely die,'"*** *Genesis 2:16-17 NKJV.*

It seems obvious, concerning the first two commands, they were easy to follow. There was nothing prohibiting about them. It almost seems God was saying, eat, drink and be merry in all you do. Who would not follow commands like them? However, the prohibited command concerning the tree of the knowledge of good, and evil was a little more difficult to follow. It seems something forbidden is something desired. There also seems to be some type of emotional recoiling to the death part of breaking the command. We can assume Adam instructed Eve about the three commandments he received from God. He also added an extra prohibition to It. He taught Eve they were not allowed to touch, or death would occur. We learn this from Eve's answer to the serpent. ***"And the woman said to the serpent, 'We may eat the fruit of the trees of the garden; but of the fruit***

of the tree which is in the midst of the garden,' God has said, 'You shall not eat it, nor shall you touch it, lest you die,'" Genesis 3:2-3 -NKJV. Responsible people know the truth and keep the truth sacred in their hearts. The truth of the command, by God, is to see if Adam and Eve would desire Him over something He forbade. We can assume God created us to be able to have desires. It is a great responsibility to understand what desires we have concerning good and evil. I would guess, Adam had a secret desire for the forbidden, and this is the reason he added an additional rule of do not touch to Eve.

Perhaps, Jesus explained this situation to James, who was possibly having difficulty with Adam and Eves disobedience. James wrote about the reward of desiring God and the penalty of desiring the forbidden. ***"Blessed is the man who endures temptation; for when he has been approved, he will receive the crown of life which the Lord has promised to those who love Him. Let no one say when he is tempted, 'I am tempted by God'; for God cannot be tempted by evil, nor does He Himself tempt anyone. But each one is tempted when he is drawn away by his own desires and enticed. Then, when desire has conceived, it gives birth to sin; and sin, when it is full-grown, brings forth death,"*** James 1:12-15 NKJV. If you are wondering why Adam never stepped in to help and protect Eve, it is because he desired the fruit from the forbidden tree ever since he was told not to eat it. Adam did not hold the command, not to eat with the proper desire to love God. He tried to protect himself from taking it with an additional warning. However, all which was needed, was a little enticement to eat it, which he got. Therefore, he fulfilled his desire and ate, and this brought forth death. The second lesson to take away from this is to make sure your desires are proper and set. Adam never settled the matter in his heart by deciding; I will not eat. His desire was for the forbidden fruit. He lost the crown of life because he did not endure temptation. When his desire was enticed and conceived, it gave birth to sin and brought forth death. ***"So all the days that Adam lived were***

nine hundred and thirty years; and he died," Genesis 5:5 NKJV.

PASSING THE BUCK SYNDROME
(How Not to Take Responsibility)

We have just seen the failure which happens when we do not take the responsibility of the commands of God seriously. We now move on in the lesson, which is, taking responsibility for our actions. How good did Adam feel when God accepted every name for each animal he gave? Let us try to answer this with a personal question, how good do you feel for an action you do, which results in praise? There is no doubt about it, you feel surprisingly good about yourself and the responsibility you exhibited in the action. Perhaps, you have false humility and say it was nothing? Maybe you try to pass the glory to God? The truth be known, we like being noticed for a job well done. We may also secretly expect people to praise us for whatever we did. Therefore, we may assume Adam felt great in obeying God and naming all the animals. This leads to the antithesis of taking responsibility for doing good, which is taking responsibility when we err, make a mistake, or sin miserably. When I say this, I do not mean the superficial, "*My bad!*" Have you ever been caught in a wrong and put the blame on someone or something else? If you have (which most of us do), then you have not taken responsibility for your bad behavior.

Adam and Eve ate the forbidden fruit. They have undergone a chemical and genetic change in their beings. Their pure minds are not pure anymore. They now see, think, and reason from a self-awareness perspective. Where there was no fear, fear abounds. Furthermore, where God was a loving friend, He is now a dangerous enemy, judge, and executioner. The historical account when God, Adam, and Eve, came face to face after Adam and Eve sinned is astonishing. God came to the garden seeking an accounting for their law-breaking action. Adam and Eve hear God walking in the garden. They fear and hide themselves. ***"And they heard the sound of the Lord God walking in the garden in the cool of the day, and Adam and his wife hid themselves from the presence of the Lord God among the trees of the garden,"*** Genesis 3:8 NKJV. God calls to them, giving them a chance to come and confess without Him having to drag the truth out of them. ***"Then the Lord God called to Adam and said to him, "Where are you?"*** (Genesis 3:9 NKJV) How silly for us to think, God does not know where we are! Nevertheless, with their newfound "godlike" understanding, Adam does not come clean but makes a statement of his now understanding the fear of the judge, ***"I heard Your voice in the garden, and I was afraid because I was naked; and I hid myself,"*** Genesis 3:10 NKJV. Well, unbeknownst to Adam, he just let the cat out of the bag! Although, he did not admit he ate the fruit, his statement and behavior show God, he did.

GOD ASKS POINTED QUESTIONS

The Lord responds to Adam's disobedience. To Adam, He asks two probing questions, which demand a truthful response. When our children were young, we took them out for pizza. I saw one of them playing with the pepper shaker. I knew this one's curiosity, so I said, *"Do not sniff the pepper shaker!"* Turning my attention to the other family members, the chitchatting between us took our attention away from the one with the pepper shaker. Suddenly, we heard coughing and commotion of agony coming from the curious one. I turned seeing his face filled with tears and redness; I said, knowing what happened by the evidence in front of me, *"Did you sniff the pepper?"* The first response was, *"No."* However, as the suffering became more intense, the truth came out, the curious one sniffed the pepper. To use a worn-out phrase, the proof was written all over the child's face.

Therefore, with the proof emanating out of Adam, God started to question him. First, He questions Adam on his fear of nakedness, which is the proof of their wrongdoing. Remember, before sin, ***"And they were both naked, the man and his wife, and were not ashamed,"*** Genesis 2:25. Now Adam said, ***"I was afraid because I was naked!"*** (Genesis 3:10)

God's question to Adam, ***"Who told you that you were naked?"***

Adam's answer to God is silence! Adam could not answer this question because, the truth is no-one told him he was naked. He knows he is naked because of the "knowledge" he gained from the fruit he ate. If Adam said something, at this point, he would be admitting his guilt. If Adam confesses, he knows the death sentence is awaiting him.

God's second question to Adam, ***"Have you eaten from the tree of which I commanded you that you should not eat?"*** Once again,

God is giving Adam the chance to take responsibility for his sin.

Adam's response, (here he passes the buck and blame for his action) ***"Then the man said, "The woman whom You gave to be with me, she gave me of the tree, and I ate."*** Many husbands say this today when things go askew in the house, it is the wife's fault for our failure.

God sees He is getting nowhere with the now shameful, fearful, and unrepentant Adam. Therefore, He turns His attention towards Eve, hoping she will give a better account of the situation.

God's question to Eve, ***"What is this you have done?"***

Eve's response, ***"The serpent deceived me, and I ate."*** Well like her husband, she passes the blame of her action onto someone else, the devil. We use this excuse today and say, *"The devil made me do it!"* (Above from Genesis 3:11-13) Unfortunately, for all of us, no one causes us to sin. Sin is our own action and responsibility.

Confessing of sin, means you take personal responsibility for what you have done. This is what God was hoping Adam and Eve would do. They, fearing the judgement of God and not knowing the mercy of God, did not take responsibility and confess their sin. They and we need to say, *"I have sinned. No one else caused me to do it. I did it."* Jesus taught about this problem of taking responsibility over our sin toward God!

"Also He spoke this parable to some who trusted in themselves that they were righteous, and despised others: 'Two men went up to the temple to pray, one a Pharisee and the other a tax collector. The Pharisee stood and prayed thus with himself, 'God, I thank You that I am not like other men—extortioners, unjust, adulterers, or even as this tax collector. I fast twice a week; I give tithes of all that I possess. 'And the tax collector, standing afar off, would not so much as raise his eyes to heaven, but beat his

breast, saying, 'God, be merciful to me a sinner! 'I tell you, this man went down to his house justified rather than the other; for everyone who exalts himself will be humbled, and he who humbles himself will be exalted," Luke 18:9-14 NKJV.

Adam failed in two ways, firstly, he did not decide, before he was tempted, not to eat from the tree of the knowledge of good and evil. Secondly, he failed to take responsibility for his eating of it. Unlike God, who before the foundation of the world, decided to be responsible for the well-being of His creation before sin, then did His responsibility after sin. ***"But when the fullness of the time had come, God sent forth His Son, born of a woman, born under the law, to redeem those who were under the law, that we might receive the adoption as sons,"*** Galatians 4:4-5 NKJV. ***"But God demonstrates His own love toward us, in that while we were still sinners, Christ died for us,"*** Romans 5:8 NKJV.

Adam and Eve had a lack of knowledge concerning God. They had not learned, ***"And there is no creature hidden from His sight, but all things are naked and open to the eyes of Him to whom we must give account,"*** Hebrews 4:13 NKJV. They thought they could run and hide from Him to escape the responsibility of their failure. Many fail to realize, even though God is not seen visibly, nevertheless, He is present spiritually. Many run and try to hide from Him under the cover, there is no God. However, there He is wherever you or I go. How foolish we must seem when we think we can cover up our sin. Solomon learned this the hard way. He lost the kingdom for his son, all because he, like Adam, did not take the responsibility of living for God seriously. He was enticed to idolatry by many ungodly wives. This shows a secret desire for other Gods even though he was given great wisdom and riches by Yahweh. He may have realized the foolishness for not taking responsibility for his idolatry too late. He wrote this problem concerning it, ***"He who covers his sins will not prosper, But whoever confesses and***

forsakes them will have mercy," Proverbs 28:13 NKJV.

We started the lesson learning how God takes responsibility very seriously; the intensity of His actions in carrying out His care and responsibility for His creation culminated in the death, burial, and resurrection of Christ. He purposed to do this before the foundation of the world.

Next, we learned how Adam, given commandments from God, broke the command not to eat. Nowhere, do we get taught, Adam purposed in his heart to be responsible to obey God. He sinned by eating something he should not have. He also teaches us how he refused to take responsibility for his disobedience.

Finally, we should personally learn; we are responsible to obey God, and if we sin, we are responsible for our sin. To blame others for our failures is not repentance. The words of Joshua teach us about the importance of deciding and keeping the decision. This is his lesson of responsibility.

"And if it seems evil to you to serve the Lord, choose for yourselves this day whom you will serve, whether the gods which your fathers served that were on the other side of the River, or the gods of the Amorites, in whose land you dwell. But as for me and my house, we will serve the Lord," Joshua 24:15 NKJV.

What Does Joshua Mean?

1. In the scheme of things, we must make a choice between two systems of existence.
2. The decision will lead to a way of behavior, whether for God or against God.
3. The facts must be examined. For Israel, it was the bondage of false gods or the freedom and delivering power of the true God, so it is for us.
4. It is a decision which should be done promptly and not put off.

5. The smart choice is the Joshua decision, ***"But as for me and my house, we will serve the Lord."***
6. It is one thing for us to accept Christ as Savior, but another thing to obey Him as Lord.
7. Jesus said the Joshua decision must be made daily. ***"If anyone desires to come after Me, let him deny himself, and take up his cross daily, and follow Me. For whoever desires to save his life will lose it, but whoever loses his life for My sake will save it,"*** Luke 9:23-24 NKJV.

The choice is ours, to be responsible, in every area of existence. We are to take responsibility over our thoughts, our words, and our deeds. This must be a decision to make beforehand, and it must become a desire of our heart. So, when we are tempted (for temptation comes to everyone, 1 Corinthians 10:13) we will not be enticed to bring forth sin, but endure the temptation, because it has already been decided in our hearts, God is our desire! No one can choose to follow God for you! You and I must decide for ourselves. Adam and Eve failed to make the choice before the temptation, let us not be like them. Christian, take responsibility seriously!

Reflections

1. What is responsibility?
2. List all your responsibilities.
3. How serious are you concerning your list?
4. Which ones are you lackadaisical towards?
5. According to 1 Peter 1: 20-21, what did God plan before He created?
6. Did sin catch God off guard? Or was God surprised by sin?
7. What are free thinking intelligent beings capable of, including you?

8. What was Christ foreordained to do?
9. How does this teach God taking responsibility for His creation?
10. What was President Truman's motto?
11. What does this mean?
12. Does God do this?
13. Do you do this?
14. Do you hold yourself accountable for your sins against God and one another?
15. What was the one prohibition given to Adam and Eve?
16. What were the permissions God gave to them?
17. Explain what Eve and Adam did. How does this affect all today?
18. Did Adam and Eve exert responsibility toward the command of God?
19. Were these two people intelligent? Why then, did they sin?
20. What are the three commands of Paradise?
21. How did Adam "enhance" the command to Eve?
22. What do responsible people do with truth and commands?
23. What are the purposes of God's commands?
24. Did God create humans to have desires?
25. How are we to handle these desires? What are we to discern about them?
26. According to James, how does a person get blessed?
27. What does God promise such a person who wins the battle over temptation?
28. How foolish is it to say, "I am tempted by God?"
29. Do you think God is tempted by evil and then tempts you?
30. Think about this, James said, ***"God cannot be tempted by evil, nor does He Himself tempt anybody!"*** Write down your conclusions to this. Point of proof, read Matthew chapter four, was Jesus, Immanuel, God with men, was Jesus tempted by evil (the devil)? Also, in the Gospels,

did Jesus ever tempt anyone? The answer demands, No! If you or I think otherwise, we are deceived.

31. Since we have desires, both good and evil, how does James teach the way we are tempted.
32. What does it mean to be enticed?
33. What does enticement conceive?
34. What happens when we are fully living in the temptation?
35. Therefore, who tempts who and who is to be blamed?
36. What does it mean to pass the buck?
37. What happens when we do not take the commands of God seriously?
38. What does it mean to take responsibility for our actions?
39. How good do you think Adam felt before the Lord when he named all the animals?
40. What does this say about Adam's intelligence?
41. How does James 1:12-15 apply to Adam's decision to eat?
42. Does saying, *"My Bad,"* mean you have taken responsibility for your errors?
43. How does thinking from a self-awareness perspective hinder a person from true repentance?
44. Before Adam and Eve ate the fruit of the knowledge of good and evil, how did they perceive God?
45. After they ate, how did they perceive God?
46. How do you perceive God?
47. Are you as silly as Adam and Eve thinking they could hide themselves and their deeds from God?
48. What are the two-pointed questions God asked Adam?
49. Do you understand, when we sin, God is asking us His pointed questions?
50. How did Adam answer these questions?
51. How did Eve answer her pointed question, *"What is this you have done?"*
52. Did Adam or Eve take responsibility of God's

command and the breaking of it?

53. How idiotic, from our hindsight, Adam, and Eve's, passing the buck seems. Have you responded to the conviction of the Holy Spirit to your sin?
54. In Luke 18:9-14, who was justified before God?
55. How did the tax collector take responsibility of his behavior?
56. What is the lesson we can learn from the Pharisee and tax collector?
57. What are the two ways Adam failed?
58. How are you failing and what can help you to turn your failing into success?
59. How does Romans 5:8 teach us; God in His responsibility and plan did not fail?
60. What knowledge of God was Adam and Eve lacking?
61. How can this knowledge help us in our temptations?
62. Can you run and hide from God?
63. What is the lesson of Proverbs 28:13? This verse should be memorized.
64. What is the lesson God taught concerning His responsibility?
65. Did God purpose His responsibility before, or after He had to carry out the giving of His Son?
66. What is the lesson Adam taught concerning his responsibilities?
67. Are you personally responsible to obey God?
68. Are you personally responsible for your failure to do so?
69. According to Joshua 24:16, what did Joshua purpose in his heart?
70. Describe the seven points of Joshua's decision.
71. How can this help you to become a responsible person?
72. What does *taking-up the cross daily* mean?
73. Is this a practice of yours?
74. Are you struggling to do this on your own?

75. If so, accept the help Jesus wants to give you. ***"And I will pray the Father, and He will give you another Helper, that He may abide with you forever—John 14:16 NKJV.***
76. Memorize and meditate on John 14:16.
77. What decisions of responsibility do you need to make in your life?

Lord Bless You!

LESSON FIVE: DEATH THE DAY MOSES DIED: A TRUTH, WE ALL WILL TOO!

DEATH: THE DAY MOSES DIED

"Then Moses went up from the plains of Moab to Mount Nebo, to the top of Pisgah, which is across from Jericho"

Deuteronomy 34:1 NKJV.

It was a beautiful bright sunny morning Moses awoke to. It was not any type of day more different than the 43,799 previous ones Moses experienced. However, this day was distinctive for Moses. It was his last day of life on earth. Moses had an appointment with death on Mount Nebo at the top of Pisgah. After saying his parting words to Israel, he faced the mount and began his ascent to his pending death. He also was climbing toward a final meeting with God, who promised to show Moses all the land his nation would inherit.

One could only wonder what was going on in the mind and heart of Moses. Was Moses experiencing fear, joy, anger, or regret, as he approached the Mount of Death? Was a kaleidoscope of his life exploding in his mind? This one point of not crossing over was a terrible area of regret Moses could not overcome. Just before his climb up the mountain he said to Israel, ***"Then I pleaded with the Lord at that time, saying: 'O Lord God, You have begun to show Your servant Your greatness and Your mighty hand, for what god is there in heaven or on earth who can do anything like Your works and Your mighty deeds? I pray, let me cross over and see the good land beyond the Jordan, those pleasant mountains, and Leban,' But the Lord was angry with me on your account, and would not listen to me. So the Lord***

said to me: 'Enough of that! Speak no more to Me of this matter," Deuteronomy 3:23-26 NKJV.

Yes, Moses was feeling anger and regret concerning a specific event in his life. This event keeps him from crossing over to the promised land. He can only get a glimpse of it. However, as he takes his first steps up to Pisgah, a panoramic of his life begins to play in his mind. There is no doubt in his mind, as he views the scenes of his life, Yahweh was with him from the beginning. The stories of his birth and boat ride on the Nile River to Pharaoh's house were clear for him to see. A pride swells up in his heart for his parents, who saved his life from Pharaoh's death sentence and for the bravery of his sister Marion as she watched over him floating down the Nile. ***"And a man of the house of Levi went and took as wife a daughter of Levi. So the woman conceived and bore a son. And when she saw that he was a beautiful child, she hid him three months. But when she could no longer hide him, she took an ark of bulrushes for him, daubed it with asphalt and pitch, put the child in it, and laid it in the reeds by the river's bank. And his sister stood afar off, to know what would be done to him,"*** Exodus 2:1-4 NKJV.

How warm the heart of Moses was as he thought about the love of two mothers in his life. The privileges he had in being called the son of Pharaoh's daughter. ***"And Pharaoh's daughter said to her, 'Go.' So the maiden went and called the child's mother. Then Pharaoh's daughter said to her, 'Take this child away and nurse him for me, and I will give you your wages.' So the woman took the child and nursed him. And the child grew, and she brought him to Pharaoh's daughter, and he became her son. So she called his name Moses, saying, 'Because I drew him out of the water,'"*** Exodus 2:8-10 NKJV.

As Moses kept climbing, he started to chuckle a little. These laughs happened as he thought of his youth and school days in the house of Pharaoh. Learning for Moses was a loving chore. He knows the daughter of Pharaoh spared no expense for training him in the wisdom of Egypt. ***"But when he was***

set out, Pharaoh's daughter took him away and brought him up as her own son. And Moses was learned in all the wisdom of the Egyptians, and was mighty in words and deeds," Acts 7:21-22 NKJV. He realized God was involved in this education for the latter purposes of his life. This memory causes Moses to stop climbing and enter a moment of worship and praise.

Moses is about one-third distance up to the summit of Pisgah. As he walks, he steps on a jagged rock. A slight pain is felt in his foot. This misstep jogs a memory in his mind, when he was forty, which he long had buried. He sees the event as clear as the day. He remembers a moment which would forever change his life. Moses felt the hand of God on him, even then. He felt he had a calling from Yahweh to deliver his brethren Israel from Egypt. Upon seeing a fellow Israelite being mistreated by an Egyptian, Moses stepped in and killed the harsh Egyptian. The next day Moses tries to stop two Israelites from beating up on each other. Moses stepped in and tried to correct the situation. With little gratitude for Moses, his fellow Israelite threatened him with exposure for the murder of the Egyptian. Into the desert he ran to escape judgement. His thoughts running wild, he thought he made a mistake thinking he was a deliverer, even though he was. ***"Now when he was forty years old, it came into his heart to visit his brethren, the children of Israel. And seeing one of them suffer wrong, he defended and avenged him who was oppressed, and struck down the Egyptian. For he supposed that his brethren would have understood that God would deliver them by his hand, but they did not understand. And the next day he appeared to two of them as they were fighting, and tried to reconcile them, saying, 'Men, you are brethren; why do you wrong one another?' But he who did his neighbor wrong pushed him away, saying, 'Who made you a ruler and a judge over us? Do you want to kill me as you did the Egyptian yesterday?' Then, at this saying, Moses fled and became a dweller in the land of Midian, where he had two sons,"*** Acts 7:23-29 NKJV. Memories of forty long years, in the land of Midian, come to mind with the meeting with his father in-law, Jethro, the marriage to his daughter Zipporah, the birth of his two sons, Gershom and Eliezer, and the lonely times shepherding the flocks. Suddenly, Moses cries out for his sons wishing they could be with him on this last journey up Pisgah.

As Moses ascends on the last half of the climb, the greatest event of his life flashes before his eyes. This was the day he encountered God! ***"Then Moses said, 'I will now turn aside and see this great sight, why the bush does not burn.' So when the Lord saw that he turned aside to look, God called to him from the midst of the bush and said, 'Moses, Moses!' And he said, 'Here I am.' Then He said, 'Do not draw near this place. Take your sandals off your feet, for the place where you stand is holy ground.' Moreover He said, 'I am the God of your father—the God of Abraham, the God of Isaac, and the God of Jacob.' And Moses hid his face, for he was afraid to look upon God,"*** Exodus 3:3-6 NKJV. Hallelujahs stream out from his mouth as he remembers the first time, he hears the voice of God. Although, the nostalgia of this moment is overwhelming, there is a little regret in Moses' mind, because he argued with the Lord there. However, he remembers accepting God's call and going off to meet Aaron to begin the deliverance of Israel out of Egypt.

The climb to the top of Pisgah is progressing rapidly and so are the memories of the last forty years of life. The battle with Pharaoh and the wonders of the plagues, flies, locust, bloody waters, and the slaying of the firstborn of Egypt are still vivid in his mind. The day of freedom and the exodus to the Red Sea was as exhilarating in the mind as in the days it happened. When Moses looked around from his vantage points on the climb, he saw rivers and lakes and the memory of God dividing the sea opened more praises to Yahweh. It was incredible to travel through the sea on dry land with walls of water making a hallway for Israel to pass through to the other side. How astonishing the sight of the waters crashing down on the onrushing army of Pharaoh. Moses cannot help but sing the horse and the rider thrown into the sea! Tears roll down his cheeks as he remembers the sweet voice of his sister Marion leading the congregation in worship.

Step by step, upward to the summit climbs Moses to his meeting with God. It feels, to him, like the travel to Mount Sinai. Hackles climb up Moses back and neck because he remembers the grumbling of Israel as they navigate to Sinai. The complaints for food and water still trouble him. The making of the golden calf for idolatrous worship brings sorrow to his heart. While I am receiving the Ten Commandments, the nation is having an orgy. He shutters as he remembers how he threw down the tablets and broke them in anger. How many miracles did God perform for them, and they would not believe? These people were unbelievably faithless in not trusting God to bring them into the promised land. How miserable was the forty years of wandering in the desert because of them? Now as he is almost to the top Moses remembers the incident which made him sin in anger against the Lord. The days, weeks, and months of constant backbiting, grumbling, and complaining hit a crescendo at the Wilderness of Zin. Here Marian died and there also was no water to drink and feed the flocks. Once again, the children of Israel grumbled. ***"And the people contended with Moses and spoke, saying: 'If only we had died when our brethren died before the Lord! Why have you brought up the assembly of the Lord into this wilderness, that we and our animals should die here? And why have you made us come up out of Egypt, to bring us to this evil place? It is not a place of grain or figs or vines or pomegranates; nor is there any water to drink,'"*** Numbers 20:3-5 NKJV."

Seeing his ascent was nearing completion, he felt more agitated because of the Wilderness of Zin experience. After all, the congregation provoked him once too many times and this caused his prohibition from crossing the Jordan into the promised land. The Lord told Moses to speak to the rock before Israel, and it would bring forth water. He was not to strike the rock like he did at Rephidim. Moses knew it was wrong to let his anger get the best of him. However, his anger was a festering wound in his heart, which needed release. ***"And Moses and Aaron gathered the assembly together before the rock; and he said to them, 'Hear now, you rebels! Must we bring water for you out of this rock?' Then Moses lifted his hand and struck the rock twice with his rod; and water came out abundantly, and the congregation and their animals drank,"*** Numbers 20:10-11 NKJV. As the scene plays out in his mind, Moses wishes he could get a redo, but it happened. Moses still hears the punishment from God as he finally finishes his climb. ***"Because you did not believe Me, to hallow Me in the eyes of the children of Israel, therefore you shall not bring this assembly into the land which I have given them,"*** Numbers 20:12 NKJV. While he waits for the Lord, Moses is grateful, for God's mercy, which will allow him to see the promised land from afar. Moses knew the deliverance from Egypt started out well, but disobedience to God was costly for him and faithlessness for the older generation. They were excluded from the land. Finally, the Lord is present on Pisgah. ***"And the Lord showed him all the land of Gilead as far as Dan, all Naphtali and the land of Ephraim and Manasseh, all the land of Judah as far as the Western Sea, the South, and the plain of the Valley of Jericho, the city of palm trees, as far as Zoar,"*** Deuteronomy 34:1-3 NKJV.

Moses is now content. ***"So Moses the servant of the Lord died there in the land of Moab, according to the word of the Lord,"*** Deuteronomy 34:5 NKJV. Moses' body, now laying on Mount Nebo, at the top of Pisgah, must be buried. God decides to bury him in a valley in the land of Moab. Therefore, He sends Michael the archangel to bury him. However, Michael coming to Pisgah sees a problem waiting for him. The devil was there, and he had plans for his enemy Moses' dead body. I bet Michael was thinking, *"There he is the accuser of the brethren. What evil does he have in mind for Moses' dead body?"* In the day, Moses died one can only imagine what took place when Michael came to carry Moses body to the awaiting gravesite. What an argument it must have been. Their words thundered down the mountain with great force. How lofty and holy were the words of Michael and disgusting and reproachable the words of the devil. The more the devil spoke his blasphemous words against God concerning Moses; the angrier Michael became. However, Michael knew better. He would not sin in anger. Therefore, he put his winning argument into the contentious battle. My guess is he said to the devil, *"You cannot have the body of Moses to defile it! Moses is saved by faith in the Son of God! His body will be preserved until the second coming of the Lord. Did not Moses instruct Israel about him?* ***The Lord your God will raise up for you a Prophet like me from your midst, from your brethren. Him you shall hear,"*** Deuteronomy 18:15 NKJV. *He whom God has called will not be taken from Him. Therefore, the Lord Rebuke You!"* With this the devil fled away and Michael, with loving care, picked up the body of Moses and brought him down from Pisgah and buried him in a valley in Moab. Jude, the Lord's brother, when he started speaking evil of people might have been corrected by Jesus with a first-person account of the day Moses died. ***"Yet Michael the archangel, in contending with the devil, when he disputed about the body of Moses, dared not bring against him a reviling accusation, but said, 'The Lord rebuke you!'"*** Jude 1:9 NKJV.

We also have a scriptural viewpoint on Moses' salvation by faith in Christ. Luke gives us this knowledge. ***"Now it came to pass, about eight days after these sayings, that He took Peter, John, and James and went up on the mountain to pray. As He prayed, the appearance of His face was altered, and His robe became white and glistening. And behold, two men talked with Him, who were Moses and Elijah, who appeared in glory and spoke of His decease which He was about to accomplish at Jerusalem,"*** Luke 9:28-31 NKJV. It is a wonderful event to see Moses enter the promised land by faith in Christ, after being blocked out because of disobedience. Moses, with Elijah, was talking to the

Lord concerning His sacrificial death for their salvation and ours. Therefore, with forceful conviction Michael could win the day and save Moses body because of Moses' faith in the Son of God.

How interesting Moses' death was, and I think our deaths will be just as engaging for us. Furthermore, Moses had a very eventful life from cradle to grave. There were many highs, and many lows he experienced. He had hardship galore, frustrations, poor judgements, along with encounters with God; mountain top grandeurs and valley lows over his one-hundred and twenty years. He was misunderstood, hated, envied, despised, and rejected by many. He also was esteemed, feared, and loved. However, the most important relationship he has was with God. This relationship was also important to God. While Moses, Aaron and Miriam were having a sibling moment, God straightened them out because He had a relationship with Moses. ***"Then He said, "Hear now My words: If there is a prophet among you, I, the Lord, make Myself known to him in a vision; I speak to him in a dream. Not so with My servant Moses; He is faithful in all My house. I speak with him face to face, Even plainly, and not in dark sayings; And he sees the form of the Lord. Why then were you not afraid to speak against My servant Moses?"*** Numbers 12:6-8 NKJV. We have to admit; Moses had a wonderful and marvelous life relationship with God. The day Moses died was an extension of his relationship with God. Here he had a face-to-face relationship in form, there he has it spiritually material. The devil did not have any chance getting the body of Moses, whom God knew.

Where are you in your life journey to the day you die? As the Scripture says, ***"And as it is appointed for men to die once, but after this the judgment,"*** Hebrews 9:27 NKJV. No matter who you are, God has given you a life like Moses. Although our lives may not be as dramatic and earth changing as Moses, we all have many of its characteristics. We are born, grow up, are educated, have parents, relationships, and events, which shape our lives and destiny. We have enemies, friends, and loved ones. What will come into remembrance, as you journey up to your personal Pisgah? I wonder why God allows us to have memories. Some memories are better not to dredge up, while others are a pleasure. Moses was truly fortunate to be able to go over the events of his life before he died. We are blessed by Moses' memories because he shared them with us, in the writing of the first five books of the Bible. My assumption is all the bad memories he wrote about were brought before the Lord and forgiven. He still dealt with the consequences, but in the day, he died, he could cross over the spiritual Jordan with a clean conscience. The life of Moses teaches us, walking with God is glorious. However, this travel on earth will be full of difficulties and problems and occasionally personal sins. Did not Jesus teach us this paradox? ***"These things I have spoken to you, that in Me you may have peace. In the world you will have tribulation; but be of good cheer, I have overcome the world,"*** John 16:33 NKJV.

How often have you heard at the time of death your life's memories pass before your eyes? Maybe, it would be a good thing for us (we do not have to write them down) to examine ourselves before we stand on Pisgah. It would be wise to straighten out all our sins, failures, and cowardice behavior, which happened after faith in Christ. The Holy Spirit will help us do this if we ask. One thing is certain; we will go over these memories after death. ***"For we must all appear before the judgment seat of Christ, that each one may receive the things done in the body, according to what he has done, whether good or bad,"*** 2 Corinthians 5:10 NKJV. The truth is God already knows everything you have done. He will not be going over them by trying to find out from you what you did. He will go over your life by playing it back to you play by play. I do not know if we see our life flash before us at the hours of death, but I do know we can go over them, anytime, before we die. Moses sets this example for us. The day Moses died was a day of joy for him,

Will it be for us? I guess it is our choice. If you do not know or have not accepted Christ as your Savior, like Moses did, do so now!

Reflections

1. What did you think about Moses before you read this?
2. How do you relate to Moses and his life?
3. Why was God angry with Moses?
4. Does this seem fair?
5. Does this event, show us the folly of acting upon the emotions of anger? From God's point of view, how does he see disobedience through anger?
6. What was Moses' punishment for his disobedience in anger? Can you get into the promise land by works or faith? Faith always leads to obedience.
7. Perhaps, you have acted in anger and have not made it right with God, and then you may wonder why is God not answering my prayers? Take time for self-reflection and work your anger out.
8. In Deuteronomy 3:23-26, is Moses like Adam, not taking responsibility for his actions and blaming others for it or just stating facts about why it happened?
9. Do you blame others for your situation? How about at church, are you always finger pointing or are you part of the problem which causes others to sin in anger?
10. Moses had a full life with God. His memories prove it. If you search your memories, with an open mind, you will be able to say you had a full life with God. Listing and listening to them may be a smart exercise to do.
11. Moses had family involvement from the good to the bad. How about you, how are you handling your family

interactions?

12. Read Acts 7:23-29, do you, like Moses, have a call from God and do the wrong thing by acting on the call in your own wisdom? How did that work out for you? What were the consequences in stepping out in your own wisdom and will?
13. Describe God's appearance in the burning bush, in Exodus three, with Moses. How did it change his life?
14. Describe God's appearance to you. How did it change your life?
15. Compare Moses climb up Pisgah towards his death, with your climb to your own Pisgah. Are you ready for the moment when God calls you out of this world?
16. How gross is the complaining of Israel in Numbers 20:3-5?
17. How gross is your complaining before God?
18. Apply Jude verse nine to Moses' death on Pisgah to Deuteronomy 34:5. What does this teach you?
19. How does Luke 9:28-31, teach about Moses saving faith in Christ?
20. How interesting will your death be? Will you face it with courage like Moses or in fear?
21. What does Hebrews 9:27 teach?
22. What does 2 Corinthians 5:10 teach?
23. Is it wise to straighten your life out before death or okay to do after?
24. Do you think it was a bed of roses for Moses and it should be for you? What did Jesus teach in John 16:33? How did Moses' life with God show this?
25. Write two life applications you can apply from Moses' life into your own.

26. Think this through about Moses concerning law and grace. ***"knowing that a man is not justified by the works of the law but by faith in Jesus Christ, even we have believed in Christ Jesus, that we might be justified by faith in Christ and not by the works of the law; for by the works of the law no flesh shall be justified,"*** Galatians 2:16 NKJV and ***"For whoever shall keep the whole law, and yet stumble in one point, he is guilty of all,"*** James 2:10 NKJV.
27. Read Romans chapter ten. How can you save your life and future destiny?
28. Was Moses prepared for death? Are you prepared for death?
29. Read the Apostle Peter's sermon; and make a decision to prepare to meet your maker forgiven.

But Peter, standing up with the eleven, raised his voice and said to them, "Men of Judea and all who dwell in Jerusalem, let this be known to you, and heed my words. For these are not drunk, as you suppose, since it is only the third hour of the day. But this is what was spoken by the prophet Joel: 'And it shall come to pass in the last days, says God, That I will pour out of My Spirit on all flesh; Your sons and your daughters shall prophesy, Your young men shall see visions, Your old men shall dream dreams. And on My menservants and on My maidservants I will pour out My Spirit in those days; And they shall prophesy. I will show wonders in heaven above And signs in the earth beneath: Blood and fire and vapor of smoke. The sun shall be turned into darkness, And the moon into blood, Before the coming of the great and awesome day of the Lord. And it shall come to pass That whoever calls on the name of the Lord Shall be saved.' "Men of Israel, hear these words: Jesus of Nazareth, a Man attested by God to you by miracles, wonders, and signs which God did through Him in your midst, as you yourselves also know— Him, being delivered by the determined

purpose and foreknowledge of God, you have taken by lawless hands, have crucified, and put to death; whom God raised up, having loosed the pains of death, because it was not possible that He should be held by it. For David says concerning Him: 'I foresaw the Lord always before my face, For He is at my right hand, that I may not be shaken. Therefore my heart rejoiced, and my tongue was glad; Moreover my flesh also will rest in hope. For You will not leave my soul in Hades, Nor will You allow Your Holy One to see corruption. You have made known to me the ways of life; You will make me full of joy in Your presence.' "Men and brethren, let me speak freely to you of the patriarch David, that he is both dead and buried, and his tomb is with us to this day. Therefore, being a prophet, and knowing that God had sworn with an oath to him that of the fruit of his body, according to the flesh, He would raise up the Christ to sit on his throne, he, foreseeing this, spoke concerning the resurrection of the Christ, that His soul was not left in Hades, nor did His flesh see corruption. This Jesus God has raised up, of which we are all witnesses. Therefore being exalted to the right hand of God, and having received from the Father the promise of the Holy Spirit, He poured out this which you now see and hear. "For David did not ascend into the heavens, but he says himself: 'The Lord said to my Lord, "Sit at My right hand, Till I make Your enemies Your footstool."' "Therefore let all the house of Israel know assuredly that God has made this Jesus, whom you crucified, both Lord and Christ." Now when they heard this, they were cut to the heart, and said to Peter and the rest of the apostles, "Men and brethren, what shall we do?" Then Peter said to them, "Repent, and let every one of you be baptized in the name of Jesus Christ for the remission of sins; and you shall receive the gift of the Holy Spirit. For the promise is to you and to your children, and to all who are afar off, as many as the Lord our God will call." Acts 2:14-39 NKJV.

Moses died and we all will too! Do you know Jesus?

LESSON SIX: THE SCRIPTURE CANNOT BE BROKEN THE BIBLE IS THE WORD OF GOD

THE BIBLE IS THE WORD OF GOD

Jesus answered them, "Is it not written in your law, 'I said, "You are gods"'? If He called them gods, to whom the word of God came (and the Scripture cannot be broken), do you say of Him whom the Father sanctified and sent into the world, 'You are blaspheming,' because I said, 'I am the Son of God'? John 10:34-36 NKJV

There is much to examine in John 10:34-36. However, there is one overlooked point in the words of Jesus, we must carefully examine and understand. He said, ***"The Scripture cannot be broken!"*** It is exceedingly difficult to determine which words, sentences or paragraphs are the most important of the Bible. Nevertheless, ***"The Scripture cannot be broken,"*** is the bedrock statement of The Law, Historical, Poetic, Prophetic, Gospel, Acts, Epistles, and Revelation, the books of the Bible. Jesus affirms this in the Sermon on the Mount, ***"For assuredly, I say to you, till heaven and earth pass away, one jot or one tittle will by no means pass from the law till all is fulfilled,"*** Matthew 5:18 - NKJV.

We learn from Strong's Concordance about the word, broken, the Lord spoke. The Greek word luo was used. "Strong's number G3089 "luo" (loo-o) a primary verb; to "loosen" (literally or figuratively): --break (up), destroy, dissolve, (un)loose, melt, put off." This word gives the general feeling of letting something go or destroying a thing to get it out of the way.

Let us use each definition in what Jesus said concerning the Scripture.

- The Scripture cannot be broken.
- The Scripture cannot be destroyed.

- The Scripture cannot be dissolved.
- The Scripture cannot be (un-)loosened.
- The Scripture cannot be melted.
- The Scripture cannot be put off.

When cannot is used by someone in a sentence, they are meaning it is not able to be done or accomplished. In other words, can (be able) I or you destroy or breakdown God's Word to a status of non-existence? No, we cannot do away with it. This is an impossibility! Nevertheless, we can ignore the Scriptures, criticize them, burn the Bible, outlaw it, and openly hate it. However, no matter what you, I, or society does to it; the Scripture CANNOT BE BROKEN! We can put the Scripture far away from and out of our mind, yet it remains on you, me, and the world as the weight of truth and justice. In a sense, the Scripture is a vow to us from God. In this reason, God emphasizes His word mightily. ***"The grass withers, the flower fades, But the word of our God stands forever,"*** Isaiah 40:8 NKJV. The Apostle Peter repeats this in his letter testifying by being a witness with Isaiah concerning God's Scripture. ***"Because 'All flesh is as grass, And all the glory of man as the flower of the grass. The grass withers, And its flower falls away, But the word of the Lord endures forever.' Now this is the word which by the gospel was preached to you,"*** 1 Peter 1:24-25 NKJV. The irony of it is man who tried to break the Scripture is broken and fades away, and the Word of God is still here! The Scripture cannot be broken. God emphasized how long His word will stand in Isaiah and 1Peter. They both said forever and forever the Scripture will stand and not be broken.

A great example to understand forever not broken is found in salvation. When you and I accept Christ as Savior, we are saved. Furthermore, we are given eternal life. Since the Scripture cannot be broken, our salvation will be good for all eternity. Why? Because our salvation is based on the word of God, and the Word is a living being. Jesus Christ is the Word, and He cannot be broken, destroyed, dissolved, (un)loosened, melted, or put off. ***"In the beginning was the Word, and the Word was with God, and the Word was God. And the Word became flesh and dwelt among us, and we beheld His glory, the glory as of the only begotten of the Father, full of grace and truth,"*** John 1:1,14 NKJV. ***"For the word of God is living and powerful, and sharper than any two-edged sword, piercing even to the division of soul and spirit, and of joints and marrow, and is a discerner of the thoughts and intents of the heart,"*** Hebrews 4:12 NKJV. Since the written word is bound to and united with the Living Word, the Scripture cannot be broken. It is indestructible and eternal!

Jesus was always cognizant about the Scriptures and the rule of them not being broken but fulfilled. He lived and based His existence on all which was written about Him. Why would this be so? Jesus cares about the Scripture because, He, being the One God, who is the Son of God in Trinity, (great is the mystery of God) has placed the word of God above His own name! ***"For You have magnified Your word above all Your name,"*** Psalm 138:2 NKJV. What an incredible statement. God is the supreme person of the whole universe, seen and unseen. Regarding this, He has made His word magnified above His name! What does this say about the Scripture not being able to be broken? God's word is the expression of who He is! It puts into words what we do not comprehend by sight. ***"For since the creation of the world His invisible attributes are clearly seen, being understood by the things that are made, even His eternal power and Godhead, so that they are without excuse,"*** Romans 1:20 NKJV. For some strange reason, also among Christians, people do not believe God created all. They have bitten the fruit of ignorance and believe a lie, the chance happening of the universe and the evolution of the species. However, the Scripture cannot be broken, and the seen world and universe proves, ***"In the beginning God created the heavens and the earth,"*** Genesis 1:1 NKJV. No matter how scientists try to explain away the magnificent creation power of God, the scriptural truth of real science cannot be broken. God created all!

How many years has it been since you have heard someone say, *"My word is my bond?"* Do we even comprehend the meaning of this phrase? How many people do you know who say something, keep it and do what they say no matter the cost? There are those who will shake your hand and make a deal with you. Their word and handshake are sufficient to trust. Nevertheless, there are more than enough people, maybe the majority, with whom you cannot trust their word. Joshua bore witness concerning God's word to Israel. He said, ***"Behold, this day I am going the way of all the earth. And you know in all your hearts and in all your souls that not one thing has failed of all the good things which the Lord your God spoke concerning you. All have come to pass for you; not one word of them has failed,"*** Joshua 23:14 NKJV. A question to consider, is it important for you to keep your word or for someone who has promised you something to keep their word? What do you think of the importance for God to keep His WORD? Since God is perfect, His word given will be faultless! Therefore, He values His word above His perfect name. If one word or verse of Scripture can be broken, how can we have faith and trust in all the Scriptures? They have lost their perfection. For example, If God did not create all, then every word in the Scripture is mute and imperfect, not trustworthy! We are in a society which uses the promise of keeping its word, only for political expediency. We need to follow Jesus' example and not trust man, but trust and live by every word, which proceeds out of the mouth of God. How did Jesus make His stand against the devil (yes, there is a devil) when the devil tempted Him by disparaging the Scripture? Jesus stood His ground by exalting the Scripture!

Let us read the event of the temptation with new vigor concerning the Scripture cannot be broken. ***"Now when the tempter came to Him, he said, 'If You are the Son of God, command that these stones become bread.' But He*** (Jesus) ***answered and said, "It is written, 'Man shall not live by bread***

alone, but by every word that proceeds from the mouth of God.'" Matthew 4:3-4 NKJV. It would be educational to read Matthew 4, to see the love Jesus had for the word of God and its power. Jesus could have destroyed the devil with a single word spewing extinction on him. Nevertheless, He stood on the Scriptures to resist and defeat Him. This would not be possible if the Scriptures were not one hundred percent true. Jesus had total trust in the writings of the Old Testament. He lived His life on the Law, Psalms, and Prophets. He exclaimed to an unbelieving religious bureaucracy which taught the Scriptures, but did not understand them, how the words of the Old Testament spoke of Him. ***"You search the Scriptures, for in them you think you have eternal life; and these are they which testify of Me,"*** John 5:39 NKJV. Furthermore, the writer of Hebrews, in the New Testament, expounds on this reality by quoting Psalm 40:7-8.

"Then I said, "Behold, I come; In the scroll of the book it is written of me. I delight to do Your will, O my God, And Your law is within my heart," Psalm 40:7-8 NKJV.

"Then I said, 'Behold, I have come— In the volume of the book it is written of Me— To do Your will, O God,'" Hebrews 10:7 NKJV.

The church has failed to understand the example Christ lived for us. He lived by what was written in the Scripture about Him. *The written word became the living Word* fulfilling all the Old Testament and bringing in the New Testament.

"In the beginning was the Word, and the Word was with God, and the Word was God. And the Word became flesh and dwelt among us, and we beheld His glory, the glory as of the only begotten of the Father, full of grace and truth," John 1:1,14 NKJV.

In the complexity of the Word, let us see the Word simply, in what God spoke and revealed about Himself in Scripture and creation; teaching who He was when He became flesh. ***The written became the living Word.*** The Scripture cannot be broken! The living Word was the evidence of the written word testifying the Scripture cannot be broken. In today's vernacular, it is the living proof! No wonder God places his Word above His name. It is the written proof of the living Word forever! The Word which became flesh cannot be broken. He is the evidence of truth concerning Scripture. If Scripture can be broken, He, Jesus, the Word, would not be so!

How can we comprehend what the Lord Jesus means when He says the Scriptures cannot be broken? Let us look at a Biblical example to understand this particularly important truth. In our first example God, said to the serpent an unbreakable scriptural truth.

> ***So the Lord God said to the serpent:***
> ***"Because you have done this,***
> ***You are cursed more than all cattle,***
> ***And more than every beast of the field;***
> ***On your belly you shall go,***
> ***And you shall eat dust All the days of your life.***
> ***And I will put enmity Between you and the woman,***
> ***And between your seed and her Seed;***
> ***He shall bruise your head,***
> ***And you shall bruise His heel."*** Genesis 3:14-15 NKJV

The section of these verses, we need to examine, concerns the woman and her seed. Let us apply the words of Jesus to them. The Scripture cannot be broken concerning the Seed of the woman. The command for Adam and Eve was not to eat from the tree of the knowledge of good and evil. The penalty for doing so would be death. It is obvious Adam and Eve are dead. Nevertheless, the death of God's penalty was not executed on them, the death of eternal damnation. This death was placed on the future Seed of the woman, who is Christ.

Adam and Eve, in lieu of the death of damnation, are sent

out of the Garden to await the Seed of the woman who will become the propitiation for their (and our) sin, dying the death promised to Adam and crushing the deceiving serpent. ***"So all the days that Adam lived were nine hundred and thirty years; and he died,"*** Genesis 5:5 NKJV. Adam and Eve, the Bible teaches had sons and daughters (see Genesis 5:5). At the end of Adam's life, he and Eve saw the world populated with, perhaps millions to billions of his offspring (see interesting sidebar on population growth at the end of study). Therefore, when Noah comes on the scene, he was born into a populated world. This is the point of Scripture not being broken coming into full effect. We must read the historical account to understand God keeping His word.

"Then the Lord saw that the wickedness of man was great in the earth, and that every intent of the thoughts of his heart was only evil continually. And the Lord was sorry that He had made man on the earth, and He was grieved in His heart. So the Lord said, 'I will destroy man whom I have created from the face of the earth, both man and beast, creeping thing and birds of the air, for I am sorry that I have made them,'" Genesis 6:5-7 NKJV.

What is the problem found in this verse? The problem is God saying He will wipe the earth clean of humans and animals. Why is this a problem? It is a problem because it will break the Scripture concerning the destruction of the devil and the salvation of mankind through the Seed of the woman. If all humans are destroyed there will be no Seed of a woman to come because there will be no women! We cannot question God on this decision, as a Sovereign, He has the legal authority to change His mind and negate His laws. However, I believe, God did want to keep the Scripture from being broken. Therefore, we read, ***"But Noah found grace in the eyes of the Lord,"*** Genesis 6:8 NKJV, and ***"This is the genealogy of Noah. Noah was a just man, perfect in his generations. Noah walked with God,"*** Genesis 6:9 NKJV. Many questions arise in the mind concerning this grace, unmerited favor, of God toward Noah. Although Noah was just and compared to the world around him, he walked with God, why would God who was disgusted with human behavior, save, and repopulate the world through Noah? God knows Noah has the DNA of Adam, which yields the behavior He detests. Therefore, those coming from Noah will behave in a manner of the people He will wipe out in the flood. Why, did God not do to Noah what He did to Enoch? ***"By faith Enoch was translated that he should not see death; and was not found, because God had translated him: for before his translation he had this testimony, that he pleased God,"*** Hebrews 11:5 KJV. Noah had the same testimony as Enoch, his great-great grandfather. Why did God save Noah on the ark because all of Enoch's other children died in the flood? They turned bad as well as Noah's offspring will. Let us boldly say, Noah, had a lot of positives for him to find favor in God's eyes, but He saved Noah in the ark and did not translate him to keep from breaking the Scripture concerning the Seed of the woman. We can deduce; from this example, God is serious about the Scriptures not being broken.

Let us look at a second example to understand the statement of the Lord, ***"The Scripture cannot be broken."*** This Scripture is directly concerned with the Seed of the woman, Himself, Jesus. This happened in the Garden of Gethsemane. Jesus was praying in the garden. The weight of the unfolding events of Scripture were heavy upon His heart. He said to Peter, James and John, ***"My soul is exceedingly sorrowful, even to death. Stay here and watch with Me,"*** Matthew 26:38 NKJV. With this anxiety now spoken, Jesus goes off to pray. ***"He went a little farther and fell on His face, and prayed, saying, 'O My Father, if it is possible, let this cup pass from Me; nevertheless, not as I will, but as You will,'"*** Matthew 26:39 NKJV. Three times our mighty Lord prays to the Father for another way to accomplish the coming passion, ***"Let this cup pass from Me,"*** is His cry, along with His prayerful submission to the Father if He did not let it pass. We do not find out The Father's answer to Jesus until the mob shows up to arrest Him.

"And suddenly, one of those who were with Jesus stretched out his hand and drew his sword, struck the servant of the high priest, and cut off his ear. But Jesus said to him, 'Put your sword in its place, for all who take the sword will perish by the sword. Or do you think that I cannot now pray to My Father, and He will provide Me with more than twelve legions of angels? How then could the Scriptures be fulfilled, that it must happen thus?'" (Matthew 26:51-54 NKJV)

The answer the Son received from the Father was, ***"The Scripture cannot be broken!"*** Therefore, Jesus was led as a lamb to the slaughter and He who knew no sin became sin for us and died on the cross to save us and crush the head of the serpent! No force found in heaven or on earth can stop what God has said through His word. Jesus' words ring true yesterday, today, and forever, ***"The Scripture cannot be broken!"***

We should have hearts filled with awe, gratitude, and thanksgiving because the Scripture cannot be broken. Jesus was not speaking for His own amusement when He taught, ***"Till heaven and earth pass away, one jot or one tittle will by no means pass from the law till all is fulfilled,"*** Matthew 5:18 NKJV. Nor was the Apostle Paul writing for his aggrandizement when he said, ***"For all the promises of God in Him are Yes, and in Him Amen, to the glory of God through us,"*** 2 Corinthians 1:20 NKJV. Gods proved He will not break His word, even to the ultimate of sacrificing His Son for us. Therefore, no matter what is happening to us, nor how long a time we are suffering a trial or illness, or persecution, we have the assurance the Scripture cannot be broken! ***"For whatever things were written before were written for our learning, that we through the patience and comfort of the Scriptures might have hope,"*** Romans 15:4 NKJV.

The importance of having a word, which is true,

trustworthy, reliable, and dependable is beyond measure. If there is no stumbling in word, the fruit shown is perfection. This point is damming to humans because not one human has been perfect in all their ways and words. ***"For we all stumble in many things. If anyone does not stumble in word, he is a perfect man, able also to bridle the whole body,"*** James 3:2 NKJV. However, the word of the Scripture which cannot be broken is of utmost importance because it reflects and proves the perfection of God. Only God is perfect in all His ways as is the Son of God and their word proves it. If it were not so the whole universe would be in chaos. If God could stumble in His word, He would not be perfect. How could the universe stay in order except by the perfect power of His word? If the Scripture can be broken, God's word is impotent and not able to save nor uphold all things by the power of the word. In fact, Hebrews 1:1-3, would be a foolish writing. ***"God, who at various times and in various ways spoke in time past to the fathers by the prophets, has in these last days spoken to us by His Son, whom He has appointed heir of all things, through whom also He made the worlds; who being the brightness of His glory and the express image of His person, and upholding all things by the word of His power, when He had by Himself purged our sins, sat down at the right hand of the Majesty on high."*** Nevertheless, these Scriptures are true, scientific, and salvational! When God spoke all that came into being and when Christ died on the cross, salvation was purchased for all. The Scripture cannot be broken!

How interesting are these words from the writer of Hebrews, ***"God, who at various times and in various ways spoke in time past to the fathers by the prophets, has in these last days spoken to us by His Son?"*** There have been written volumes of books concerning the Bible from the believing to the disbelieving sides. It is a book loved and revered by millions and misunderstood and hated by others. The strange problem is, there are those unbelievers who vigorously tried to disprove the Scriptures and have ended up believing in it and there are those who believed the Bible and have ended up hating it. God's Word, the Bible, does not need anyone to defend it for it can defend itself. We have already learned it will last forever. If you read it, you will learn the secret to how it came about.

THE SECRET

1. ***"All Scripture is given by inspiration of God, and is profitable for doctrine, for reproof, for correction, for instruction in righteousness, that the man of God may be complete, thoroughly equipped for every good work,"*** *2 Timothy 3:16-17.*
2. ***"Knowing this first, that no prophecy of Scripture is of any private interpretation, for prophecy never came by the will of man, but holy men of God spoke as they were moved by the Holy Spirit,"*** *2 Peter 1:20-21.*

The secret, God is the writer and author of the 66 books of the Bible. He is the one, who through His Spirit, directed and moved various people to write them and councils to rally around these sacred writings. A just man named Simeon warned Mary concerning, her Son, Jesus. ***"Then Simeon blessed them, and said to Mary His mother, 'Behold, this Child is destined for the fall and rising of many in Israel, and for a sign which will be spoken against,"*** Luke 2:34 NKJV. Jesus, the living Word, was, and still, until the end of time, is destined for the rise and fall of many. Without hesitation, we can apply this warning to the written word, the Holy Bible. This book was, is, and will be destined for the rise and fall of many. The Scripture cannot be broken. Those who love them will rise and those who hate them will fall. The Scripture, though factually, historically, and archaeologically provable, must be accepted by faith. This is a Scriptural principle which cannot be broken. ***"But without faith it is impossible to please Him, for he who comes to God must believe that He is, and that He is a rewarder of those who diligently seek Him,"*** Hebrews 11:6 NKJV. Paul warned Timothy to beware of the haters of Scripture and Jesus Christ. ***"But shun profane and idle babblings, for they will increase to more ungodliness,"*** 2 Timothy 2:15-16. The believers in Thessalonica, understood the secret of the Scriptures shared by the Apostle Paul to them, and he commended them for it. ***"For this reason we also thank God without ceasing, because when you received the word of God which you heard from us, you welcomed it not as the word of men, but as it is in truth, the word of God, which also effectively works in you who believe,"*** 1 Thessalonians 2:13 NKJV.

In summary, the truth of the Bible is dependent on the words of Jesus, ***"The Scripture cannot be broken!"*** God commands us not to lie, ***"You shall not bear false witness against your neighbor,"*** Exodus 20:16. If the Scripture can be broken, then God has borne false witness against us, making the Bible false. However, the Bible is true. The choice is yours to believe the Bible, reject the Bible, or after believing it is the Word of God, to walk away from it or continually keep it. I hope this lesson strengthens you to trust and keep the Word of God.

Reflections

1. What is your opinion or understanding of what the Bible is?
2. How do you respond to it?
3. In John 10:34-36, what is Jesus implying about the Scripture?
4. Do you agree, Jesus's statement, ***"The Scripture cannot be broken,"*** is the bedrock statement of the books of the Bible? If yes, what is your conclusive argument for it or no, what is your argument against it?
5. How does Matthew 5:18 concur with John 10:34-36?
6. According to Strong's Concordance, number G3089, give the various meanings for the Greek word luo, translated broken.
7. How do these words enhance the understanding of the Scripture not being broken?

8. How can you apply this in your life?
9. What does cannot mean?
10. Why does Jesus use such a strong word concerning the Scripture?
11. Can the Bible be broken down to a false teaching?
12. Can mankind destroy the word of God?
13. Can the Scripture be dissolved?
14. Can the word of God be loosened?
15. Can the Scriptures be melted away?
16. Can the Bible be put off?
17. How does Isaiah 40:8 and 1 Peter 1:24-25 address and defines the word of God?
18. How does this cannot be broken teaching apply to salvation?
19. How does this cannot be broken teaching apply to the Word, Jesus, see John 1:1&14?
20. How was Jesus cognizant about the Scriptures and the rule of them in His life?
21. Where has God placed His word according to Psalm 138:2?
22. Why is this an incredible statement?
23. What does creation say about God, according to Romans 1:30?
24. How does this apply to Genesis 1:1? Is this real science? Or is the theory of evolution real science?
25. If God did not create according to the Biblical account than His word is not true, and it is broken and untrustworthy. Do you concur, yes or no? Explain your reasoning.
26. Is your word trustworthy? Do people who know you believe your word is your bond? If so, why? If not, why? If you are not trustworthy, what steps can you take to become trustworthy?
27. Should every Christian's word be their bond?
28. How important is it for our God to be trustworthy and a person whose word is their bond?

29. How did Jesus resist the devil? Did the devil flee after Jesus' successful resistance?
30. What roll did the word of God play in this battle of Jesus v devil?
31. How essential is it for you to follow Jesus' example of implicitly trusting the Scripture?
32. Would you conclude; Jesus genuinely believes the Scripture cannot be broken?
33. How did Jesus live His life, His own way, or the way of the Word?
34. How does Jesus explain the Central Point and topic of the Scriptures in John 5:39?
35. How does Psalm 40:7-8 and Hebrews 10:7 concur with John 5:39?
36. If the Scripture can be broken, could we trust Psalm 40:7-8, Hebrews 10:7, and John 5:39?
37. Have you failed to see and understand how Christ lived His life according to the Scriptures?
38. If Christ lived this way, then and lives in you now, will He not live the same way in you?
39. Did God, the Son, reveal God in the flesh by exemplifying the written Word, in becoming the living Word, John 1:1&14?
40. Write a detailed account of how God kept the Scripture, ***"And I will put enmity Between you and the woman, And between your seed and her Seed; He shall bruise your head, And you shall bruise His heel,"*** from being broken.
41. How did He do this from Adam to Noah to Christ?
42. How does this speak to you?
43. What does James say about perfection in James 3:2?
44. How does this point to the perfection of God?
45. How does this teach the stability of the creation?
46. How does the perfect Word, in Hebrews 1:1-3, give evidence of the Scripture not being able to be broken? What would the consequences be if it can be broken?

47. What ways, does Hebrews 1:1-3 teach concerning the ways God spoke?
48. What is the expressed secret about how the Bible came into being according to 2 Timothy 3:16-17 and 2 Peter 3:16-17?
49. What is the modern application of Luke 2:34, concerning the Word, Jesus Christ and indirectly the Scriptures?
50. How are we to receive the Word of God according to Hebrews 11:6?
51. How did the Thessalonians receive the preaching of Paul according to 1 Thessalonians 2:13?
52. Summarize, how this lesson changes your perspective of the Bible.

God Bless You!

LESSON SEVEN: FOUNDATIONS TRUTHS FOR INDIVIDUALS, CHURCHES, AND NATIONS TO BUILD ON

TRUTHS FOR INDIVIDUALS, CHURCHES, AND NATIONS TO BUILD ON

"For no other foundation can anyone lay than that which is laid, which is Jesus Christ." 1 Corinthians 3:11 NKJV

There is no need, here, to explain the importance of foundations concerning building an edifice. There is a need to understand the ramifications of the two foundations, one concerning the philosophy throughout the world and the other God. The Lord points out the two differing foundations in the world. The one foundation is strong because it is built upon the rock of truth, Christ, and Scripture. The other foundation is weak because it is built upon a lie. The lie which states, there is no God, it is man who is a god who has evolved out of the primordial soup. The foundation of God builds a house based on truth, absolutes, and consequences for forsaking Him. The foundation of evolutionary man is based on lies, falsehoods, distorted science, and no consequences for behavior contrary to moral law. The rock is the place to build the foundation whose foundational material is God and His word. The sand is not the place to build your foundation whose material is man and his word.

Jesus taught this Scriptural truth. In fact, it is the last four verses of the Sermon on the Mount. We can look at these four verses as a spiritual place to build or a worldly place, not to build. It is an incredible summary of His whole sermon. ***"Therefore whoever hears these sayings of Mine, and does them, I will liken him to a wise man who built his house on the rock: and the rain descended, the floods came, and the winds blew and beat on that house; and it did not fall, for it was founded on the rock. 'But everyone who hears these sayings of Mine, and does not do***

them, will be like a foolish man who built his house on the sand: and the rain descended, the floods came, and the winds blew and beat on that house; and it fell. And great was its fall,'" Matthew 7:24-27 NKJV.

Examination of the Verses

Have we really examined these verses and understood the profound truth of them?

1. The first house laid its foundation on solid rock and built the house upon it.
2. The house's foundational rock was strong and stable. It seems, in this illustration, no force of nature could destroy the rock and foundation to bring a collapse of the house built on it.
3. The spiritual application of the strong rock, foundation, and house is about an individual person or any group, from churches to nations, who know; Jesus is the rock, and His sayings are the framework to live by. They build their lives on Him.
4. The forces of wind, floods, and rains are the difficulties of life and the antichrist warfare against those who live in faith.
5. The summary is, those who are wise trust in Christ and His words, the Bible, weather the storm, no matter how violent towards them and come out standing strong! The clarion call is, ***"God has said!"***
6. The second house is the exact opposite of the first. The house's foundation was built on sandy earth devoid of solid anchoring rock base.
7. The sandy earth was very weak and a foolish place to build a house. The owner did not dig deep into the earth to find stability. It seems, in this illustration, any force of nature beating against the house can cause it to collapse, no matter how big the outward

appearance is.

8. The spiritual application for the house built on sand is about individuals, groups, or nations, which scorn God and build their lives on the lie of human wisdom devoid of God and Scriptural absolutes. Their clarion call is, ***"Has God said?"***
9. The forces of wind, floods, and rains beating the sand the house is built on are the absolute truths of God, His judgements, and righteousness.
10. The summary is, over time, the foolish whose house was not built on Christ, and His word finally collapse under the pounding storms from God, destroying the lying foundation.

If you think, the foolish man illustration is silly and the Lord is exaggerating, think again. How many times did Israel collapse? What happened to Nadab and Abihu? What did the Lord do to Egypt in Exodus? Where is Babylon, Assyria, Rome, who ruled the world? What happened to the Aztec and Mayans? How big was the collapse of the Soviet Union? How many people were saved with Noah? How sorrowful is the collapsing of the British Empire? How horrible it is watching the falling of America? How fearful it is watching the Lord remove the lampstand from once powerful denominations! How many individuals, who seemed invincible, have fallen, and collapsed? Where are Sodom and Gommorrah? These all suffered the storm because they moved to sandy soil and built themselves on lies.

You may be wondering, why it takes a long time before God storms on the house or empires built on sand? What did God tell Abraham about getting the land? Listen to the conversation, ***"Now as for you, you shall go to your fathers in peace; you shall be buried at a good old age. But in the fourth generation they shall return here, for the iniquity of the Amorites is not yet complete,"*** Genesis 15:15-16 NKJV. God, who is merciful, gives people and nations the time to repent or the time to complete their evil to its fullest! However, be assured, sooner or later, the foolish house will fall.

"For the wrath of God is revealed from heaven against all ungodliness and unrighteousness of men, who suppress the truth in unrighteousness, because what may be known of God is manifest in them, for God has shown it to them. For since the creation of the world His invisible attributes are clearly seen, being understood by the things that are made, even His eternal power and Godhead, so that they are without excuse, because, although they knew God, they did not glorify Him as God, nor were thankful, but became futile in their thoughts, and their foolish hearts were darkened. Professing to be wise, they became fools, and changed the glory of the incorruptible God into an image made like corruptible man—and birds and four-footed animals and creeping things," Romans 1:18-23 NKJV.

Do you see the simple demonic phrase, *"Has God said,"* explained in the above quote? Also, do you understand the foundation explained here, about the foolish man who did not acknowledge Christ and His words, but denies the existence of God? Their foundation is a lie. The evolutionary man was not created but is here by chance (they became fools). Since there is no God, there are no absolutes. Since there are no absolutes, there is no moral authority, there are no rights or wrongs (and changed the glory of the incorruptible God for corruptible behaviors and realities). The earth and its creatures are to be worshiped for we evolved from and through them. Laws, rules, regulations, and moral behaviors are puritanical. Only certain life is valuable. The wise foundation built on God created the heavens and the earth and made us in his image is firm. Since there is a God, He is accountable to. He Has moral absolutes, which cannot be denied. There are consequences for breaking His authority and commands. Therefore, laws, rules, regulations, and moral behaviors are imperative. Since God is, all life is important to Him. There is no confusion over when life begins, or what sex a person may be, or who may marry who. These all have absolutes in God's creation. The foolish foundation questions these absolutes and breaks them. Sooner or later, this foolishness will collapse on itself, and It will collapse on you, your city, your church, or your country. Jesus said so, and history proves it. The wise foundation built on Christ leads to truth, justice, order, liberty, life, and happiness. The foolish foundation brings in lies, injustice chaos, bondage, corruption, sorrow, and death.

Moses (who existed and did write the Pentateuch, contrary to modern-day scholarship, which denies him, and is foolish) summarizes the above paragraph and the Lord's statement of the wise and foolish builders beautifully. ***"Behold, I set before you today a blessing and a curse: the blessing, if you obey the commandments of the Lord your God which I command you today; and the curse, if you do not obey the commandments of the Lord your God, but turn aside from the way which I command you today, to go after other gods which you have not known,"*** Deuteronomy 11:26-28 NKJV.

The Psalmist teaches there will be a day of reckoning for the foolish.

"The Lord brings the counsel of the nations to nothing; He makes the plans of the peoples of no effect. The counsel of the Lord stands forever, The plans of His heart to all generations" Psalm 33:10-11 NKJV.

As the Lord said, the rain will fall, the floods will come, and the winds will blow on all houses. When He sends His storms, on the foolish house, it will collapse and fall.

Modern Dilemma

(To the revisionist, secular and religious, you are the fool of Jesus' teaching. Therefore, in this section we will talk with truth in history and ignore you. The revisionists are bringing us into the storms of God.)

"Blessed is the nation whose God is the Lord,

The people He has chosen as His own inheritance,"

Psalm 33:12 NKJV.

The Declaration of Independence gives us the key to the foundation of the American building.

"We hold these Truths to be self-evident, that all Men are created equal, that they are endowed by their Creator with certain unalienable Rights, that among these are Life, Liberty, and the Pursuit of Happiness"

True American history teaches this Creator is the God of the Bible. Independence was founded on this rock. Furthermore, (if we remember our history lessons) in the establishment of a governing Constitution, James Madison declared the three branches of government were designed according to Isaiah 33.

http://americanpatriotseries.blogspot.com/2011/07/faith-of-our-fathers.html

(Go there for more proofs.)

"For the Lord is our Judge, The Lord is our Lawgiver, The Lord is our King; He will save us," Isaiah 33:22.

Furthermore, our history lessons teach the Constitution is full of Biblical precepts for governing. See,

https://nccs.net/blogs/articles/parallel-concepts-between-the-u-s-constitution-the-bible

To the dismay of the revisionist, no-God moving away from the Constitution and Bible crowd, cancel culture, the document called the Constitution is founded on the rock. With all your storms, you throw against it; you cannot cause it to collapse. The Constitution and Declaration of Independence are always in your way. Therefore, you want to do away with them. You may disparage them, but woe to your foundation. This is your dilemma.

Who can forget the history lessons we learned in school

(when it was taught truthfully), which taught us what Karl Marx believed, "Religion is the opiate of the people?" How happy was the socialist and communist Marx to get his God-void dogma foundation from Charles Darwin's "On the Origin of Species?" He was extremely merry. This gave him the impetus to deny creational-scientific truths for human based assumptions. This, no-God, philosophy gave birth to the Communist revolution. Merrily this perverse philosophy became the death, downfall, and enslavement of hundreds of millions of humans made in the image of God. Instead of promised liberty and financial provision, it brought about the enslavement of souls to tyrannical elite government and dictators who became demigods. The tools of their change are lies, fear, censorship, degradation of human worth, perversions, idolatry, sorcery, hatred, contentions, jealousies, wrath, theft, and murder. This socialist-communist way of government is incompatible with God ordained government. Those who practice such things must destroy and replace any person, place, morals, or government, which is in their way to political power and control. Marxism is demonic, and, built on the foolish thoughts of man. (This is a summary of the foolish system, the beast, which is marching around the globe and will become subject to God's wrath. You need to investigate the depth of it yourself.) How important is it for a society to have its foundation on the Rock, holding fast to it with virtue? This type of people can withstand the storm from the ungodly. This is our dilemma! (This paragraph is written from my historical perspective from the 1950s to today.)

Although Jesus said those who do not build their lives on Him are foolish, He acknowledges these fools have power. He said this to their stupid faces when they came to arrest Him. ***"Then Jesus said to the chief priests, captains of the temple, and the elders who had come to Him, 'Have you come out, as against a robber, with swords and clubs? When I was with you daily in the temple, you did not try to seize Me. But this is your hour, and***

the power of darkness,'" Luke 22:52-53 NKJV. Christians should not be deceived concerning the power and cunningness of the foolish builders. Sometimes, the house of fools seems to be an all-powerful giant (This is so if we take our eyes off Jesus). This happened to Israel on the report and fear of the ten spies, who took their eyes off God. They said the giants of the promised land were too mighty for them to defeat. We need to go back to Egypt, was their cry. Only Joshua and Caleb kept their eyes on Yahweh and said the giants were just a nuisance. Through God, they will fall! They knew they were wise men whose building was on the rock, and the giants were foolish men whose building was on sand. The giants must collapse before them (Read Numbers 13-14 for the account).

Listen to the difference between faithful wise people and faithless fools.

The Faithful

"Then Caleb quieted the people before Moses, and said, 'Let us go up at once and take possession, for we are well able to overcome it,'" Numbers 13:30 NKJV.

The Unfaithful

"But the men who had gone up with him said, 'We are not able to go up against the people, for they are stronger than we.' And they gave the children of Israel a bad report of the land which they had spied out, saying, 'The land through which we have gone as spies is a land that devours its inhabitants, and all the people whom we saw in it are men of great stature. There we saw the giants (the descendants of Anak came from the giants); and we were like grasshoppers in our own sight, and so we were in their sight,'" Numbers 13:31-33 NKJV.

The results of this, back and forth battle were dramatic. All the generation of delivered Israelites, except two, did not have faith in the Rock and His promises, they collapsed and fell across the desert. Only the two who believed in the Rock and built their lives on His words entered the promise land. Their house did not collapse nor fall before the fear of giants.

The Dilemma in Action: How are we moving to a foolish foundation?

This section, again, will be troubling and quarrelsome to the foolish of Matthew 7:26, both in the church and in secular American society. Nevertheless, through summary, let us examine a problem which we are living through, the problem of a foundation switch.

The work of the foolish, we call them leftist, progressives, liberals, Democrats, Republicans, socialist, Marxist, communist, globalists, climatologists, or any religion or system not founded in and on Christ, is to belittle, denigrate, question, cast aspersions and doubts on God and His Word, the Holy Bible. By destroying trust in God and proper interpretation of His Word, they can move us and our building from the rock to their sand. In the case of America, since they cannot destroy it, they seek to move us away from it to humanistic, socialistic, Godless communism. In the case of the Church, since the gates of hell cannot prevail against it, they seek to undermine and destroy faith in the interpretation of the Word, with always pronouncing, ***"Has God Said."*** Therefore, moving us away from the Rock, ***"Jesus said to him, 'I am the way, the truth, and the life. No one comes to the Father except through Me,'"*** John 14:6 NKJV, to all roads lead to God. God's way is exclusively narrow while the foolish way is extremely broad and wide. In the end only the Rock building of God will stand, while the other will totally collapse. ***"Then Death and Hades were cast into the lake of fire. This is the second death. And anyone not found written in the Book of Life was cast into the lake of fire,"*** Revelation 20:14-15 NKJV.

The Constitution is good. However, the reality is, it always governed sinful men. (What is written here is a summary, it would take a fearless scholar to unravel the works of the foolish in our time.) Nevertheless, working through sin the Constitution has been a bulwark against evil. Therefore, the Constitution founded on the Rock cannot fall. The foolish know this, which led to evil or foolish people trying and just about succeeding in moving America away from its foundation, because this is the only way to change the nation. As former President Obama said, he wanted to, "Fundamentally change America." The foolish started their assault on the Constitution, bit by bit, court decision by court decision, legislation by legislation, immorality by immorality, lie upon lies, evil on evil, perversion upon perversion ... the rain, floods, and winds of darkness. These, unconstitutionally, took control of money through the unconstitutional Federal Reserve Bank. They instituted welfare through various legislative actions and the Supreme Court, under false constitutional premises, ushered in abortion, pornography, abolishment of traditional marriage. Not only did they usher in immorality they also had the nerve to kick God out of American civilization. They outlawed prayer and Bible from all things public. The educational system under siege and takeover since the signing of the Humanist Manifesto, has almost completely fallen into the hands of the foolish and their Godless foundation. The foolish have stepped-up their building through raw power and intimidation and violence causing cities to crumble and harsh censorship and canceling culture. These things have also been directed at the church, and much of the church has moved away from its stormproof Rock. Many in church do not believe the Bible but trust in philosophies of the world, from militant feminism, humanism, critical racist theory, and perversions. The Constitution still stands, but we do not govern on it anymore. The Bible still stands, but we do not believe it anymore. We have exchanged rock for sand. The giants of the sand buildings are enormous, octopus-creatures who have their tentacles involved in every aspect of American life (also, in most of the nations of the world, if not all) and institutions. It seems immovable, unbeatable, and super powerful. Nevertheless, it is a building which is erected on sand. There is a big difference between an awakening (from God) and wokeness (from man). Their wisdom seems superb, yet not in the eyes of God, ***"For it is written: 'I will destroy the wisdom of the wise, And bring to nothing the understanding of the prudent,'"*** 1 Corinthians 1:19 NKJV. The understanding knows sooner or later, either separately or with the whole nation, the foolish, in church and out of church, will fall, they have a Godless foundation.

LESSONS TO LEARN

There are many lessons we can learn from the Lord's words in Matthew 7:24-27.

- The Lord breaks down belief systems (house) into two simple categories. The first one is the truth, which is, the thought set of the mind stayed on Christ and His words. The second system (house) is false, which is the antichrist mindset of the world. Each human has the choice of which system they will build their lives, culture, nation, and church on.
- Both "houses" will experience great storms. The house on the Rock will experience the wrath of man (the foolish). As Jesus said, ***"And from the days of John the Baptist until now the kingdom of heaven suffers violence, and the violent take it by force,"*** Matthew 11:12 NKJV. However, Jesus promised us, though, we might be beaten, battered, or bruised by the rain, floods, and wind we would not fall or collapse!
- Only people who accept Christ and follow His teachings are considered wise and receive His promise of standing tall when all storms are quelled.
- People outside of Christ who spurn Him, and His words are considered by Him as fools.
- The fool has or is building their lives foundation on a lie, which says, there is no God, and for the apostate church, has God said!
- Contrary to popular belief, storms of various types will hit the foolish. The rain of truth, the floods of judgement, and the winds of righteousness from the throne of God will happen. The result will be the

complete fall and collapse of the foolish.

- A major problem with Christians, when they are confronted with the house built on sand by the foolish, are they forget their foundation is Almighty God, and they fear the building of fools whose foundation is not God.
- The foolish building might be strong, but its base is sand, and its foundation is a lie! In simple words, we see the giants, feel, and experience their storms and forget our God is the almighty God, and our truth is absolute!
- We must remember the foolish, from Adam and Eve to today, have built or are building their houses on sand. Today's foolish builders will not and have not learned from the historical evidence, all who choose the lie have fallen and great was their fall.
- The foolish are wise in their own eyes, and they will storm against anyone or anything opposing them. However, the wise keep their eyes on Christ, stand on the infallible truths of His Word, endure and in the end watch the fall of the fool.
- A sorrowful truth for the wise to remember, we once were fools also. Only the grace of God made us wise unto salvation. Therefore, we must be alert and not be sucked down again into sinking sand.
- Let us not be deceived, the foolish will storm against the wise in Christ. The wise in Christ, through the weapons of our warfare in God, must storm upon the foolish and our aim must be their sandy soil foundation. We preach Christ crucified, the wisdom of God and this is a mighty truth to aim at the unbeliever's foolish foundation.
- Buildings have a facade which enables it to be

identified. Most people in New York know the Empire State Building by sight. They may not know what is transpiring on the inside, but they know there is an activity in it. The spiritual principle is the same with the wise man's building and the foolish man's building. Each building, the wise and foolish, can be seen by the other. The activity inside each is understood and seen by the other. However, the wise does not understand the secret motives of the foolish nor does the foolish comprehend the motives of the wise. Nevertheless, Jesus said at the end of the storms of rain, floods, and winds, the wise and foolish motives will be revealed. ***"For there is nothing hidden which will not be revealed, nor has anything been kept secret but that it should come to light. If anyone has ears to hear, let him hear,"*** Mark 4:22-23 NKJV. The funny truths about storms are they are cleansing, revealing, and sometimes destructive.

- Finally, the wise need to understand, today in America, the foolish are storming against God, the Constitution, and the Church. This storm has been raining, flooding, and blowing for years. The question is, when the storm moves into calm, will the wise still worship their God, have the Constitution, and be the body of Christ? God knows the answer, soon we will know it also! We are going to learn how deep we are in Christ.

Therefore, let the words of Psalm One encourage and strengthen our understanding of Matthew 7:24-27.

"Blessed is the man Who walks not in the counsel of the ungodly, Nor stands in the path of sinners, Nor sits in the seat of the scornful; But his delight is in the law of the Lord, And in His law he meditates day and night. He shall be like a tree Planted by the rivers of water, That brings forth its fruit in its season, Whose leaf also shall not wither; And whatever he does shall

prosper. The ungodly are not so, But are like the chaff which the wind drives away. Therefore the ungodly shall not stand in the judgment, Nor sinners in the congregation of the righteous. For the Lord knows the way of the righteous, But the way of the ungodly shall perish."

Furthermore, as children of the King of Kings, in whom we are already sitting in the heavenly places, we declare, "The foolish workers against the Kingdom of Heaven shall and will fall and collapse."

Joshua 24:14-24 NKJV

"Now therefore, fear the Lord, serve Him in sincerity and in truth, and put away the gods which your fathers served on the other side of the River and in Egypt. Serve the Lord! And if it seems evil to you to serve the Lord, choose for yourselves this day whom you will serve, whether the gods which your fathers served that were on the other side of the River, or the gods of the Amorites, in whose land you dwell. But as for me and my house, we will serve the Lord." So the people answered and said: "Far be it from us that we should forsake the Lord to serve other gods; for the Lord our God is He who brought us and our fathers up out of the land of Egypt, from the house of bondage, who did those great signs in our sight, and preserved us in all the way that we went and among all the people through whom we passed. And the Lord drove out from before us all the people, including the Amorites who dwelt in the land. We also will serve the Lord, for He is our God." But Joshua said to the people, "You cannot serve the Lord, for He is a holy God. He is a jealous God; He will not forgive your transgressions nor your sins. If you forsake the Lord and serve foreign gods, then He will turn and do you harm and consume you, after He has done you good." And the people said to Joshua, "No, but we will serve the Lord!" So

Joshua said to the people, "You are witnesses against yourselves that you have chosen the Lord for yourselves, to serve Him." And they said, "We are witnesses!" "Now therefore," he said, "put away the foreign gods which are among you, and incline your heart to the Lord God of Israel." And the people said to Joshua, "The Lord our God we will serve, and His voice we will obey!"

Make the Apostles' Creed your Christian foundation.

This should be memorized and spoken once a day.

I believe in God, the Father almighty, creator of heaven and earth.

I believe in Jesus Christ, God's only Son, our Lord, who was conceived by the Holy Spirit, born of the Virgin Mary, suffered under Pontius Pilate, was crucified, died, and was buried; He descended to the dead.

On the third day He rose again; He ascended into heaven, He is seated at the right hand of the Father, and He will come to judge the living and the dead.

I believe in the Holy Spirit, the holy catholic Church, the communion of saints, the forgiveness of sins, the resurrection of the body, and life everlasting. Amen.

(Note: catholic means the one universal-ekklesia-church of Jesus Christ, it is not a denomination.)

"And they continued steadfastly in the apostles' doctrine and fellowship, in the breaking of bread, and in prayers," Acts 2:42.

"If the foundations are destroyed, What can the righteous do?" (Psalm 11:3)

"They do not know, nor do they understand; They walk about in

darkness; All the foundations of the earth are unstable," Psalm 82:5.

"Righteousness and justice are the foundation of Your throne," Psalm 89:14.

"Behold, I lay in Zion a stone for a foundation, A tried stone, a precious cornerstone, a sure foundation; Whoever believes will not act hastily," Isaiah 28:16.

"When the enemy comes in like a flood, The Spirit of the Lord will lift up a standard against him," Isaiah 59:19.

Reflections

1) What is a foundation?
2) Are foundations only important for physical edifices or also for human belief systems?
3) What foundation is your life based on?
4) Breakdown and explain the Lord's statement in Matthew 7:24-27.
    - A. Why does Jesus want us to hear what He is saying?
    - B. What is the importance of doing what He says?
    - C. What does He liken a person who obeys Him to?
    - D. What does a wise man build His house on?
    - E. Are the sayings of Jesus, bedrock for our beliefs and morals?

F. What does He mean for the rain to descend?

G. What does He mean for the floods to come?

H. What does He mean by the winds blowing?

I. What does He mean by the beating on the house by these elements of nature?

J. What does He mean by the storms not prevailing on the house because it was founded on the rock?

K. What does Jesus call the person who hears His sayings but ignores them?

L. Is Jesus being mean, calling someone a fool?

M. Where did the fool build his house?

N. What does Jesus say happened to this house after the rains, floods, and winds beat on it?

O. What does a great fall mean?

5) Is Jesus really talking about building edifices or mindsets (attitudes, beliefs, moralities, mentalities)?

6) Do you agree with these explanations of Matthew 7:24-27? If so, why? If not, why not?

A. The first house laid its foundation on solid rock and built the house upon it.

B. The house's foundational rock was strong and stable. It seems, in this illustration, no force of nature could destroy the rock and foundation to bring a collapse of the house built on it.

C. The spiritual application of the strong rock, foundation, and house is about an individual person or any group, from churches to nations, who know; Jesus is the rock, and His sayings are the framework to live by. They build their lives on Him.

D. The forces of wind, floods, and rains are the difficulties of life and the antichrist warfare against those who live in faith.

E. The summary is, those who are wise trust in Christ and His words, the Bible, weather the storm, no matter how violent towards them and come out standing strong! The clarion call is, ***"God has said!"***

F. The second house is the exact opposite of the first. The house's foundation was built on sandy earth devoid of solid anchoring rock base.

G. The sandy earth was very weak and a foolish place to build a house. The owner did not dig deep into the earth to find stability. It seems, in this illustration, any force of nature beating against the house can cause it to collapse, no matter how big the outward appearance is.

H. The spiritual application for the house built on sand is about individuals, groups, or nations, which scorn God and build their lives on the lie of human wisdom devoid of God and Scriptural absolutes. Their clarion call is, ***"Has God said?"***

I. The forces of wind, floods, and rains beating the sand the house is built on are the absolute truths of God, His judgements, and righteousness.

J. The summary is, over time, the foolish whose house was not built on Christ, and His word finally collapse under the pounding storms from God, destroying the lying foundation.

7) Do you think Jesus' illustration is silly?

8) What is He trying to tell us to build on?

9) Do a little research and answer these questions?

A. How many times did Israel collapse when it strayed from the Law?

B. What happened to Nadab and Abihu?

C. What did the Lord do to Egypt in Exodus? How did He rain, flood, and windstorm on the Egyptians foundational beliefs?

D. What happened to Babylon, Assyria, Rome, and other historical world powers, who were idolatrous in nature?

E. Where are the Aztec and Mayan civilizations?

F. How many people were saved in Noah's day?

G. How big was the collapse of the Soviet Union?

H. How are the British Empire and United States of America collapsing?

I. What happen to Sodom and Gommorrah?

J. What is happening to once powerful denominations?

10) Why does it take God such a long time to collapse evil?

11) In Genesis 15: 15-16, how did God explain His judgements to Abraham?

12) What does it mean to repent of your or a nations' house built on an anti- Biblical foundation?

13) Have you really understood the hard truths of Romans 1:18-23?

A) What is revealed about the wrath of God?

B) Describe the foundation of ungodliness, unrighteousness, and falsehoods.

C) What does creation teach us? What is the false conclusion of evolution?

D) Why are we all without excuse?

E) Where do people become futile?

F) What happens to foolish hearts?

G) How does professing to be wise, they became fools agree with Jesus' teaching of the foolish builder?

H) What does a fool turn the image of God into?

I) How do you see this in today's world?

14) Do you understand the demonic phrase, ***"Has God said,"*** Genesis 3:1?

15) How has this question destroyed foundations, which should be built on a rock?

16) Describe the foundation of evolutionary societies.

17) Describe the foundation of societies build on Genesis 1:1.

18) What is your foundation? What is your country's foundation? There is no gray area concerning the two foundations.

19) When the storms of judgements rain down and flood and blow across society, which one will stand or collapse, the evolution-based or creation-based society?

20) Why are laws, rules, regulations, and moral behavior imperative?

21) How do behavioral actions declare a person or a nation's foundational principles?

22) How does Deuteronomy 11:26-28, describe or give the foundation for Matthew 7:24-27?

23) What does Psalm 33:10 teach concerning the fool who built the house on the sand?

24) How does Psalm 33:12 describe a happy nation?

25) How does these words, in The Declaration of Independence, ***"We hold these Truths to be self-evident, that all Men are created equal, that they are endowed by their Creator with certain unalienable Rights, that among these are Life, Liberty, and the Pursuit of Happiness,"*** agree with Psalm 33:12 and Matthew 7:24-27?

26) How does Isaiah 33:22 fit into the foundation of American government?

27) Is this standing true today, or being eroded away?

28) How has Marxism attacked the God-foundation of countries and what are its results? Is this a good foundation or foolish?

29) Do a history search and count the number of political murders under, Lenin, Stalin, Mao, and the rest of these godless foundational countries?

30) How does this prove Jesus' acknowledgement of their corrupt power, according to Luke 22:52-53?

31) A problem with Christians is their ability to be deceived because of a lack of Biblical knowledge. Can you name areas in Christianity where the power and cunningness of the foolish builders have taken over and replaced Biblical doctrines?

32) How did giants in the promised land cause Israel to stumble?

33) How many spies were sent to the promised land (read Numbers 13)?

34) What happened when the spies came back to camp with their report?

35) What evidence of a God-foundation did Joshua and Caleb exhibit?

36) What evidence of a no-God-foundation did the other ten spies exhibit?

37) According to Matthew 7:24-27, what types of people

were Joshua and Caleb? What was their situation at the end of forty years in the wilderness? Did they collapse and fall or stand and prosper?

38) According to Matthew 7:24-27, what types of people were the ten bad reporter people? What was their situation at the end of forty years in the wilderness? Did they collapse and fall or stand and prosper?

39) According to Matthew 7:24-27, what types of people were all those who came out of Egypt with Moses after the report of the ten spies? What was their situation at the end of forty years in the wilderness? Did they collapse and fall or stand and prosper?

40) According to the section, The Dilemma in Action, how are we in our modern society moving to a foolish foundation?

41) Why is the Bible under constant attack and doubt?

42) What happens (like the nation of Israel) to people when faith in God is destroyed?

43) Can the Word of God be destroyed? Therefore, what strategy is used by evil to move people away from a sure foundation to sandy soil?

44) What is the narrow way of God, which leads to a building on the rock?

45) What is the broad way of the foolish, which leads to a building on sandy soil?

46) In the end, according to Revelation 20:14-15, which of the two will still be standing strong?

47) In the section, The Constitution is good, without looking at the country through political eyes but through Biblical eyes, what is your conclusions concerning those I listed on the moving away of the country from its Christian foundation to a new humanistic-evolution foundation?

48) What is the current foundation of America, is it built on the sayings of Jesus anymore or the words of men?

49) According to Matthew 7:24-27, what will be the end of America if it does not return to the sayings of Jesus? What will be the end of that church which has also left the sayings of Jesus?

50) According to 1 Corinthians 3:11, what is the foundation of foundations?

51) What does God declare He will do to all other foundations in 1 Corinthians 1:19?

52) Are you a wise person or foolish?

53) In the Lessons section, go over each lesson and in your own words, summarize each lesson. Try to see, which apply to you. What needs strengthening in your life? What is strong in your life concerning the sayings of Jesus? What is weak in your life concerning the sayings of Jesus?

54) What does Psalm 1 teach about following the sayings of Jesus?

55) What does Joshua say for us to do in Joshua 24:14-24?

56) How can the Apostles' Creed strengthen our Christian building?

57) What does Acts 2:42 teach?

58) What does Psalm 11:3 teach?

59) What does Psalm 82:5 teach?

60) What does Psalm 89:14 teach?

61) What does Isaiah 28:16 teach?

62) What does Isaiah 59:19 teach?

63) Have you ever considered the importance of the Scriptural foundation?

In summary, God wants us to build our life on His Son, the sure foundation! If you or I have been lukewarm concerning this, we need to make a life correction.

God Bless You!

LESSON EIGHT: PRIDE THE SIN WHICH PRECEDES A FALL

PRIDE

The Sin Which Precedes a Fall

Pride goes before destruction,
And a haughty spirit before a fall.
Better to be of a humble spirit with the lowly,
Than to divide the spoil with the proud.
Proverbs 16:18-19 NKJV

Is pride a curse or blessing, possibly both? On the one hand, there is the haughtiness of pride based in one's perception of self as superior to others. On the other hand, there is the pride associated with humility in satisfaction of personal accomplishments. The haughty pride is spoken about in this manner by those affected by it, "Who the hell, does he/she think they are?" Whereas the person who is industrious and just has the satisfaction of a job well done is spoken in this manner, "What a fine person he/she is!"

Two admonishments for us:

1. Concerning, the pride of satisfaction, ***"But let each one examine his own work, and then he will have rejoicing in himself alone, and not in another. For each one shall bear his own load,"*** Galatians 6:4-5 NKJV.
2. Concerning, the pride of arrogance, ***"For if anyone thinks himself to be something, when he is nothing, he deceives himself,"*** Galatians 6:3 NKJV.

An important point to consider here, Paul was admonishing Christians about the proper use of pride. A prideful Christian is more intolerable to bear than an unregenerate lordly person. A good example to follow is John the Baptist. He had a special calling in his life. He was secure in himself and had a healthy pride in his call.

"Now this is the testimony of John, when the Jews sent priests and Levites from Jerusalem to ask him, 'Who are you?' He confessed, and did not deny, but confessed, 'I am not the Christ.' And they asked him, 'What then? Are you Elijah?' He said, 'I am not.' 'Are you the Prophet?' And he answered, 'No.' Then they said to him, 'Who are you, that we may give an answer to those who sent us? What do you say about yourself?' He said: 'I am The voice of one crying in the wilderness: Make straight the way of the Lord,' as the prophet Isaiah said." John 1:19-23 NKJV

The Baptist did not consider himself something other than what he was. He was not roaming the desert tooting his own horn, *"Look at me; I am special!"* When asked he humbly stated who he was and his mission. His mission was to exalt the name of the Savior, not his own. When his disciples complained, people were following Jesus and not John, a pride of satisfaction was his answer. ***"He must increase, but I must decrease,"*** John 3:30 NKJV.

The voice crying in the wilderness was not shining a light of pride on himself. He is an example for us to follow today. Although John the Baptist was famous, he did not let fame get to his head. He obeyed God, exalted the Christ, and spoke out against sin and evil. Nevertheless, his death was not a death of the pride which goes before destruction, but a suffering of death for the sake of righteousness.

Let us look at the damaging effects caused by the spiritual pride of arrogance. This pride was running amok in the church at Corinth.

Let us briefly look at two examples.

The First Example, of The Arrogance of Pride

"Now I say this, that each of you says, 'I am of Paul,' or 'I am of Apollos,' or 'I am of Cephas,' or 'I am of Christ.' Is Christ divided? Was Paul crucified for you? Or were you baptized in the name of

Paul?" (1 Corinthians 1:12-13 NKJV)

This admonishment of Paul towards the Corinthians is pointed towards their spiritual pride of arrogance in the attitude of superiority. This church divided itself into factions. The pride of superiority caused this. One clique said, ***"I am of Paul!"*** The implication of this is simple. The followers of Paul were strutting around the other believers claiming their Christianity was superior to their inferior Christianity. They were haughty and divisive. Their nostrils were flared in distaste towards those who were not of their group. In fact, they were looking down their noses towards them. There were three more fractious groups, which were exhibiting their pride of superiority and behaving as bad as the followers of Paul. The pride of superiority is a gross and heinous sin. This sin has its roots in the devil himself. Lucifer thought he was something special, even more special than God. His pride knew no limits, and it was his downfall and impending destruction.

"How you are fallen from heaven, O Lucifer, son of the morning! How you are cut down to the ground," Isaiah 14:12 NKJV.

"The devil, who deceived them, was cast into the lake of fire and brimstone where the beast and the false prophet are. And they will be tormented day and night forever and ever," Revelation 20:10 NKJV.

The boastful arrogant pride of the fractious Corinthians, those who think they are superior because they are of Paul or Apollos, or Cephas, or using Christ as a weapon of pride, are playing with a fall and destruction. Paul warned the Galatians how this destruction would come about. He said, ***"But if you bite and devour one another, beware lest you be consumed by one another!"*** (Galatians 5:15 NKJV) The arrogance of haughty pride in Corinth was about to become a self-consuming destruction if they did not repent. This is much like our denominationalism today.

The Second Example, of The Arrogance of Pride

In the Corinthian church, the arrogance of pride and its haughtiness knew no limits. The Corinthians did not only think who they were, but they were proud and strutting around rejoicing over a distasteful sin. The Apostle Paul was disgusted over it. Listen to what he said about this.

"It is actually reported that there is sexual immorality among you, and such sexual immorality as is not even named among the Gentiles—that a man has his father's wife! And you are puffed up, and have not rather mourned, that he who has done this deed might be taken away from among you," 1 Corinthians 5:1-2 NKJV.

You may think this is not true, the church being "puffed up" over sexual immorality is stupid. Nevertheless, it was genuine in Corinth, as it is real today. How many denominations of our time have fallen into the arrogance of pride over sexual immorality? The sad truth is many have gone after the sin of sexual immorality. They are ordaining the practice of this as something wholesome and consecrated by God. This is the arrogance of pride to the nth degree. It is frightening to think of the destruction and fall of the church to come if there is no repentance.

The Danger to Be Prideful Can Come Upon You

Individually speaking, we must all be aware, on guard, and watching, we do not let the arrogance of pride into our lives. This lesson is vividly taught in the Book of Esther. We read about a certain person, Haman, the son of Hammedatha the Agagite. King Ahasuerus promoted Haman to be his highest official. In our language, he made him the top dog. As his name indicates, Haman was a descendant of Agag, the king of the Amalekites[1]. With this pedigree we can ascertain, Haman was a proud person. Although he was a captive subject, he rose to a great prominence in the land of his captivity. The question is, how did Haman's pride handle this promotion? Did he let his pride reign in haughtiness by agreeing with it saying, I am a superior person or by humility of satisfaction; he was chosen to the position?

The Destruction Because of Pride

Let us allow Haman to answer the question himself. King Ahasuerus wanted to honor Mordecai for saving his life. Therefore, he asked Haman what should be done to honor a person whom the king delights in. Listen to what Haman thinks about himself.

"The king's servants said to him, 'Haman is there, standing in the court.' And the king said, 'Let him come in.' So Haman came in, and the king asked him, 'What shall be done for the man whom the king delights to honor?' Now Haman thought in his heart, 'Whom would the king delight to honor more than me?'" (Esther 6:5-6 NKJV)

Unfortunately, Haman thought he was by far, more superior than anyone else. His pride knew no humility. He was a very haughty person.

We are studying Proverbs 16:18-19.

"Pride goes before destruction,
And a haughty spirit before a fall.
Better to be of a humble spirit with the lowly,
Than to divide the spoil with the proud."

Many of us wonder if this Proverb is true. We see many prideful haughty people strutting around seeming to be blessed and growing with power. We wonder, where is their destruction? Where is their fall? The answer to these questions can be found in the life of Haman.

Do you know prideful people have an insatiable desire for praise and acknowledgement of their grandeur from the people around them? Secondly, do you not know, when a prideful person does not receive the worship and adulation from others, they will do everything in their power to destroy those who do not worship them? Haman had this problem. He needed the adoration of others. This provided proof to him and his opinion of self; he was someone incredibly special. Now the king commanded everyone to bow and give Haman homage. Esther chapter three verse two confirms this.

"And all the king's servants who were within the king's gate bowed and paid homage to Haman, for so the king had commanded concerning him."

Haman ate up this praise! He thought he deserved it. His pride was being fed and strengthened. How do we know this? We understand this, by the way; he behaved when one man refused to bend the knee to him. Esther 3:2 confirms this also, ***"But Mordecai would not bow or pay homage."***

When Haman found out about Mordecai the Jew not paying him homage, he was filled with rage! His pride was called into question, how dare anyone would do this to him.

"When Haman saw that Mordecai did not bow or pay him homage, Haman was filled with wrath," Esther 3:5 NKJV.

A prideful person cannot deal with such a thing. They will do everything to correct this situation even to the destruction of those who do not pay homage to them. Look how Haman reacted.

"But he disdained to lay hands on Mordecai alone, for they had told him of the people of Mordecai. Instead, Haman sought to destroy all the Jews who were throughout the whole kingdom of Ahasuerus—the people of Mordecai," Esther 3:6 NKJV.

The writer of Esther tells us of his detailed plan to do this. Furthermore, we learn of his plans for Mordecai. Listen to his wounded pride and plans of vengeance over it.

"Moreover Haman said, 'Besides, Queen Esther invited no one but me to come in with the king to the banquet that she prepared; and tomorrow I am again invited by her, along with the king. Yet all this avails me nothing, so long as I see Mordecai the Jew sitting at the king's gate.' Then his wife Zeresh and all his friends said to

him, 'Let a gallows be made, fifty cubits high, and in the morning suggest to the king that Mordecai be hanged on it; then go merrily with the king to the banquet.' And the thing pleased Haman; so he had the gallows made," Esther 5:12-14 NKJV.

Oh, what an irritant Mordecai was to the glory seeking Haman. If Haman had the pride of satisfaction over what he had accomplished, Mordecai's slights of him would little matter. However, Mordecai wounded his haughty pride beyond Haman's ability to handle the slight rationally. Haman's ego was totally bent out of joint. His pride needed justice. Therefore, to assuage his hurt ego, he set out to murder Mordecai and destroy all the Jews in the empire. The sad thing is Haman had the power to do it.

"Then Haman said to King Ahasuerus, 'There is a certain people scattered and dispersed among the people in all the provinces of your kingdom; their laws are different from all other people's, and they do not keep the king's laws. Therefore it is not fitting for the king to let them remain. If it pleases the king, let a decree be written that they be destroyed, and I will pay ten thousand talents of silver into the hands of those who do the work, to bring it into the king's treasuries.' So the king took his signet ring from his hand and gave it to Haman, the son of Hammedatha the Agagite, the enemy of the Jews. And the king said to Haman, 'The money and the people are given to you, to do with them as seems good to you.'" (Esther 3:8-11 NKJV)

Haman was a haughty and arrogant prideful person. He would not let anyone, or anything get in his way. If you think little of him, Haman will destroy you. Are you a person like Haman? Has your pride been insulted? Who are you trying to destroy?

Well, it looks like the exalting pride of Haman is going to win, however, Proverbs teaches his fall and destruction is coming. This will happen to all prideful people, sooner or later. The truth about Haman is about to be exposed. The facade of his falseness is going to be torn down by Queen

Esther, Mordecai's niece and adopted daughter, a Jew. News of the pending slaughter of the Jews by Haman spread quickly through society. It seems the only one who did not know was Esther. Mordecai informs Esther. After much worry and concern, Esther begins her plan to uncover the evil plot to King Ahasuerus.

"Then Esther told them to reply to Mordecai: 'Go, gather all the Jews who are present in Shushan, and fast for me; neither eat nor drink for three days, night or day. My maids and I will fast likewise. And so I will go to the king, which is against the law; and if I perish, I perish!'" (Esther 4:15-16 NKJV)

The Queens plan was simple but brilliant. She planned two banquets to soften the king's heart and expose the evil Haman. She used Haman's pride against himself by only asking for him to be a guest. ***"So Esther answered, 'If it pleases the king, let the king and Haman come today to the banquet that I have prepared for him,'"*** Esther 5:4 NKJV. The first banquet went well, and she asked the king and Haman to come back for another the next day. Haman is feeling like a super top dog.

"So Haman went out that day joyful and with a glad heart; but when Haman saw Mordecai in the king's gate, and that he did not stand or tremble before him, he was filled with indignation against Mordecai," Esther 5:9 NKJV.

Judgement day is very soon for Haman. His egocentric pride and hate for Mordecai will subsequently bring his destruction and fall. The night of the first banquet Haman builds the gallows for Mordecai. Little did he know that noose would become his. Let us remember, ***"Pride goes before destruction, And a haughty spirit before a fall."*** Here is the account of God fulfilling this verse in the life of Haman. The night before the second banquet King Ahasuerus is disturbed and wants to know if the man who saved his life received anything. ***"Then the king said, 'What honor or dignity has been bestowed on Mordecai for this?' And the king's servants who***

attended him said, 'Nothing has been done for him,'" Esther 6:3 NKJV.

Haman is called in for his opinion on honoring someone the king delights in. Haman thinking the king wants to honor him, his pride not accepting it could be for someone else, gives the king his advice on how to honor himself, the great Haman. However, to Haman's surprise, the person to be honored is the one he hates, Mordecai. Furthermore, Haman is chosen to do the honoring. This is a mighty first blow of destruction to Haman and his pride.

"Afterward Mordecai went back to the king's gate. But Haman hurried to his house, mourning and with his head covered. When Haman told his wife Zeresh and all his friends everything that had happened to him, his wise men and his wife Zeresh said to him, 'If Mordecai, before whom you have begun to fall, is of Jewish descent, you will not prevail against him but will surely fall before him,'" Esther 6:12-13 NKJV.

The Fall of a Haughty Spirit

Haman is in grave danger. His pride is bringing upon him destruction, and his haughtiness are causing his fall. Before Haman could think of a way out of his predicament, the day of the queen's second banquet was ready. ***"While they were still talking with him, the king's eunuchs came, and hastened to bring Haman to the banquet which Esther had prepared,"*** Esther 6:14 NKJV. Haman is off to the banquet and is probably thinking he is going to a safe space. After all, he was invited by the queen herself! However, Queen Esther is ready to spring into action and expose the haughty Haman the Agagite.

"So the king and Haman went to dine with Queen Esther. And on the second day, at the banquet of wine, the king again said to Esther, 'What is your petition, Queen Esther? It shall be granted you. And what is your request, up to half the kingdom? It shall be done!' Then Queen Esther answered and said, 'If I have found favor in your sight, O king, and if it pleases the king, let my life

be given me at my petition, and my people at my request. For we have been sold, my people and I, to be destroyed, to be killed, and to be annihilated. Had we been sold as male and female slaves, I would have held my tongue, although the enemy could never compensate for the king's loss.' So King Ahasuerus answered and said to Queen Esther, 'Who is he, and where is he, who would dare presume in his heart to do such a thing?' And Esther said, 'The adversary and enemy is this wicked Haman!'" (Esther 7:1-6 NKJV)

The end verse tells us exactly how the prideful and haughty Haman now feels. ***"So Haman was terrified before the king and queen!"*** (Esther 7:1-6 NKJV) How did King Ahasuerus feel about this?

"Then the king arose in his wrath from the banquet of wine and went into the palace garden; but Haman stood before Queen Esther, pleading for his life, for he saw that evil was determined against him by the king" Esther 7:7 NKJV.

Now comes the verdict and the end of Haman's destruction and fall. ***"When the king returned from the palace garden to the place of the banquet of wine, Haman had fallen across the couch where Esther was. Then the king said, 'Will he also assault the queen while I am in the house?' As the word left the king's mouth, they covered Haman's face. Now Harbonah, one of the eunuchs, said to the king, 'Look! The gallows, fifty cubits high, which Haman made for Mordecai, who spoke good on the king's behalf, is standing at the house of Haman.' Then the king said, 'Hang him on it!' So they hanged Haman on the gallows that he had prepared for Mordecai. Then the king's wrath subsided."*** Esther 7:8-10 NKJV. (Underlined for emphasis.)

The Exaltation of the Humble

How is one to feel about the destruction and fall of Haman? I think we need to view this with a sense of awe and fear. Our awe centered on the justice of God. Our fear centered in our own mindset, where is my pride leading me? A second lesson for us in Proverbs 16:19, ***"Better to be of a humble spirit with the lowly, Than to divide the spoil with the proud,"*** is shown in the life of Mordecai, the object of Haman's wrath. The proud and haughty will be destroyed and fall, although in their exaltation, they cause untold tragedies and problems. For the person who stands for God against the wickedly proud, although he/she may suffer much, perhaps death, they will be exalted. They will take possession of all the wicked have. Look what happened to the lowly Mordecai.

"On that day King Ahasuerus gave Queen Esther the house of Haman, the enemy of the Jews. And Mordecai came before the king, for Esther had told how he was related to her. So the king took off his signet ring, which he had taken from Haman, and gave it to Mordecai; and Esther appointed Mordecai over the house of Haman," Esther 8:1-2 NKJV.

And ...

"So Mordecai went out from the presence of the king in royal apparel of blue and white, with a great crown of gold and a garment of fine linen and purple; and the city of Shushan rejoiced and was glad,"
Esther 8:15 NKJV.

He, who was prideful became destroyed and he who was humble was exulted. Perhaps, you are in a similar situation? Maybe, you are Mr. or Ms. Peacock strutting around, exalting yourself and putting others down? You need to be aware of the danger you face. Conversely, you may be humble and on the end of someone's prideful wrath? Nevertheless, endure until God rectifies the situation.

Lesson to Be Learned

1. Pride is a two-edged sword. Wrongly used, it is damaging, rightly used; it is edifying.
2. Dealing with prideful and haughty people is difficult.

This is especially so, with the prideful who are in a seat of authority.

3. In dealing with authoritative pride requires a God based response.
   - A. Sinful pride must be understood and exposed God's way.
   - B. This requires prayer and fasting by the individual or groups affected by the pride of wrath.
   - C. The endurance of the humble must be strong to the end.
   - D. Trusting in the truths of Proverbs 16:18, ***"Pride goes before destruction, And a haughty spirit before a fall,"*** is essential for a proper response.
   - E. If God gives you a plan on how to win in your situation, do not jump ahead of His timing to execute it.

4. Examine yourself, make sure you do not have a beam in your own eye such as the same pride of someone you are upset with. God will use such a person to correct you from your sin.

5. Sinful pride, especially in churches, is extremely dangerous and destructive to the Gospel of Christ.

Life's Applications

1. We all tend to have sinful pride. We must be aware of it.
2. We must have the same attitude of Jesus Christ. ***"Let this mind be in you which was also in Christ Jesus, who, being in the form of God, did not consider it robbery to be equal with God, but made Himself of no reputation, taking the form of a bondservant, and coming in the likeness of men. And being found in appearance as a man, He humbled Himself and became obedient to the point of death, even the death of the cross. Therefore God also has highly exalted Him and given Him the name which is above every name,"*** Philippians 2:5-9 NKJV.
3. Understanding of how serious God feels about the sin of pride, and haughtiness are essential for a proper

mindset.

4. Follow the examples of Esther and Mordecai.
5. It is your choice to choose the proper use of *pride*.

Reflections

1. Define the word pride.
2. Do you know someone who is prideful?
3. Have you been affected by someone who is prideful?
4. How did they affect you?
5. How long has the effect lasted in your life?
6. Do you get a knot in your heart when you think of the person?
7. Describe how you have properly or improperly handled the situation of pride.
8. Do you have areas in your life where you exhibited pride?
9. Have you hurt someone else with your pride?
10. Memorize Proverbs 16:18-19.
11. What does Solomon mean by Pride goes before destruction?
12. What is a haughty spirit? Is this something good to have?
13. What does Solomon mean by a haughty spirit before a fall?
14. Why is it better to be of a humble spirit with the lowly? Who are the lowly? Who do you spend your time with?
15. Why is it bad to divide the spoil with the proud?

What is the spoil to be divided? Who are the proud?

16. Is pride a curse or a blessing?
17. What is the haughtiness of pride? Why is this sinful before the eyes of God?
18. What is humility of pride or pride of satisfaction?
19. How does Galatians 6:4-5 explain this for the believer?
20. Concerning the pride of arrogance, what does Paul say about this in Galatians 6:3?
21. Are you a Galatians 6:4-5 Christian or a Galatians 6:3 Christian?
22. Why is a prideful Christian more intolerable than an unsaved person?
23. What type of Prophet was John the Baptist, a Galatians 6:4-5 or a Galatians 6:3 person?
24. Write a small commentary on John the Baptist, according to John 1:19-23, concerning his attitude. How did he handle his ministry, pridefully or humbly?
25. According to John 3:30, how did the Baptist handle himself concerning Jesus? How do you do in this area?
26. According to 1 Corinthians 1:12-13, what was happening in Corinth?
27. Why is this an example of contentious arrogant pride?
28. Why did the sin of pride cause the sin of sectarianism in the congregation at Corinth? What is sectarianism? Is sectarianism alive in the "church" of today?
29. Is a clique in churches today a kind of inter-

sectarianism? Is this behavior prideful?

30. What is an attitude of superiority? How is this a manifestation of pride?
31. How does this cause cliques in churches? Why does a clique exclude others from joining it? How does James 2:1-13 explain this?
32. Where does the pride of superiority have its roots from?
33. How does Isaiah 14:12 and Revelation 20:10 describe the fall and pending destruction of the devil?
34. How does Paul describe the pending fall and destruction people in the church acting pridefully? Would repentance and change of attitude prevent this?
35. How prideful were the Corinthians according to 1 Corinthians 5:1-2?
36. How is the behavior of sexual deviancy becoming a source of pride in today's denominations?
37. According to Revelation 2:12-29, what prideful conditions were abounding in the church at Pergamos and Thyatira?
38. What was Jesus going to do about these problems?
39. Is the judgement of the Lord a frightening specter to receive?
40. Why must we as individuals be continually aware and on guard against the sin of pride?
41. Take twenty minutes of time and read the Book of Esther. Why were the Jews in captivity? Who was the King? How did Esther become Queen? Who was Mordecai? Who was Haman?

42. How did Haman emotionally handle his promotion with humility or pride?
43. What did Mordecai cause Haman to feel?
44. What did the thought in Haman's heart reveal about himself in Esther 6:5-6?
45. What plan did Haman bring to the King because of his wounded pride concerning Mordecai?
46. How irrational is it to let one person get "under your skin" and wound your pride? What does this say about Haman?
47. In Esther 3:2, we read Mordecai would not bow or pay homage to Haman. Was Mordecai correct in his action?
48. Why would Haman be filled with wrath since only one person did not give him homage?
49. Why do prideful people get angry when they are not recognized?
50. What was the nuclear reaction of Haman according to Esther 3:6? Is this reasonable? If you have ever been involved in church splits or an emptying church, could it be because some people have a Haman complex? In your workplace or even in your home, is the Haman complex alive? How sinful is this?
51. How high did Haman plan to hang Mordecai?
52. Would you say Haman was narcissistic?
53. Would you say Haman was a megalomaniac?
54. How does Haman's response to Mordecai, promote the fear of him among people and the exalting of his self-aggrandizement?
55. How did God disrupt the king's sleep to

start Haman's downfall and destruction, in Esther 6:1-10?

56. What did the humble Esther request, before she entered the battle to expose Haman in Esther 4:15-16?
57. If Esther needed prayer and fasting for God's help in confronting a prideful person, how about you? Do you confront pride before you pray and get the answer of God's help? My guess, from personal experience, is you lost the confrontation, did you?
58. What was Esther's plan to soften the king's heart to bring about the fall of Haman, the saving of her uncle, and the Jews?
59. How did Esther appeal to the king, knowing his pride, to get the desired answer she needs in Esther 7:1-6?
60. How important, in confronting a sinful prideful person, is it to bring the facts before all involved with grace and humility? How did Esther do this? This is an important lesson for a Christian to learn. Remember, it is not wise to add fuel to the fire, but to extinguish the fire!
61. When Haman was exposed by Esther, how did the king respond to her revelation?
62. What was the prideful Haman's reaction?
63. What was the king's verdict on Haman?
64. Where did he have Haman executed?
65. What happened to his possessions?
66. What happened to the humble God-fearing Mordecai concerning the position Haman had?
67. How does this book prove Proverbs 16:18-19?

68. What is the warning for a disciple of Jesus in this lesson?
69. Comment on *Lesson to be Learned* numbers 1 to 5 and *Life's Applications* 1-5.
70. Please do a self-examination under the guidance of the Holy Spirit and ask Him to point out the sin of pride in your life?
71. Read John 13:1-17, compare Christ and Haman in their mindset. Which one should you follow and why?

Pride is a serious and deadly sin. This issue must be dealt with in the life of a believer. May humility be your way of life.

May God Help Us All!

LESSON NINE: JESUS CHRIST OUR LORD AND STRENGTH A LIVING RELATIONSHIP WITH CHRIST

LESSON ONE

THE NAME OF THE LORD

"Therefore God also has highly exalted Him and given Him the name which is above every name, that at the name of Jesus every knee should bow, of those in heaven, and of those on earth, and of those under the earth, and that every tongue should confess that Jesus Christ is Lord, to the glory of God the Father."
Philippians 2:9-11 NKJV

"For all people walk each in the name of his god,
But we will walk in the name of the Lord our God
Forever and ever."
Micah 4:5 NKJV

Every parent has the wonderful right to give a name to the child who is born to them. This child automatically has the surname of the parents, describing who the child belongs to and what family lineage they are of. This giving of names began with the first created human. ***"Then God said, 'Let Us make man*** (Adam) ***in Our image,'"*** Genesis 1:26 NKJV. God created him, naming him man. The Hebrew word for man is Adam, see Strong's word H120, *'adam, aw-dawm' (ruddy i.e., a human being (an individual or the species, mankind, etc.): -man (mean, of low degree), person).* Thus, our lineage, before political correctness and woke ideology, was and is mankind. This is a designation made by God. ***"He created them male and female, and blessed them and called them Mankind in the day they were created,"*** Genesis 5:2 NKJV. It seems, God conferred the honor of naming to Adam, when He created the woman from one of Adam's ribs. ***"And Adam called his wife's name Eve, because she was the mother of all living,"*** Genesis 3:20 NKJV. Adam and Eve had children and gave them names. The giving of names was established by God, who then expected the parents to name their offspring.

JESUS NAMED BY GOD

However, when it came to naming God's only begotten Son, God did not give this naming right to Mary and Joseph. He kept the privilege of naming and conferred the name He wanted for His Son to Joseph, the name which is above all names.

"Now the birth of Jesus Christ was as follows: After His mother Mary was betrothed to Joseph, before they came together, she was found with child of the Holy Spirit. Then Joseph her husband, being a just man, and not wanting to make her a public example, was minded to put her away secretly. But while he thought about these things, behold, an angel of the Lord appeared to him in a dream, saying, 'Joseph, son of David, do not be afraid to take to you Mary your wife, for that which is conceived in her is of the Holy Spirit. And she will bring forth a Son, and you shall call His name Jesus, for He will save His people from their sins,'" Matthew 1:18-21 NKJV.

Joseph obeys God and calls the newborn babe, Jesus! ***"Then Joseph, being aroused from sleep, did as the angel of the Lord commanded him and took to him his wife, and did not know her till she had brought forth her firstborn Son. And he called His name Jesus,"*** Matthew 1:24-25 NKJV.

Jesus, born of the Virgin Mary, was placed under the authority of Joseph by God the Father, who moved His family to Nazareth. Therefore, Jesus was known as Jesus of Nazareth.

"Philip found Nathanael and said to him, "We have found Him of whom Moses in the law, and also the prophets, wrote—Jesus of Nazareth, the son of Joseph," John 1:45 NKJV.

The title of Christ belonged to Jesus because He is the Messiah promised in the Old Testament. Therefore, Jesus is known by the town He grew up in, Nazareth, and by His redemptive work of salvation, Christ. Even Pilate, whom Jesus suffered under, acknowledged Jesus was called Christ.

"Therefore, when they had gathered together, Pilate said to them, "Whom do you want me to release to you? Barabbas, or Jesus who is called Christ?" (Matthew 27:17 NKJV)

JESUS THE HIGHEST NAME

Another way of knowing who Jesus is, comes by His identity of being called the son of someone. Since God is the Father of Jesus, Jesus is known as, Jesus the Son of God! What did the angel say to Mary concerning this identifier?

"And the angel answered and said to her, 'The Holy Spirit will come upon you, and the power of the Highest will overshadow you; therefore, also, that Holy One who is to be born will be called the Son of God,'" Luke 1:35 NKJV.

Even the demons named Jesus this way.

"When He had come to the other side, to the country of the Gergesenes, there met Him two demon-possessed men, coming out of the tombs, exceedingly fierce, so that no one could pass that way. And suddenly they cried out, saying, 'What have we to do with You, Jesus, You Son of God? Have You come here to torment us before the time?'" (Matthew 8:28-29 NKJV)

Jesus is the highest name because it is the name of God.

Concerning the kingly or royal heritage of Jesus, He is rightfully called king because He was of the household of David. Jesus, although He is the Son of God, comes from the lineage of David through Mary and His stepfather Joseph. (See the genealogical lines written in Matthew One and Luke Three)

Joseph's Line:

"The book of the genealogy of Jesus Christ, the Son of David, the Son of Abraham ..." (Matthew 1:1 NKJV).

Mary's Line (As was supposed Joseph's son, but understood to be Mary's son and line and God is His Father):

"Now Jesus Himself began His ministry at about thirty years of age, being (as was supposed) the son of Joseph, the son of Heli ... the son of David, the son of Enosh, the son of Seth, the son of Adam, the son of God," Luke 3:23 to 38 NKJV.

Jesus is known as the Son of David throughout Israel:

"Now they came to Jericho. As He went out of Jericho with His disciples and a great multitude, blind Bartimaeus, the son of Timaeus, sat by the road begging. And when he heard that it was Jesus of Nazareth, he began to cry out and say, 'Jesus, Son of David, have mercy on me!' Then many warned him to be quiet; but he cried out all the more, 'Son of David, have mercy on me!'" (Mark 10:46-48 NKJV)

The Apostle Paul affirms the titles and lineage of Jesus of Nazareth, as Christ, God's Son, and the seed of David.

"Paul, a bondservant of Jesus Christ, called to be an apostle, separated to the gospel of God which He promised before through His prophets in the Holy Scriptures, concerning His Son Jesus Christ our Lord, who was born of the seed of David according to the flesh, and declared to be the Son of God with power according to the Spirit of holiness, by the resurrection from the dead," Romans 1:1-4 NKJV.

HIS NAME

Jesus is the name which is above all names. The Lord's name has great meaning. The root of His name is the Hebrew, Yeshua, from Strong's H3091, *Joshua (Yhowshua {yeh-ho-shoo'-ah}: Jehovah-saved; Jehoshua, i.e., Joshua).* In the Koine Greek language of the New Testament gives us Strong's G2424 *'Iησοῦς, pronounced, ee-ay-sooce: of Hebrew origin (H3091); Jesus (i.e., Jehoshua), the name of our Lord.* Therefore, the power of the name of Jesus is its declaring Jehovah (Yahweh) Saves. Jesus saves because He is the promised seed of Eve, through the promised seed of Abraham, in which the entire world is saved or redeemed. Furthermore, add the title Christ to Jesus and no other name can match it. Christ from Strong's G5547, *χριστός, pronounced Christos (Khris-tos): anointed, i.e., the Messiah, an epithet of Jesus: --Christ.* The roots of this are in the Hebrew H4899, מָשִׁיחַ *pronounced mashiyach (maw-shee-akh): anointed; usually a consecrated person (as a king, priest, or saint); specifically, the Messiah: --anointed, Messiah.* Therefore, the Name, which is above all names, Jesus Christ, means The Anointed Savior! As the angel declared, ***"Call His name Jesus, for He will save His people from their sins."***

The prophet Isaiah received great insight into the name which is above all names. He prophesied about the birth of Jesus and explains or defines the greatness of His name, Anointed Savior, Jesus Christ.

"For unto us a Child is born,
Unto us a Son is given;
And the government will be upon His shoulder.
And His name will be called Wonderful, Counselor,
Mighty God, Everlasting Father, Prince of Peace.
Of the increase of His government and peace

There will be no end,
Upon the throne of David and over His kingdom,
To order it and establish it with judgment and justice
From that time forward, even forever.
The zeal of the Lord of hosts will perform this,"
Isaiah 9:6-7 NKJV.

Isaiah teaches us about a Child, a Son who will be born and given to us. He also says His name will have incredible meaning. A question to ask, what is the Child and Son's name? The angel of God told Joseph this prophesied name. The name the Son will be called is Jesus, ***"You shall call His name Jesus."*** There are professors who say this verse, in Isaiah, teaches His name will be Wonderful, or His name will be Counselor, or His name will be Mighty God, or Everlasting Father, or Prince of Peace. I do concur with this point of view. However, another aspect to consider is the name God gave His Son at His birth. His name shall be called Jesus. The name Jesus, described by Isaiah in these ways, is to teach why the name Jesus Christ is above all names. Isaiah's five names for Him could be adjectives to Jesus, describing who Jesus is. This is so because His very being is Wonderful, His wisdom will be greater than the wisdom of Solomon to counsel, because being conceived by the Holy Spirit, Jesus is the Mighty God, since all was created through Him, He is the Everlasting Father, and finally because the government is on His shoulder, He has the authority to be the Prince of Peace. Therefore, His name, Jesus, will be called ***"Wonderful Jesus, Counselor Jesus, Mighty God Jesus, Everlasting Father Jesus, Prince of Peace Jesus."***

PAUL'S SUMMARY OF JESUS AND HIS NAME

"He is the image of the invisible God, the firstborn over all creation. For by Him all things were created that are in heaven and that are on earth, visible and invisible, whether thrones or dominions or principalities or powers. All things were created through Him and for Him. And He is before all things, and in Him all things consist. And He is the head of the body, the church, who is the beginning, the firstborn from the dead, that in all things He may have the preeminence," Colossians 1:15-18 NKJV.

- Jesus is the image of the invisible God–As Isaiah said, the Everlasting Father.
- Jesus is the firstborn over all creation–As the angel said, the Son of God.
- Jesus is the creator, as Isaiah said, the Mighty God.
- Jesus is the head of the body, the church, in which He has the preeminence, as Isaiah said, Counselor, the government is on His shoulder.
- In fact, how Paul describes Jesus in Colossians 1:15-18 can be summed up in one word from Isaiah–***Wonderful.***

There really is not a name that is greater than the Lord's name, Jesus.

NO OTHER NAME HAS THE TOTAL AUTHORITY LIKE THE NAME JESUS

If we understand Philippians 2:9-11, we can gain the knowledge and reverence of the name of Jesus. Let us understand the fact, God the Father Almighty, creator of heaven and earth, the ultimate ruler of the creation, is the one who has highly exalted Jesus. Jesus the Son exalted and sitting at the right hand of the Father. There is no other place of seating which is higher than the seat at the right hand of God and only Jesus sits there. Therefore, the name of the Son of God, who is seated at the right hand of the Father, at the seat of ultimate authority, Jesus, is above every name. As the Psalmist wrote:

'But My faithfulness and My mercy shall be with him,
And in My name his horn shall be exalted.
Also I will set his hand over the sea,
And his right hand over the rivers.
He shall cry to Me, 'You are my Father, My
God, and the rock of my salvation.'
Also I will make him My firstborn, The
highest of the kings of the earth."
Psalm 89:24-27 NKJV

Jesus is the firstborn Son of God. The firstborn son is the heir to the throne. In accordance with Jesus being the firstborn of God, He inherits the position of the highest king of the earth!

"Therefore God also has highly exalted Him and given Him the name which is above every name, that at the name of Jesus every knee should bow, of those in heaven, and of those on earth, and of those under the earth, and that every tongue should confess that Jesus Christ is Lord, to the glory of God the Father," Philippians

2:9-11 NKJV.

Since Jesus is King of kings, God will cause every knee to bow down at the name of Jesus and every tongue will confess the LORD Jesus Christ.

THERE IS POWER IN THE NAME OF JESUS

THE SAVING POWER

There is power in the name of Jesus because the person, Jesus, is the name. Remember, the angel said, ***"His name will be Jesus!"*** This is the Son of God, the highest name of all. There are marvelous powerful facts and benefits tied up in the name of Jesus. The incredible fact of the Lord having the name which is above all names is because His name, Jesus, is the only name which can save our souls. In a fierce argument with the rulers of Israel, Peter acknowledges the saving power of believing in the name of Jesus in an argument with the unbelieving rulers of Israel. Why is this so? This is so because Jesus, Himself, died for our sins and forgiveness. No other named person in heaven or earth or under the earth has a name which died for our sins. Only the name, which is above all names, Jesus, can save. He is the only Savior, there is no other. This is the highest of God's priorities for mankind, to save us from our sins. Christ Jesus, the Anointed Savior, the name above all names saves.

"Then Peter, filled with the Holy Spirit, said to them, "Rulers of the people and elders of Israel: If we this day are judged for a good deed done to a helpless man, by what means he has been made well, let it be known to you all, and to all the people of Israel, that by the name of Jesus Christ of Nazareth, whom you crucified, whom God raised from the dead, by Him this man stands here before you whole. This is the 'stone which was rejected by you builders, which has become the chief cornerstone.' Nor is there salvation in any other, for there is no other name under heaven given among men by which we must be saved," Acts 4:8-12 NKJV.

Did you notice what the Spirit filled Peter said? If you think there are other saviors other than the Highest Name in heaven and earth, you need to think again. Peter said, ***"Nor is there salvation in any other, for there is no other name under***

heaven given among men by which we must be saved." The phrase, ***"No Other name under heaven,"*** means exactly this, only Jesus saves.

"And it shall come to pass That whoever calls on the name of the Lord Shall be saved," Acts 2:21 NKJV.

"For the Scripture says, 'Whoever believes on Him will not be put to shame.' For there is no distinction between Jew and Greek, for the same Lord over all is rich to all who call upon Him. For 'whoever calls on the name of the Lord shall be saved,'" Romans 10:11-13 NKJV.

In the annals of history, with all the names of great men and women recorded, is there one name found among them which can save and make a person right with God? In all those who lived, claiming to be great, are they alive today with the power to save by faith in their name? Of all the religious movements from time immemorial is there one system of belief which will save your soul? The honest answer to all three questions is no. Only the resurrected Son of God, Jesus, the name above all names saves. Jesus is the only name who died and has come back to life to bring the healing balm of salvation to the entire world. ***"I am He who lives, and was dead, and behold, I am alive forevermore. Amen."*** (Revelation 1:18 NKJV). The name which is above all names saves!

THE ADMITTANCE POWER

I do not think I am wrong to say, the religions of the world require great works of human effort to even think they may have an audience with their so-called gods. The power of the name of Jesus gives us instant and free and personal boldness to enter the throne room of God for audience with Him. We enter in through the merits of Christ, His name, it is powerful. This is a permission Jesus, Himself, gives us. He has the authority to give us this permission.

The Apostle John wrote about Jesus' knowledge of Himself at the last supper concerning the authority He has.

"Now before the Feast of the Passover, when Jesus knew that His hour had come that He should depart from this world to the Father, having loved His own who were in the world, He loved them to the end. And supper being ended, the devil having already put it into the heart of Judas Iscariot, Simon's son, to betray Him, Jesus, knowing that the Father had given all things into His hands, and that He had come from God and was going to God," John 13:1-3 NKJV.

Jesus has been given all things into His hands. This means He has all authority as He explained to the disciples after the resurrection. ***"And Jesus came and spoke to them, saying, 'All authority has been given to Me in heaven and on earth,'"*** Matthew 28:18 NKJV. Therefore, Jesus, with the knowledge of His authority and the power of His name, in the middle of the supper, invites the disciples to use His name in prayer. It is an authoritative invitation.

"Most assuredly, I say to you, he who believes in Me, the works that I do he will do also; and greater works than these he will do, because I go to My Father. And whatever you ask in My name, that

I will do, that the Father may be glorified in the Son. If you ask anything in My name, I will do it," John 14:12-14 NKJV.

And again He says:

"And in that day you will ask Me nothing. Most assuredly, I say to you, whatever you ask the Father in My name He will give you. Until now you have asked nothing in My name. Ask, and you will receive, that your joy may be full," John 16:23-24 NKJV.

And again He says:

"In that day you will ask in My name, and I do not say to you that I shall pray the Father for you; for the Father Himself loves you, because you have loved Me, and have believed that I came forth from God. I came forth from the Father and have come into the world. Again, I leave the world and go to the Father," John 16:26-28 NKJV.

The name above all names, who has all authority and power in His name, grants to us His name to enter the throne room of the Father to pray and receive in His name. This is not a Carte-Blanche check signed by Jesus for you or me to get anything we want. Some teach Jesus gives us a check with His signature on it and all we need to do is fill the amount in and cash it with the Father. His name is a royal pass or ticket to allow you and me to enter into the throne room. Our personal name or being or goodness does not have the power to allow us to enter in. We get into the throne room of God only by Jesus' permission and admittance power. Therefore, we can ask boldly for anything according to the guidelines set forth in the whole of scripture. We must remember, when we enter in by the name of Jesus, we have a responsibility to enter in properly and pray according to the will of God. Selfish use of the name of Jesus will get one nowhere with God.

Let us understand proper use of prayer. It is possible, when James the brother of Jesus was growing up watching

Jesus pray and receive answers to prayer, he tried to emulate Jesus in prayer. It is easy to say James' prayer life was not as fulfilling as his brother's prayer life. Naturally, he goes to Jesus and complains. Why do you get your prayers answered and I do not! I wonder if Jesus said these words to James, ***"You ask and do not receive, because you ask amiss, that you may spend it on your pleasures,"*** James 4:3 NKJV. Nevertheless, let us still go into the throne room as Jesus has given us permission because He will be there to help us to ask rightly. The book of Hebrews declares this help.

"Seeing then that we have a great High Priest who has passed through the heavens, Jesus the Son of God, let us hold fast our confession. For we do not have a High Priest who cannot sympathize with our weaknesses, but was in all points tempted as we are, yet without sin. Let us therefore come boldly to the throne of grace, that we may obtain mercy and find grace to help in time of need," Hebrews 4:14-16 NKJV.

THE HEALING POWER

One of the most blessed gifts tied up with the name of Jesus is healing. This blessing is also the hardest to understand. Nevertheless, the name of Jesus brings healing. To be honest, we do not understand this healing as the apostles understood it. We use the name of Jesus flippantly proclaiming, *"You are healed,"* and when the person is not healed, we blame their faithlessness. Personally, I have experienced healing in Jesus' name and also no healing in it. I have prayed for healing in Jesus' name for some people and some were healed while others were not. The experience is both exhilarating and depressing. The only reasonable statement I can express concerning the difficulties of healing in the name of Jesus is, the name is His name, and He will invoke the power of His name as He sees fit. However, we are to trust in the Lord with all our hearts and not lean to our own understanding (See Proverbs 3:5) in the way the Lord heals but continue to seek healing in His name.

"Now Peter and John went up together to the temple at the hour of prayer, the ninth hour. And a certain man lame from his mother's womb was carried, whom they laid daily at the gate of the temple, which is called Beautiful, to ask alms from those who entered the temple; who, seeing Peter and John about to go into the temple, asked for alms. And fixing his eyes on him, with John, Peter said, 'Look at us.' So he gave them his attention, expecting to receive something from them. Then Peter said, 'Silver and gold I do not have, but what I do have I give you: In the name of Jesus Christ of Nazareth, rise up and walk.' And he took him by the right hand and lifted him up, and immediately his feet and ankle bones received strength. So he, leaping up, stood and walked and entered the temple with them—walking, leaping, and praising God. And all the people saw him walking and praising God. Then

they knew that it was he who sat begging alms at the Beautiful Gate of the temple; and they were filled with wonder and amazement at what had happened to him," Acts 3:1-10 NKJV.

DELIVERANCE POWER

Why are we afraid of the demon world as Christians? Since Jesus is the authority over everything in heaven, on the earth and under the earth we should be strong in His name.

"Now there was a man in their synagogue with an unclean spirit. And he cried out, saying, 'Let us alone! What have we to do with You, Jesus of Nazareth? Did You come to destroy us? I know who You are—the Holy One of God!' But Jesus rebuked him, saying, 'Be quiet, and come out of him!' And when the unclean spirit had convulsed him and cried out with a loud voice, he came out of him. Then they were all amazed, so that they questioned among themselves, saying, 'What is this? What new doctrine is this? For with authority He commands even the unclean spirits, and they obey Him,'" Mark 1:23-27 NKJV.

The Apostle Paul had many struggles with demons. He had personal struggles in his life with them as well. A struggle which he had to live with by the grace of Christ. One thing about it, Paul was not afraid of them no matter how strong they were. This lesson in Jesus' name proves it. We should learn it also!

"Now it happened, as we went to prayer, that a certain slave girl possessed with a spirit of divination met us, who brought her masters much profit by fortune-telling. This girl followed Paul and us, and cried out, saying, 'These men are the servants of the Most High God, who proclaim to us the way of salvation.' And this she did for many days. But Paul, greatly annoyed, turned and said to the spirit, 'I command you in the name of Jesus Christ to come out of her.' And he came out that very hour," Acts 16:16-18 NKJV.

No matter how scary the battle is against darkness we must be strong in the delivering name of Jesus. The Apostle

John said, ***"You are of God, little children, and have overcome them, because He who is in you is greater than he who is in the world,"*** 1 John 4:4 NKJV.

We have briefly examined the authority of the name of Jesus pertaining to the Lord's saving power, admittance power, power in prayer, healing power, and deliverance power from evil. These areas are of the utmost importance for a Christian to grow in. The Apostle Peter admonishes us, ***"But grow in the grace and knowledge of our Lord and Savior Jesus Christ,"*** 2 Peter 3:18 NKJV. While the Apostle Paul commands us to, ***"Work out your own salvation with fear and trembling,"*** Philippians 2:12 NKJV. Therefore, how are we to grow in the Name of The Lord and work out the *Name Of The Lord* in our salvation daily? This is a growth which we must all undertake in His name.

OLD TESTAMENT POWER OF THE NAME TEACHINGS

There is a true saying, The Old Testament is the New Testament concealed and the New Testament is the Old Testament revealed. Remember what we claimed about the Name? Let us learn how to grow in Christ and His Name through the working of the Name in the life of individuals and the nation of Israel written in the Old Testament. ***"For whatever things were written before were written for our learning, that we through the patience and comfort of the Scriptures might have hope,"*** Romans 15:4 NKJV. Let us examine a few sections of the Old Testament to increase our faith in the Name of Jesus.

Remember what we claimed about the Name? *There is power in the name of Jesus because the person, Jesus, is the name.* The Old Testament revelation of God appearing to Moses (Read Exodus Chapter 3) amplifies the eternal existence of the Name of Jesus.

LEARNING BY THE NAME I AM

"Then Moses said to God, 'Indeed when I come to the children of Israel and say to them, The God of your fathers has sent me to you,' and they say to me, 'What is His name?' what shall I say to them? And God said to Moses, 'I AM WHO I AM.' And He said, 'Thus you shall say to the children of Israel, 'I AM has sent me to you,'" Exodus 3:13-14 NKJV.

The Lord Jesus is the existing one! He is the I AM. He was not ashamed to proclaim His name before the disbelieving Jews.

"Then the Jews said to Him, 'You are not yet fifty years old, and have You seen Abraham?' Jesus said to them, 'Most assuredly, I say to you, before Abraham was, I AM,'" John 8:57-58 NKJV.

Jesus is the great I AM! The God of the burning bush, our Lord and Savior. The revelation of God to Moses and to us! Moses experienced all the blessings and power of the Name I AM. A thorough reading of Exodus to Deuteronomy will show us the life we can experience with Jesus by Moses' experiences with I AM.

- He experienced salvation.
- He was admitted into the presence of God.
- He had power in prayer.
- He was healthy.
- He was victorious over the demonic idols of Egypt.
- He came out of bondage and led the Nation of Israel to freedom.

Moses had a relationship with I AM, Jesus, all believers can have in their life. Furthermore, I AM did prove to Moses He is the name which is above all names and at His name every knee will bow. What did I AM do to the nation of Egypt in delivering the Israelites? If you know your Biblical history, I AM destroyed Egypt to deliver His people. Moses went down from Mount Sinai in the name of I AM, the name above all names in heaven, on earth, and below the earth. With I Am for Moses no one could stand against him. The power of God in the Exodus story is supreme. No human nor demon was able to withstand or defeat I AM. ***"Jesus Christ is the same yesterday, today, and forever,"*** Hebrews 13:8 NKJV. God's dealings with Moses proves there is power in the name of Jesus. We are to grow in this and work it out in our salvation. All the names of the Lord in the Old Testament are the further revelation of I AM.

Learning By the Name "You-Are-The-God-Who-Sees" El Roi

We can live in the name of Jesus because we can trust He knows everything going on in our life. He sees us and when necessary, He intervenes to protect us and establish His plan for us. After Hagar became pregnant from Abraham, Sarah mistreated her. Therefore, because of mistreatment, Hagar ran away (Read Genesis 16). In this moment of time for Hagar she needed divine intervention. Really, what was a pregnant woman with no resources going to do in a hostile environment. She needs the safety and protection of her family. Hagar, unable to think correctly because of the stress of her situation with Sarah, gets a mental adjustment from The-God-Who-Sees! He tells her to go home! Therefore, Hagar in amazement of the care of God for her declares,

"Then she called the name of the Lord who spoke to her, You-Are-the-God-Who-Sees; for she said, 'Have I also here seen Him who sees me?' Therefore the well was called Beer Lahai Roi; observe, it is between Kadesh and Bered," Genesis 16:13-14 NKJV.

Hagar called the name of the Lord, ***"You-Are-the-God-Who-Sees."*** Jesus, the Name above all names, is ***the-God-Who-Sees***! He sees you and all your life and situations. Through Hagar's problem, Jesus shows us He sees and cares for everyone. Jesus, the everlasting Father, teaches in the Sermon on the Mount the seeing eye of God for you and me. ***"Therefore do not worry, saying, 'What shall we eat?' or 'What shall we drink?' or 'What shall we wear?' For after all these things the Gentiles seek. For your heavenly Father knows that you need all these things,"*** Matthew 6:31-32 NKJV. God's dealings with Hagar proves there is power in the name of Jesus. We are to grow in this and work it out in our salvation.

Learning By the Name "For I Am the Lord Who Heals You" Yahweh Rophe

"If you diligently heed the voice of the Lord your God and do what is right in His sight, give ear to His commandments and keep all His statutes, I will put none of the diseases on you which I have brought on the Egyptians. For I am the Lord who heals you," Exodus 15:26 NKJV.

How does the life of Moses teach us this valuable name of the Lord? After Moses burning bush experience, where he placed his faith in, I AM, Moses lived a faithful obedient life. He only had one sin when he disobeyed God and struck the rock instead of speaking to it to get water at Kadesh (Read Numbers 20). This sin kept Moses from leading Israel into the promised land. However bad this was, it may have been a release of the bitterness built in Moses' heart because of the rebellious people he was leading. Although God was firm in His decision, Moses was forgiven and continued to lead the nation and have a relationship with God. His epitaph shows the power of Yahweh

Rophe, The Lord Who Heals, on the obedient life of Moses. ***"So Moses the servant of the Lord died there in the land of Moab, according to the word of the Lord. Moses was one hundred and twenty years old when he died. His eyes were not dim nor his natural vigor diminished,"*** Deuteronomy 34:5,7 NKJV. Jesus is Yahweh Rophe, the Lord Who Heals. God's dealings with Moses proves there is power in the name of Jesus to heal and keep us strong all our life. We are to grow in this and work it out in our salvation.

Learning by the Name "The Lord Will Provide" Yahweh Yireh

The Lord will provide is of great importance to everyone. The prayer bowls of heaven are constantly being filled with requests for God's blessing of prosperity. How would you like to have been Abraham? After going childless with Sarah at the age of one-hundred God fulfills His promise to them and Isaac is born. Abraham is happy but out of nowhere, he gets a strange command from God!

"Now it came to pass after these things that God tested Abraham, and said to him, 'Abraham!' And he said, 'Here I am.' Then He said, 'Take now your son, your only son Isaac, whom you love, and go to the land of Moriah, and offer him there as a burnt offering on one of the mountains of which I shall tell you,'" Genesis 22:1-2NKJV.

What is this all about? Imagine you are Abraham, would you be saying, *"God, you gave me a son and now you want me to sacrifice him?"* However, we may be thankful we are not Abraham, because Abraham was not worried about the command like we would be. His dealings with God gave him a faith of trust no matter how difficult a situation God brought him to. It seems Abraham reasoned in his heart based on the promises of God. ***"Then God said: 'No, Sarah your wife shall***

bear you a son, and you shall call his name Isaac; I will establish My covenant with him for an everlasting covenant, and with his descendants after him,'" Genesis 17:19 NKJV. Based on this promise Abraham came to this conclusion, ***"Concluding that God was able to raise him up, even from the dead,"*** Hebrews 11:19 NKJV.

Therefore, when Isaac questioned Abraham concerning where the lamb was for the burnt offering, Abraham could confidently declare to Isaac. ***"My son, God will provide for Himself the lamb for a burnt offering. So the two of them went together,"*** Genesis 22:8 NKJV. The momentous sacrifice was about to happen. Abraham got Isaac ready for the sacrifice. The knife was in Abraham's hand lifted and ready to strike.

"But the Angel of the Lord called to him from heaven and said, 'Abraham, Abraham!' So he said, 'Here I am.' And He said, 'Do not lay your hand on the lad, or do anything to him; for now I know that you fear God, since you have not withheld your son, your only son, from Me.' Then Abraham lifted his eyes and looked, and there behind him was a ram caught in a thicket by its horns. So Abraham went and took the ram, and offered it up for a burnt offering instead of his son."

The faith of Abraham and his trust in God pays off. Isaac is alive and a ram from the Lord took Isaac's place.

"And Abraham called the name of the place, The-Lord-Will-Provide; as it is said to this day, 'In the Mount of the Lord it shall be provided,'" Genesis 22:10-14 NKJV.

A second example of the provision of the Lord is found in Exodus. The children of Israel are in the desert, and they need food. Unlike their grandfather Abraham, they did not have faith nor trust in God. Abraham experienced God and believed. The children of Israel experienced God and did not believe. Abraham trusted the Lord would provide. Abraham's grandchildren did not. In fact they were a bunch of complaining babies. However, the Lord who began an excellent work in them was working to complete it.

"And the Lord spoke to Moses, saying, 'I have heard the complaints of the children of Israel. Speak to them, saying, At twilight you shall eat meat, and in the morning you shall be filled with bread. And you shall know that I am the Lord your God.' So it was that quail came up at evening and covered the camp, and in the morning the dew lay all around the camp. And when the layer of dew lifted, there, on the surface of the wilderness, was a small round substance, as fine as frost on the ground. And the house of Israel called its name Manna. And it was like white coriander seed, and the taste of it was like wafers made with honey. Then Moses said, 'This is the thing which the Lord has commanded: Fill an omer with it, to be kept for your generations, that they may see the bread with which I fed you in the wilderness, when I brought you out of the land of Egypt.'" Exodus 16:11-14,31-32 NKJV.

What is the point of this section? The point is, the Lord will provide!

The Name above all names is Jesus and Jesus is Jesus Yahweh Yireh. He is the provision for our sins. ***"The next day John saw Jesus coming toward him, and said, 'Behold! The Lamb of God who takes away the sin of the world!'"*** (John 1:29 NKJV) He also is the manna, the bread of life for us. ***"And Jesus said to them, 'I am the bread of life. He who comes to Me shall never hunger, and he who believes in Me shall never thirst,'"*** John 6:35 NKJV. As Paul declares, ***"And my God shall supply all your need according to His riches in glory by Christ Jesus,"*** Philippians 4:19 NKJV.

God's dealings with Abraham and Israel prove there is power in the name of Jesus to provide. We are to grow in this and work it out in our salvation.

Learning By The Name "The Lord

My Shepherd" Yahweh Raah

The 23rd Psalm grants us a beautiful picture of how a shepherd experienced being shepherded by God. David shouts out the first verse with a magnificent exclamation, "The Lord *is* my Shepherd." He then teaches us the many ways and benefits he experienced the shepherding ways of God. The Psalm speaks of this quite simply and emphatically. It is a great invitation to all souls to enter the sheepfold of Jesus to receive His shepherding provision, guidance, and protection.

"The Lord is my shepherd;
I shall not want.
He makes me to lie down in green pastures;
He leads me beside the still waters.
He restores my soul;
He leads me in the paths of righteousness
For His name's sake.
Yea, though I walk through the valley of the shadow of death,
I will fear no evil;
For You are with me;
Your rod and Your staff, they comfort me.
You prepare a table before me in the presence of my enemies;
You anoint my head with oil;
My cup runs over.
Surely goodness and mercy shall follow me
All the days of my life;
And I will dwell in the house of the Lord Forever."

Psalm 23 NKJV

What a blessing for us because Jesus, the name above all names, is our Yahweh Raah, our shepherd. ***"Then Jesus said to them again, 'Most assuredly, I say to you, I am the door of the sheep. All who ever came before Me are thieves and robbers, but the sheep did not hear them. I am the door. If anyone enters by Me, he will be saved, and will go in and out and find pasture. The***

thief does not come except to steal, and to kill, and to destroy. I have come that they may have life, and that they may have it more abundantly.' 'I am the good shepherd. The good shepherd gives His life for the sheep. I am the good shepherd; and I know My sheep, and am known by My own,'" John 10:7-11,14 NKJV.

Let us remember all power and authority has been given to Jesus, by the Father, and as a good shepherd He can do for us what He did for David in the 23rd Psalm! God's dealings with King David prove there is power in the name of Jesus to shepherd. We are to grow in this and work it out in our salvation. This is a lifelong process.

SUMMARY OF LEARNING BY THE NAMES

Through this lesson we have begun to study the name above all names, the greatest name in the Bible, Jesus. A problem we must fix in Christianity is our respect for Jesus Christ. The personal friendly way of the Lord has caused His church to forget who He really is. He is the resurrected LORD, the ultimate authority. Perhaps, in order to understand this meaning, we need to say it in a simple modern term. Jesus is the boss, the headman, the one who can hire (save) you or fire you (cast you into hell)! No other person or being has this authority. Therefore, our relationship with Him must first of all be reverent worship and obedience. Secondly, in our reverence and obedience, we find a friend who enables and cares for us to become the best we can be. We find this friendship and care through the descriptive names about Jesus revealed in the Old and New Testaments. This is so because He is who He is, the great I AM!

We are learning about who Jesus is (not was), because ***"Jesus Christ is the same yesterday, today, and forever,"*** Hebrews 13:8 NKJV. Therefore, all the revealed names of Him are pertinent to us today and forever. The names of Jesus are the descriptors of His very essence. They are the revelation of God on how He will express Himself to us and how we can relate to Him. Jesus is the greatest name given among men. No one else using the name of Jesus will be considered above all. Only Jesus Christ of Nazareth can claim this. The wonder of this name also enables us to be personable with God. Jesus has called us His friends and has allowed sinners to address Him simply as Jesus. By this allowance, when we address Jesus, we enter into the presence of all His names and all Jesus is, becomes personal to us. Therefore, we know the Lord Jesus, through all His names in full. ***"For in Him dwells all the fullness of the Godhead bodily,"*** Colossians 2:9 NKJV.

An important name of Jesus we need to discuss, in our summary, is ***Immanuel.*** The prophet Isaiah wrote about Immanuel.

"Therefore the Lord Himself will give you a sign: Behold, the virgin shall conceive and bear a Son, and shall call His name Immanuel," Isaiah 7:14 NKJV.

The Apostle Matthew explains this prophecy for us.

"But while he (Joseph) ***thought about these things, behold, an angel of the Lord appeared to him in a dream, saying, 'Joseph, son of David, do not be afraid to take to you Mary your wife, for that which is conceived in her is of the Holy Spirit. And she will bring forth a Son, and you shall call His name Jesus, for He will save His people from their sins.' So all this was done that it might be fulfilled which was spoken by the Lord through the prophet, saying: 'Behold, the virgin shall be with child, and bear a Son, and they shall call His name Immanuel,' which is translated, 'God with us,'"*** Matthew 1:20-23 NKJV.

Immanuel, Jesus Christ, conceived by the Holy Spirit and born of the Virgin Mary, becoming God with us. As the Nicene Creed states, *"God from God, Light from Light, true God from true God; begotten not made, one in being with the Father. Through Him all things were made. For us men and for our salvation He came down from heaven. By the power of the Holy Spirit He was born of the Virgin Mary and became man."* Who is Immanuel? He is God becoming man, to save man and reestablish our relationship with Him. The Apostle John explains the importance of Immanuel, God with us, in his gospel.

"And the Word became flesh and dwelt among us, and we beheld His glory, the glory as of the only begotten of the Father, full of

grace and truth," John 1:14 NKJV.

By the name Immanuel, Jesus, brings God to us and most importantly, us to God. Without, this name we would be lost forever. Isaiah is correct when he said, ***His name is Wonderful!*** All the incredible qualities of God are expressed in all the names of Jesus, who will forever be our intercessor before God the Father. How extremely important the revelation of Immanuel, Jesus Christ is for us. Through Him we have an everlasting relationship with God.

"Then I, John, saw the holy city, New Jerusalem, coming down out of heaven from God, prepared as a bride adorned for her husband. And I heard a loud voice from heaven saying, 'Behold, the tabernacle of God is with men, and He will dwell with them, and they shall be His people. God Himself will be with them and be their God,'" Revelation 21:2-3 NKJV.

Jesus our Immanuel the greatest name of all!

THE FULLNESS OF JESUS

What All of His Name Is

- I AM
- The-God-Who-Sees
- I am the Lord who heals you
- The Lord will provide
- The Lord My Shepard
- Wonderful
- Counselor
- Mighty God
- Everlasting Father
- Prince of Peace
- Immanuel
- Son of David
- Son of God
- Jesus of Nazareth
- Christ
- Jesus!

All of the above are many names describing the one name, Jesus, who is Our Lord and Savior. There are many more names of Him in Scripture, not included in this study, such as ***Elohim, El Shaddai, Alpha and Omega.*** These will be left to each of us to discover in Jesus, the Creator, Almighty and the Beginning and End. The point for all of us to understand concerning Jesus, the name above all names, is He relates and expresses Himself to us by all the names of His in the scripture. He meets us in the narrow way fraught with difficulties always helping us through each moment. He in Himself, has all abilities to do so. The names of Jesus prove it.

WALK IN HIS NAME

"For all people walk each in the name of his god,
But we will walk in the name of the Lord
our God Forever and ever."
Micah 4:5 NKJV

As born-again believers in the name of Jesus Christ, who was crucified for our sins and resurrected on the third day, we are admonished to ***"Walk in the name of the Lord our God Forever and ever!"*** The church at Antioch was recognized by the unbelievers in their city as people who walked in the name of the Lord. This happened after Barnabas brought Saul to Antioch. ***"And when he*** (Barnabas) ***had found him*** (Saul-Paul), ***he brought him to Antioch. So it was that for a whole year they assembled with the church and taught a great many people. And the disciples were first called Christians in Antioch,"*** Acts 11:26 NKJV. The disciples had a powerful walk in Antioch. These were believers who walked in the name of the Lord in a mighty way. So great was their witness of walking in the name of the Lord Jesus Christ, they earned the name of Christian.

How interesting the disciples were called Christ with the suffix -ian added. Those who saw these disciples knew they were those who followed and belonged to Jesus. Hence, they were called Christians, followers of Christ! Christians, from Strong's G5546 "Christianos, *a Christian, i.e. follower of Christ: --Christian."* They were the Church at Antioch, but the individual members of the church body were known as Christians. This is a prophecy of Isaiah coming to existence.

"Even to them I will give in My house And within My walls a place and a name Better than that of sons and daughters; I will give them an everlasting name That shall not be cut off," Isaiah 56:5 NKJV.

"The Gentiles shall see your righteousness, And all kings your glory. You shall be called by a new name, Which the mouth of the Lord will name," Isaiah 62:2 NKJV.

"You shall leave your name as a curse to My chosen; For the Lord God will slay you, And call His servants by another name," Isaiah 65:15 NKJV.

This new name came into existence in Antioch, ***"And the disciples were first called Christians in Antioch."***

We are prophesied to walk in the name of the Lord our God forever and ever. The name of the Lord our God given to walk in is Jesus Christ, our Lord and Savior. Remember, the angel told Joseph to name Mary's child, *Jesus*. This name was God's chosen name for His Son. We, believers in Jesus, are also given a prophetic chosen name to walk in forever and ever. This name is Christian! We are those who belong to Jesus and walk in the fullness of Jesus Himself. This is why we are called Christians. It does not matter that I grew-up in the Catholic Church, worshipped in the Episcopal Church, was ordained in the Church of Christ, also ordained in the Christian and Missionary Alliance. What matters is, I am a Christian and anyone who calls Jesus Lord, is my fellow Christian. No matter what church or denomination they attend. ***"Therefore I make known to you that no one speaking by the Spirit of God calls Jesus accursed, and no one can say that Jesus is Lord except by the Holy Spirit,"*** 1 Corinthians 12:3 NKJV. By this name, Christian, the world will know we are one. Therefore, let us never forget, ***"God also has highly exalted Him and given Him the name which is above every name, that at the name of Jesus every knee should bow, of those in heaven, and of those on earth, and of those under the earth, and that every tongue should confess that Jesus Christ is Lord, to the glory of God the Father,"*** Philippians 2:9-11 NKJV. This name is upon us as Christian. Let us be always walking in the name of the Lord!

HOW DO WE DO THIS?

There are no laws or regulations to follow which enable a person to walk in the name of the Lord. The walk in the name of the Lord is a walk of faith. The faith in Christ, believed in the mind or heart, confessed by our mouths, obeyed in our deeds. ***"But that no one is justified by the law in the sight of God is evident, for 'the just shall live by faith,'"*** Galatians 3:11 NKJV. Furthermore, ***"That if you confess with your mouth the Lord Jesus and believe in your heart that God has raised Him from the dead, you will be saved. For with the heart one believes unto righteousness, and with the mouth confession is made unto salvation. For the Scripture says, 'Whoever believes on Him will not be put to shame,'"*** Romans 10:9-11 NKJV. Walking in the name of the Lord is accomplished by having a believing heart, confessing mouth, then obeying what we believe and confess. This way of walking in the name of the Lord, must apply to all His names culminating in the name Jesus! A Christian's walk should amplify Christ in all His fullness. Knowledge is power but the knowledge of the LORD is the highest of powers. In our walk of faith, Christians ought to magnify the name above all names, Jesus.

"Some trust in chariots, and some in horses; But we will remember the name of the Lord our God,"
Psalm 20:7 NKJV.

Reflections

1. In Philippians 2:9-11, what has God done to Jesus?
2. What will happen, by all creatures, at the name of Jesus?
3. What will every tongue confess concerning Jesus

Christ?

4. How do you apply this knowledge in your life and relationship with God?
5. Where did the origination of naming begin?
6. What lineage name did God give to humans?
7. Why do you think today's politically correct movement is against anything with the name man in it?
8. How does this compare to evolution?
9. Who named Jesus, Mary and Joseph, or God the Father?
10. How significant is this? (Concerning parentage)
11. Joseph and Mary were obedient to God. How do you compare to them?
12. How did the town of Nazareth get attached to Jesus' name?
13. Why is Jesus given the name Christ?
14. Who is Jesus' Father in Luke 1:35? How is this expressed?
15. What do the demons know about Jesus in Matthew 8:28-29?
16. Since Jesus is the Son of God, explain why this makes His name above everyone and everything. How is this a reality in your life?
17. Why is Jesus considered a King? What is His earthly lineage? How is this a reality in your life?
18. According to Strong's Concordance, what does Jesus Christ's name mean? How is this a reality in your life?
19. What are the five names Isaiah 9:6-7 calls the Child and Son given to us?
20. Describe each of these names of Jesus.
21. How can Jesus meet you in these names? How is this a reality in your life?
22. How do these names affirm the greatest name of all, Jesus?
23. Describe Paul's summary of Jesus and His name in

Colossians 1:15-18.

24. How should these truths of Jesus affect your life?
25. According to Philippians 2:9-11, how much authority does Jesus have?
26. According to Psalm 89:24-27, what does God say He will give to His firstborn Son Jesus?
27. How should this truth be active in your life?
28. How does the name of Jesus have the power to save?
29. According to Acts 4:8-12, what name has the power to save?
30. What does this power to save mean?
31. Has the power of His name saved you?
32. What does it mean concerning the name of Jesus that has admittance power?
33. How does this admittance power of Jesus name work in prayer?
34. According to James 4:3, what is the proper use of the admitting name of Jesus in prayer?
35. How should this truth of admittance be active in your life?
36. Why is the healing power in the name of Jesus the most difficult to understand?
37. How has healing or the lack of healing in Jesus' name affected you and your faith?
38. Who is greater, Jesus or the demon world?
39. Are you afraid of these evil beings?
40. What does Mark 1:23-27 teach us about faith in Jesus over the demons?
41. What does 1John 4:4 teach concerning you, Jesus, and the demons?
42. How should this truth of Jesus affect your life?
43. What does Romans 15:4 teach about the Old Testament?
44. How can this teach us about the greatness of the name of Jesus and about who He is?
45. What is the significance of the name I AM in Exodus

3:13-14?

46. In John 8:57-58, who does Jesus say He is?
47. Is Jesus saying He was the one in the burning bush?
48. What were the experiences of Moses with I AM?
49. What does this teach you about the experiences you can have with I AM?
50. How should this truth of Jesus affect your life?
51. What can we learn about the name Jesus, I AM, who was called, *"You-Are-The-God-Who-Sees?"*
52. What can we learn about the name Jesus, I AM, who called Himself, *"For I Am the Lord Who Heals You?"*
53. What can we learn about the name Jesus, I AM, who was called by Abraham, *"The-Lord-Will-Provide?"*
54. What can we learn about the name Jesus, I AM, who was called by David, *"The Lord My Shepard?"*
55. What other names of Jesus are there in Scripture which teach about the greatest name of all?
56. What is the meaning of Hebrews 13:8?
57. How can we apply the meaning of Hebrews 13:8, with all the revealed names of Jesus?
58. How will Jesus react to us in the meaning of Hebrews 13:8?
59. What is the importance of the name Immanuel, concerning Jesus? How does this give Him the name above all names?
60. How should you live before Immanuel?
61. According to Colossians 2:9, what dwells in Jesus?
62. How does the name Immanuel bring God to us and more importantly, us to God?
63. What are we admonished to do in Micah 4:5?
64. According to Acts 11:26, what name were the believers called in Antioch?
65. How does this fulfill Isaiah 65:15?
66. How are you walking in the name of the LORD?

LESSON TWO

THE LORD OUR STRENGTH

FINDING HIS STRENGTH

"Not that I speak in regard to need, for I have learned in whatever state I am, to be content: I know how to be abased, and I know how to abound. Everywhere and in all things I have learned both to be full and to be hungry, both to abound and to suffer need. I can do all things through Christ who strengthens me," Philippians 4:11-13 NKJV.

As I contemplate the use of this scripture, ***"I can do all things through Christ who strengthens me,"*** I am amazed at the reality of the vast majority of ***"Christians"*** who have left the faith because they could not do all things through Christ who is our strength. The proof of this is seen in the wreckage of Christian lives shipwrecked from the failure to handle the adversities of the difficult narrow way of Christianity. This shows we are not more than conquerors, but the conquered. Paul states through Christ we conquer. ***"Who shall separate us from the love of Christ? Shall tribulation, or distress, or persecution, or famine, or nakedness, or peril, or sword? As it is written: 'For Your sake we are killed all day long; We are accounted as sheep for the slaughter.' Yet in all these things we are more than conquerors through Him who loved us. For I am persuaded that neither death nor life, nor angels nor principalities nor powers, nor things present nor things to come, nor height nor depth, nor any other created thing, shall be able to separate us from the love of God which is in Christ Jesus our Lord."*** Romans 8:35-39 NKJV

Paul teaches Christians may face and experience many difficulties.

THE DIFFICULTIES

- Tribulations
- Distresses
- Persecutions (These are troubles from people or problems of many sorts)
- Famines (Hunger)
- Financial difficulties resulting in nakedness (The inability to provide for oneself or family)
- Peril (Paul faced perils in the sea, he was shipwrecked, and on land, from robbers, for example)
- The sword representing the danger of physical attacks
- Being a martyr
- Battling governmental persecution
- Battling Satanical oppression

In these teachings of Paul, he gives us the clue of his victory in them. This clue further explains Philippians 3:13, doing all things through Christs' strength. The clue is in how we go through the difficulties. He said*, **"Yet in all these things we are more than conquerors through Him who loved us!"***

It is interesting how Paul states he has needs. He said to the Philippians, ***"Not that I speak in regard to need."*** The Apostle is human, just like us. He has needs, just like us. Just like us, he did not receive an answer to all his prayers the way he requested them. In Paul's problem with the demons, we are taught something mysterious through the strength of Christ. ***"And lest I should be exalted above measure by the abundance of the revelations, a thorn in the flesh was given to me, a messenger of Satan to buffet me, lest I be exalted above measure. Concerning this thing I pleaded with the Lord three times that it might depart from me. And He said to me, 'My grace is sufficient for you, for***

My strength is made perfect in weakness.' Therefore most gladly I will rather boast in my infirmities, that the power of Christ may rest upon me," 2 Corinthians 12:7-9 NKJV. Paul said, ***"For I have learned in whatever state I am, to be content."*** In his "with the demon," Paul had to rely on Christ's grace for relief. He had to learn how-to live-in grace and be content with that! Paul, like us, prays and pleads over and over, "Lord, heal me, make this thing depart from me!" Nevertheless, the Lord does not heal nor take it away, but wants us to overcome it through His grace. Hence, in His grace we do all things through Christ who strengthens us. This is a learning experience. Sometimes this learning is difficult or hard to accept.

How, strange to hear the words of Jesus, ***"My strength is made perfect in weakness."*** How opposite is this to the way we think? The world glories in the strong, but God glories in the weak. Paul explains the concept of God glorying in the weak in 1 Corinthians 1:27-29, ***"But God has chosen the foolish things of the world to put to shame the wise, and God has chosen the weak things of the world to put to shame the things which are mighty; and the base things of the world and the things which are despised God has chosen, and the things which are not, to bring to nothing the things that are, that no flesh should glory in His presence."*** Furthermore, concerning how we look at things and glory in strength, God said to Isaiah, ***"For My thoughts are not your thoughts, Nor are your ways My ways, says the Lord. For as the heavens are higher than the earth, So are My ways higher than your ways, And My thoughts than your thoughts,"*** Isaiah 55:8-9 NKJV. We really do not accept this line of reasoning from God. We prove this in the most pathetic of statements, "God helps those who help themselves!" What are we saying? We are saying, God helps the strong, not the weak. Furthermore, He helps the wise, not those who are insufficiently intelligent according to the standards of the world. This pathetic statement almost implies, God saves those who help themselves. Contrary to the prosperity gospel, Paul, a remarkably successful and influential intellectual Pharisee, was humbled by God. This humbling brought humility and weakness to Paul. What did Jesus say to Ananias concerning Paul's Christian journey? Jesus said, ***"For I will show him how many things he must suffer for My name's sake,"*** Acts 9:16 NKJV. Paul was definitely assigned for great moments. Nevertheless, even in those moments he needed Christ because of the sufferings coming his way. God knew Paul was a strong and intelligent person. However, spiritually he was very weak. The countless hours of rabbinical training made him worldly wise not scripturally wise. Therefore, from the moment God knocked him off his horse (Acts 9) Paul gave up his human strength for the strength of Christ and his worldly wisdom for the wisdom of God. How else can you explain what happened at his conversion? All of Paul's formal education in the Torah did him no avail. May I possibly say, Paul was quite foolish in his understanding of the Old Testament Scriptures. There was Christ in their midst, fulfilling all the prophets, living the law righteously, performing miracles only God could do and Paul and his fellow scholars missed it. In fact, they were incensed over Christ to the point of jealous insanity. After Paul lost the wisdom of the world, his former colleagues hated him too.

THE MARVEL OF THE STRENGTH AND WISDOM FROM CHRIST

Paul had to be made weak by God to be saved. As he was traveling in human strength and wisdom to Damascus to imprison Christians, God met him. In this encounter, Paul became weak and then he was made strong by accepting Christ as his savior. ***"As he journeyed he came near Damascus, and suddenly a light shone around him from heaven. Then he fell to the ground, and heard a voice saying to him, 'Saul, Saul, why are you persecuting Me?'"*** (Acts 9:3-4 NKJV) At this moment of Paul's humbling to weakness before God, Paul could be saved. ***"So he, trembling and astonished, said, 'Lord, what do You want me to do?' Then the Lord said to him, 'Arise and go into the city, and you will be told what you must do,'"*** Acts 9:6 NKJV. How wonderful the transformation of ignorance to Godly wisdom is the testimony of Paul. The one who was terrifying believers because of scriptural stupidity and arrogance became wise and humble, in Christ, with power. ***"Immediately he preached the Christ in the synagogues, that He is the Son of God. Then all who heard were amazed, and said, 'Is this not he who destroyed those who called on this name in Jerusalem, and has come here for that purpose, so that he might bring them bound to the chief priests?' But Saul increased all the more in strength, and confounded the Jews who dwelt in Damascus, proving that this Jesus is the Christ,"*** Acts 9:20-22 NKJV. Paul went from human strength to Christ's strength. He went from human wisdom to the wisdom of God, in the understanding of the Scriptures.

LEARNING CHRIST

The Apostle Paul does not teach a Christianity devoid of problems with only supernatural riches in a believer's life. Paul teaches the Christian life with all its needs, up and downs. He does not stray from the Lord's teaching, ***"These things I have spoken to you, that in Me you may have peace. In the world you will have tribulation; but be of good cheer, I have overcome the world,"*** John 16:33 NKJV. He finds his ability to endure and enjoy all with contentment through Christ, no matter what state he is in. He does not leave the Lord's teaching, "***And in that day you will ask Me nothing. Most assuredly, I say to you, whatever you ask the Father in My name He will give you. Until now you have asked nothing in My name. Ask, and you will receive, that your joy may be full,"*** John 16:23-24 NKJV. He does not deny, with a head in the sky attitude, concerning his personal needs. He states he has concerns and deep problems. Nevertheless, he is able to go through all with the hidden strength of Christ because he has the assurance of God's answers to his prayers.

PAUL'S TESTIMONY

"From the Jews five times I received forty stripes minus one. Three times I was beaten with rods; once I was stoned; three times I was shipwrecked; a night and a day I have been in the deep; in journeys often, in perils of waters, in perils of robbers, in perils of my own countrymen, in perils of the Gentiles, in perils in the city, in perils in the wilderness, in perils in the sea, in perils among false brethren; in weariness and toil, in sleeplessness often, in hunger and thirst, in fastings often, in cold and nakedness— besides the other things, what comes upon me daily: my deep concern for all the churches. Who is weak, and I am not weak? Who is made to stumble, and I do not burn with indignation?" (2 Corinthians 11:24-29 NKJV)

I say with conviction, Paul was more than a conqueror in his "difficulties," through Christ who strengthened him. This type of Christian life is far from the minds of many modern day "Christians." However, it may be the reality for us again. Did you read Paul's statement in verse 29, ***"Who is weak, and I am not weak?"*** The mighty Saul before conversion; has become the weak Paul after conversion. What did it take from God to make Paul this way? It took many difficulties to take Paul from a position of self-sufficiency to Christ-dependency. Let us examine Philippians 4:11-13, in order to get the content and context for receiving Christs' strength.

"Not that I speak in regard to need, for I have learned in whatever state I am, to be content: I know how to be abased, and I know how to abound. Everywhere and in all things I have learned both to be full and to be hungry, both to abound and to suffer need. I can do all things through Christ who strengthens me."

Do you find it interesting, Paul had to learn how to live Biblically in different types of life states? The Lord taught Paul to apply the Scriptures in the normal course of daily activities. Truly, it is one thing to know the Bible and another thing to live and apply the Bible. Also, it is one thing to preach Christ and another thing to live through and by Christ and His strength. The key to understanding and knowledge of when someone applies the Scripture and lives through Christ is their contentment. How did God teach Paul to be content? Did God spare Paul from life or did God immerse or baptize Paul into all of life?

WHAT GOD ALLOWED

God allowed Paul many experiences to help Paul learn contentment in Christ.

- He allowed Paul to be abased (Abase, from Strong's G5014: to depress; figuratively, to humiliate (in condition or heart):--abase, bring low, humble (self)). See how in above 2 Corinthians 11:24-29.
- He allowed Paul to abound (Abound, from Strong's G4052: to superabound (in quantity or quality), be in excess, be superfluous; also (transitively) to cause to superabound or excel:--(make, more) abound, (have, have more) abundance (be more) abundant, be the better, enough and to spare, exceed, excel, increase, be left, redound, remain (over and above)). How? ***"It is doubtless not profitable for me to boast. I will come to visions and revelations of the Lord: I know a man in Christ who fourteen years ago—whether in the body I do not know, or whether out of the body I do not know, God knows—such a one was caught up to the third heaven. And I know such a man—whether in the body or out of the body I do not know, God knows— how he was caught up into Paradise and heard inexpressible words, which it is not lawful for a man to utter,"*** 2 Corinthians 12:1-4 NKJV. Paul had the super wealthy experience of visions and revelations of the Lord.

WHAT DID PAUL LEARN

- He learned to be full (Full, from Strong's G5526: to fodder, i.e. (generally) to gorge (supply food in abundance):--feed, fill, satisfy).
- He learned to be hungry (Hungry, from Strong's G3983: (through the idea of pinching toil; "pine"); to famish (absolutely or comparatively); figuratively, to crave:--be an hungered.).
- He learned how to abound (See above Strong's G4052).
- He learned to suffer need (Suffer Need, from Strong's G5302: to be later, i.e. (by implication) to be inferior; generally, to fall short (be deficient):--come behind (short), be destitute, fail, lack, suffer need, (be in) want, be the worse).

The result of God's teaching methods in Paul was, Paul learned to be content in the abundance and poverty of life. How did Paul arrive to the state of contentment? He says, through Christ who strengthened him in all the states he was in. How else can you explain Paul's ability to endure, whippings, being beat by rods, being stoned to death, shipwrecked and everything else he went through? Only the strength of Christ, who endured whipping and crucifixion, could enable Paul to be content. He explained this way of life to the Galatians in chapter 2 verse 20. Let us study it in three versions.

PAUL FINDS CHRISTS' STRENGTH IN THE EXCHANGED LIFE

"I have been crucified with Christ; it is no longer I who live, but Christ lives in me; and the life which I now live in the flesh I live by faith in the Son of God, who loved me and gave Himself for me." NKJV

"I am crucified with Christ: nevertheless I live; yet not I, but Christ liveth in me: and the life which I now live in the flesh I live by the faith of the Son of God, who loved me, and gave himself for me." KJV

"I have been crucified with Christ [that is, in Him I have shared His crucifixion]; it is no longer I who live, but Christ lives in me. The life I now live in the body I live by faith [by adhering to, relying on, and completely trusting] in the Son of God, who loved me and gave Himself up for me." AMP

PAUL'S REALITY

- He is crucified (and put to death) with Christ in Christ's crucifixion.
- Even though he is dead in Christ, He lives.
- He claims it is not his life's life which is alive, but Christ's life living in him.
- This is how he gets the strength of Christ to do all things; he lives by a faith of complete trust in Christ's loving Life in him.

The Apostle Paul had the strength of Christ because he learned the exchanged life through faith. For Paul, being born again was a reality of faith. He walked according to a higher law. ***"For the law of the Spirit of life in Christ Jesus has made me free from the law of sin and death,"*** Romans 8:2 NKJV. The Apostle grasped the two principles of the mystery of being born again to gain the strength of Christ in this higher law of God.

1. First Principle: Christ is in Us: ***"The mystery which has been hidden from ages and from generations, but now has been revealed to His saints. To them God willed to make known what are the riches of the glory of this mystery among the Gentiles: which is Christ in you, the hope of glory,"*** Colossians 1:26-27 NKJV.
2. Second Principle: Christ is our life: ***"When Christ who is our life appears, then you also will appear with Him in glory,"*** Colossians 3:4 NKJV.

The Apostle Paul learned the reality of Christ in us through His Spirit. Jesus said this happens by faith in Him. ***"Jesus answered, Most assuredly, I say to you, unless one is born of water and the Spirit, he cannot enter the kingdom of***

God," John 3:5 NKJV. The question for us is, do we believe in our being born again and the new life we have in Christ? Paul states another important fact concerning John 3:5. ***"Therefore, if anyone is in Christ, he is a new creation; old things have passed away; behold, all things have become new,"*** 2 Corinthians 5:17 NKJV. Paul's Christ strength came by a deep faith in what God said. This came to him through much struggle. In his Christian walk he once was frustrated. In anxiety he cried, ***"O wretched man that I am! Who will deliver me from this body of death?"*** (Romans 7:24) After learning through faith the Christ strength, Paul spoke jubilantly of the deliverance, ***"I thank God —through Jesus Christ our Lord! So then, with the mind I myself serve the law of God, but with the flesh the law of sin,"*** Romans 7:25 NKJV. Finally, in Paul's mind the higher law of the Spirit of life became his dominant mindset. The Spirit of life in Christ, imparted to him the strength of Christ in all situations.

THE KEY TO PAUL'S SECRET STRENGTH

What is the key in activating Christs' strength enabling a person to do all things? It is the decision to go through the state we are in, to its conclusion by ***faith***, ***trusting*** Christ's love in us. Paul had a willingness to finish all life's events for the sake of Christ. ***"Now when we heard these things, both we and those from that place pleaded with him not to go up to Jerusalem. Then Paul answered, 'What do you mean by weeping and breaking my heart? For I am ready not only to be bound, but also to die at Jerusalem for the name of the Lord Jesus,'"*** Acts 21:12-13 NKJV. He testifies of this in a farewell to his friend Timothy. ***"For I am already being poured out as a drink offering, and the time of my departure is at hand. I have fought the good fight, I have finished the race, I have kept the faith,"*** 2 Timothy 4:6-7 NKJV. Paul is facing execution and his testimony is, he kept the faith.

Paul chose to live by faith in the Son of God over faith in his own strengths. This was a difficult lesson to learn. However, he learned it. Therefore, his learned behavior, to be content no matter how difficult the narrow way became, is a testimony of Christ's strength in him. If one learns to be content he shows he trusts Christ entirely. It does not mean you are happy with starving, persecutions or diseases, but you are happy and satisfied because Christ is your life. Therefore, He becomes your strength to be a conqueror over whatever state you are in. How horrible it is, when we let our circumstances conquer us through use of our own failing strength. The scars of defeat, in being conquered, hurt for a lifetime and the results do too. The joy of finding Christ's strength and the victory to conquer any state uplifts one always. The truth of being in various states, as Paul puts it in Philippians 3:11-12, is the revealing of the kind of faith and trust we have in God and His Word, the Bible. Paul's testimony is wonderful. How about our testimony of Christ in us, is it vivid or dull?

PAUL TEACHES GOD WORKS THROUGH FAITH

"But without faith it is impossible to please Him, for he who comes to God must believe that He is, and that He is a rewarder of those who diligently seek Him," Hebrews 11:6 NKJV

This verse is overlooked by the church to its detriment. Paul is teaching us the key to obtaining the strength of Christ. This key is faith. Let us look at this verse and try to comprehend what it says.

- If we have no faith, it is impossible to please God. Impossible, is Strong's G102: unable, i.e. weak (literally or figuratively); passively, impossible:--could not do, impossible, impotent, not possible, weak.

Literally speaking, a person, who does not have faith, is without power or have the capability to please God. We do not realize how much faith we really live by and do not apply spiritually. An example of faith exhibited is by drivers of cars, who trust their fellow drivers to stay on their side of the road. If we did not have this faith we probably would not drive. Many people have a faith saying, "There is a God," but their faith is insufficient to please God. The faith needed to please God is a seeking faith of people who honestly believe He is God. The seeking faith is in believing God's word and work in Christ. James explains this point this way: ***"But someone will say, 'You have faith, and I have works.' Show me your faith without your works, and I will show you my faith by my works. You believe that there is one God. You do well. Even the demons believe—and tremble! But do you want to know, O foolish man, that faith without works is dead?"*** (James 2:18-20 NKJV) The faith God is looking for is a belief in Him and trust in His Word and action on it. Paul learned this and found Christ's strength through faith and believing in Jesus. Therefore, he learned contentment in all states of life.

Furthermore, concerning faith, Paul said, ***"For in it the righteousness of God is revealed from faith to faith; as it is written, 'The just shall live by faith,'"*** Romans 1:17 NKJV. Paul is teaching the New Testament life from an Old Testament principle. The prophet Habakkuk taught the faith principle in Habakkuk chapter 2:4: ***"Behold the proud, His soul is not upright in him; 'But the just shall live by his faith.'"*** Paul explains in Romans 1:16 and 17:

- The righteousness of God is revealed in the gospel of Jesus Christ.
- This revealing is the power of God to salvation to everyone who believes.
- We enter salvation by faith and then we live saved by faith.
- This living is a moment-by-moment faith to faith existence, believing Christ dwells in the heart.

Paul prayed for the Ephesian Christians to learn this secret. He prayed, ***"That Christ may dwell in your hearts through faith,"*** Ephesians 3:17 NKJV. Paul learned to live by faith, trusting Christ was dwelling in His heart. He did not trust feelings concerning the reality of it. His vibrant faith gave him the ability to receive Christ's strength in whatever state he was in.

PETER—THE EXAMPLE OF LIVING BY FAITH AND LIVING BY SIGHT

How amazing, the Apostle Peter in a matter of minutes, went from a walk of faith, getting strength from Christ to a walk by sight and losing the strength of Christ. This all happened in a matter of moments. Therefore, we need to hold on to faith moment by moment. How did Peter accomplish this inglorious feat; faith to faithlessness? This event in Peter's life is complex. Nevertheless, the lesson is easy to understand. According to Matthew chapter 14, Jesus feeds the five thousand people from a few loaves of bread and fishes. He then sends the crowds away. The Lord, having a desire to be alone and pray, sent His disciples away on their fishing boat. After a while, Jesus looking out towards the boat, which was in the middle of the Sea of Galilee, saw His disciples struggling against the wind.

"And when He had sent the multitudes away, He went up on the mountain by Himself to pray. Now when evening came, He was alone there. But the boat was now in the middle of the sea, tossed by the waves, for the wind was contrary. Now in the fourth watch of the night Jesus went to them, walking on the sea. And when the disciples saw Him walking on the sea, they were troubled, saying, 'It is a ghost!' And they cried out for fear," Matthew 14:23-26 NKJV.

What a complex situation this is. We see the Lord walking on a stormy sea and the disciples storm tossed in their boat. It is at this point we see the reverse metamorphosis of Peter from faith to faithlessness.

"But immediately Jesus spoke to them, saying, 'Be of good cheer! It is I; do not be afraid.' And Peter answered Him and said, 'Lord,

if it is You, command me to come to You on the water.' So He said, 'Come.' And when Peter had come down out of the boat, he walked on the water to go to Jesus," Matthew 14:27-29 NKJV.

Who can deny the great faith and quickening strength of Jesus upon Peter, at this moment? The proof is Peter had faith in the command of Christ and walked on water! What a thrill of faith this must have been for him. I wonder if he yelled to the other disciples in the boat, "Hey, guys look at me walking on water!" Well, the bragging did not last too long because Peter quickly lost faith. In losing faith, he lost the strength of Christ to walk on water.

LOSING FAITH BRINGS A SINKING FEELING

"But when he saw that the wind was boisterous, he was afraid; and beginning to sink he cried out, saying, 'Lord, save me!'" (Matthew 14:30 NKJV)

We have just watched the eyewitness account of the reverse metamorphosis of Peter from being full of faith and the strength of Christ to faithlessness and weakness in human strength. In losing faith, Peter a great swimmer, (see John 21) became weak and fearful and began to sink into the sea for drowning. This behavior haunted him many times after, but as Paul learned to live by Christ's strength through many trials, so did Peter. When you lose faith, take a lesson, from the sinking Peter and cry out, ***"Lord, save me!"***

THE WONDERFUL GRACE OF JESUS

We may marvel at the loss of faith by Peter (even though we are all without excuse concerning this). Nevertheless, Peter had the clarity of thought to reestablish faith by crying out to Christ and His strength to save him.

"And immediately Jesus stretched out His hand and caught him, and said to him, 'O you of little faith, why did you doubt?' And when they got into the boat, the wind ceased," Matthew 14:31-32 NKJV.

How wonderful it is when we rest in the Lord and the power of His strength. If we go through the states of life, with Christ's strength, we can be safely in the boat free from the howling winds around us. John writes an amazing thing concerning going through rough seas with Christ. ***"Then they willingly received Him into the boat, and immediately the boat was at the land where they were going,"*** John 6:21 NKJV. The disciples willingly received Jesus into the boat by faith. The joy and contentment they experienced by having Jesus with them, made the trip to their destination seem like nothing. The lesson of Peter's trip from faith to faithlessness must be a warning to us all. The cure for this is to not listen to the boisterous waves whirling around us in whatever state we are in. We must have one hundred percent focus of faith on Christ. We must not obsess over the problem but go through the problem trusting Christ. He said, ***"And lo, I am with you always, even to the end of the age. Amen,"*** Matthew 28:20 NKJV. ***"So we may boldly say: 'The Lord is my helper; I will not fear. What can man do to me?'"*** (Hebrews 13:6)

The Apostle John puts his stamp of approval on finding the conquering strength of Christ. He wrote, ***"For whatever is born of God overcomes the world. And this is the victory that***

has overcome the world— our faith. Who is he who overcomes the world, but he who believes that Jesus is the Son of God?" (1 John 5:4-5 NKJV) When we learn to live by faith, as Paul, Peter, John and countless other believers, we will be content in the strength of God to overcome all life's states.

THE FAITH HALL OF FAME

SAINTS WHO LIVED BY THE STRENGTH OF CHRIST

Hebrews chapter eleven is a fantastic writing for education, information, and encouragement for the life of faith. This chapter teaches how to go through all of life's states. Take a moment, open your Bible, and read the whole chapter. It is interesting to note Adam and Eve are not listed in the hall of faith. They chose not to live by faith believing and obeying the word of God. Faithfulness began with Abel, who sacrificed according to the will of God. His brother Cain was like his parents, faithless in his sacrifice. ***"By faith Abel offered to God a more excellent sacrifice than Cain, through which he obtained witness that he was righteous, God testifying of his gifts; and through it he being dead still speaks,"*** Hebrews 11:4 NKJV. The secret of Abel was, he believed God and acted accordingly.

Enoch teaches the righteousness and power of faith. It is written, he pleased God (Hebrews 11:5). We learned in Hebrews 11:6 without faith we cannot please God, Therefore, Enoch was a man of faith fully pleasing God. He received the strength of Christ and was raptured to heaven. The secret of Enoch was, he believed God and acted accordingly.

Noah had faithful reverence and believed God's command. ***"By faith Noah, being divinely warned of things not yet seen, moved with godly fear, prepared an ark for the saving of his household, by which he condemned the world and became heir of the righteousness which is according to faith,"*** Hebrews 11:7 NKJV. By faith and through the wisdom and strength of God, he built an immense ark. Noah did not live by sight, but by faith. It takes a strong willful faith to believe in things to come which were never experienced before. Noah was five hundred years old when he started having children. He was six hundred years old when that which was not seen came to sight, the great rain of flood waters. Between five hundred years to six hundred years old, Noah heard God. He had to keep faith and build the ark. Truly, Noah lived by faith and we are here because of him. The secret of Noah is, he believed God and acted accordingly.

Abraham did not do anything as spectacular as Noah. God told him to move to a place not seen by him before and he moved there. ***"By faith Abraham obeyed when he was called to go out to the place which he would receive as an inheritance. And he went out, not knowing where he was going,"*** Hebrews 11:8 NKJV. Abraham and his wife, Sarah, were having trouble conceiving. They were childless. Nevertheless, God promised Abraham a child by Sarah and through her a mighty nation. Abraham believed God and had faith in the promise. ***"For what does the Scripture say? "Abraham believed God, and it was accounted to him for righteousness,"*** Romans 4:3 NKJV. Therefore, Sarah and Abraham received the strength of Christ to have a baby in advanced old age. ***"By faith Sarah herself also received strength to conceive seed, and she bore a child when she was past the age, because she judged Him faithful who had promised. Therefore from one man, and him as good as dead, were born as many as the stars of the sky in multitude—innumerable as the sand which is by the seashore,"*** Hebrews 11:11-12 NKJV. The secret of Abraham and Sarah is, they believed God and acted accordingly.

Let us not forget Abraham's greatest act of obedient faith. This act was the offering to God of his son Isaac, whom he deeply loved. Few of us could pass this test of faith. How beautiful the foreshadowing of God who actually did offer His Son for an atonement for all. "***By faith Abraham, when he was tested, offered up Isaac, and he who had received the promises offered up his only begotten son, of whom it was said, 'In Isaac your seed shall be called,' concluding that God was able to raise***

him up, even from the dead, from which he also received him in a figurative sense," Hebrews 11:17-19 NKJV. What can we conclude from this? We can deduce one important fact. A person who knows God intimately, trusts God, and can do all things through Christ who strengthens them. Abraham proved it in a difficult state. He proved faith in God brings the provisions of strength from God. ***"And He said, 'Do not lay your hand on the lad, or do anything to him; for now I know that you fear God, since you have not withheld your son, your only son, from Me.' Then Abraham lifted his eyes and looked, and there behind him was a ram caught in a thicket by its horns. So Abraham went and took the ram, and offered it up for a burnt offering instead of his son. And Abraham called the name of the place, The- Lord-Will-Provide; as it is said to this day, "In the Mount of the Lord it shall be provided,"*** Genesis 22:12-14 NKJV. The secret of Abraham is, he believed God and acted accordingly.

Furthermore, the Hall of Fame talks about the faith of Isaac, Jacob, and Joseph, who all trusted in the strength of Christ, to believe God and act accordingly! This is summed up in the faith of Moses. ***"By faith Moses, when he became of age, refused to be called the son of Pharaoh's daughter, choosing rather to suffer affliction with the people of God than to enjoy the passing pleasures of sin, esteeming the reproach of Christ greater riches than the treasures in Egypt; for he looked to the reward,"*** Hebrews 11:24-26 NKJV.

Did you notice what the faith of Moses (and all the saints of old) looked forward to by faith? Moses looked forward to the reward of God's promises according to His word! Moses went through many states of events in his life. Like us he had his ups and downs, joys and frustrations, but he never lost sight of his strength. Here are a few events proving this and setting forth the faith we need to develop. ***"By faith he forsook Egypt, not fearing the wrath of the king; for he endured***

as seeing Him who is invisible. By faith he kept the Passover and the sprinkling of blood, lest he who destroyed the firstborn should touch them. By faith they passed through the Red Sea as by dry land, whereas the Egyptians, attempting to do so, were drowned," Hebrews 11:27-29 NKJV. The Egyptians tried to cross the Red Sea after Israel but their faith was not in God and His promises. They had self-faith which always will fail no matter how great a person or country can become. They did not please God. Hence, the Red Sea closed in and drowned them. The secret of Moses is, he believed God.

THE REALITIES OF A VIBRANT FAITH LIFE

Faith is a wonderful life to live when we keep our focus on Christ. The writer of Hebrews summarizes the many states of life requiring faith to receive the strength of Christ. Since I believe, Paul wrote Hebrews, he understood this and learned to be content in all the states of human affairs which came his way.

"By faith the walls of Jericho fell down after they were encircled for seven days. By faith the harlot Rahab did not perish with those who did not believe, when she had received the spies with peace. And what more shall I say? For the time would fail me to tell of Gideon and Barak and Samson and Jephthah, also of David and Samuel and the prophets: who through faith subdued kingdoms, worked righteousness, obtained promises, stopped the mouths of lions, quenched the violence of fire, escaped the edge of the sword, out of weakness were made strong, became valiant in battle, turned to flight the armies of the aliens. Women received their dead raised to life again. Others were tortured, not accepting deliverance, that they might obtain a better resurrection. Still others had trial of mockings and scourgings, yes, and of chains and imprisonment. They were stoned, they were sawn in two, were tempted, were slain with the sword. They wandered about in sheepskins and goatskins, being destitute, afflicted, tormented— of whom the world was not worthy. They wandered in deserts and mountains, in dens and caves of the earth. And all these, having obtained a good testimony through faith, did not receive the promise, God having provided something better for us, that they should not be made perfect apart from us," Hebrews 11:30-40 NKJV.

How marvelous is this section of scripture? The truths

of a life of faith are exhibited to the fullest. This is real Christianity and the walk of faith. What will be written about you and me in the Book of Life concerning our faith and adherence to it? ***"And anyone not found written in the Book of Life was cast into the lake of fire,"*** Revelation 20:15 NKJV. If we want what God has provided for us, we must live the life of faith. Faith is what conquers fear and enables us through the strength of Christ to be more than conquerors. Paul said he could do all things through Christ who strengthened him. Therefore, Paul found contentment in this. This also must become our reality and declaration.

THE STRENGTH OF CHRIST

We have traveled a long road in showing the truth of being strengthened by Christ through faith. As it was for the saints of old it is also for us today, Christ can strengthen us. One good piece of information for us from Jesus, will help us to not be intimidated to start a journey of faith. The giants of faith also had to begin with a small seed of faith. ***"Then He said, 'To what shall we liken the kingdom of God? Or with what parable shall we picture it? It is like a mustard seed which, when it is sown on the ground, is smaller than all the seeds on earth; but when it is sown, it grows up and becomes greater than all herbs, and shoots out large branches, so that the birds of the air may nest under its shade,'"*** Mark 4:30-32 NKJV. We begin our faith journey to the strength of Christ by starting to believe and trust the Bible. We plant the Word in our heart and have faith in it, applying it to our state of affairs.

ENCOURAGEMENTS FOR CHRIST'S STRENGTH FOR US

GOD PROMISED HE WOULD STRENGTHEN US

- *"Fear not, for I am with you; Be not dismayed, for I am your God. I will strengthen you, Yes, I will help you, I will uphold you with My righteous right hand," Isaiah 41:10* NKJV.
- *"Have you not known? Have you not heard? The everlasting God, the Lord, The Creator of the ends of the earth, Neither faints nor is weary. His understanding is unsearchable. He gives power to the weak, And to those who have no might He increases strength. Even the youths shall faint and be weary, And the young men shall utterly fall, But those who wait on the Lord Shall renew their strength; They shall mount up with wings like eagles, They shall run and not be weary, They shall walk and not faint," Isaiah 40:28-31* NKJV.

JESUS TELLS US

- *"Come to Me, all you who labor and are heavy laden, and I will give you rest. Take My yoke upon you and learn from Me, for I am gentle and lowly in heart, and you will find rest for your souls. For My yoke is easy and My burden is light,"* Matthew 11:28-30 NKJV.
- *"I am with you always, even to the end of the age. Amen,"* Matthew 28:20 NKJV.
- *"If you love Me, keep My commandments. And I will pray the Father, and He will give you another Helper, that He may abide with you forever— the Spirit of truth, whom the world cannot receive, because it neither sees Him nor knows Him; but you know Him, for He dwells with you and will be in you. I will not leave you orphans; I will come to you,"* John 14:15-18 NKJV.

The promises are a positive of God's assurance to be with us and strengthen us.

JESUS TEACHES HOW THE SPIRIT WILL HELP US

- ***"He will glorify Me, for He will take of what is Mine and declare it to you. All things that the Father has are Mine. Therefore I said that He will take of Mine and declare it to you,"*** John 16:14-15 NKJV.

The Spirit works in us by imparting to us what belongs to Jesus. Therefore, strength belongs to Jesus and this is one of Jesus' belongings the Holy Spirit gives us.

PAUL SHOWS THROUGH THE PRAYER OF FAITH HOW THE STRENGTH OF CHRIST COMES

- ***"That He would grant you, according to the riches of His glory, to be strengthened with might through His Spirit in the inner man, that Christ may dwell in your hearts through faith; that you, being rooted and grounded in love, may be able to comprehend with all the saints what is the width and length and depth and height— to know the love of Christ which passes knowledge; that you may be filled with all the fullness of God,"*** Ephesians 3:16-19 NKJV.

Educational Points of the Prayer

1. We may petition God for Christ's strength.
2. God has plenty of riches in His glory to answer the prayer.
3. The strength of Christ is released through the Holy Spirit in our inner man (our heart).
4. Faith is the key which allows Christ to dwell in our hearts.
5. Love (our love for God) is the essential grounding from which to base our petitions.
6. Finally, Paul wants us to really comprehend and know Christ's love and God intimately, by being filled with the fullness of God.

WHAT MUST WE DO?

What must we do to receive the strength of Christ in our life? There is no formula for this to happen. It happens when we simply have faith, trust and acceptance of what God says and promises. Accepting is a vital part of faith, which consents to receive what God says and says yes to it! How did Israel fail to receive the strength of Christ in their history? They failed because they did not have faith. Therefore, they did not please God!

"But Israel, pursuing the law of righteousness, has not attained to the law of righteousness. Why? Because they did not seek it by faith, but as it were, by the works of the law. For they stumbled at that stumbling stone." Romans 9:31-32 NKJV

We must not fall into the trap like Israel did. The trap for us is living by feelings and sight. We must heed the warning of not having an evil heart of unbelief. ***"Beware, brethren, lest there be in any of you an evil heart of unbelief in departing from the living God,"*** Hebrews 3:12 NKJV. Having no faith, trust, and acceptance of the Word of God will give us nothing from heaven. Therefore, as you and I travel through the various states of life with its highs and lows, we must develop the trusting faith which declares, ***"I can do all things through Christ who strengthens me!"***

Reflections

1. *According to Paul's testimony in Philippians 4:11-13, what did the Lord teach Paul concerning the life of a Christian in this present world?*
2. *How does this verse give problems to the prosperity gospel?*

3. *Do these verses teach how God disciplines His children?*
4. *Are you a casualty of misunderstanding Bible verses? Do you know others who have left the faith because they feel God let them down?*
5. *What is the difficult narrow way of Christianity (See Matthew 7:13-19)?*
6. *List the difficulties of the narrow way anyone can encounter in the Christian life according to Paul in Romans 8:35-39.*
7. *How do we conquer these adversities?*
8. *How does this mesh with Philippians 3:13?*
9. *Are you startled by the very human needs and difficulties of the Apostle Paul?*
10. *How is Paul taught to handle the demon world in 2 Corinthians 12:7-9?*
11. *Where does God's strength become perfect?*
12. *Take a minute and examine yourself according to questions 1 to 11. How is Christ strengthening you in your difficult walk?*
13. *How does 1 Corinthians 1:27-29 explain how God glories in the weak?*
14. *What is the difference between being a Christian in your own strength and being a Christian through the strength of Christ?*
15. *What is the difference between the mind of God and our minds, in Isaiah 55:8-9?*
16. *What does this mean If we think scripturally, we will understand properly, and walk accordingly? How is this manifested in your life?*
17. *How does God's statement about what He was going to do to the extremely strong and intellectual giant Paul in Acts 9:16, line up with your theology?*
18. *How did Paul's countless hours of rabbinical training compare to the tough love school of God for Paul? What about you?*

19. *Let us examine Acts 9;3-6: What happened to the powerhouse Saul on the road to Damascus? How did God weaken Saul to save him? Did this get Saul's attention? Compare yourself with Saul and his "Damascus Road Experience," is Christ trying to get your attention somehow?*
20. *How did Saul, the terror to Christians because of scriptural stupidity and arrogance, become the humble and wise Christian Apostle?*
21. *Did Paul preach, A) Christianity is a life of supernatural riches or B) Christianity is a life of problems which can be solved through Christ?*
22. *How does Paul live John 16:33 and John 16:23-24?*
23. *List the tribulations of Paul's life from his autobiography written in 2 Corinthians 11:24-29. Does this make you appreciate the grace of God in your life?*
24. *Was Paul more than a conqueror in these tribulations? What does Paul's statement "Who is weak, and I am not weak" mean?*
25. *Describe the difference between self-sufficiency and Christ-dependency. Where are you in this conversion in salvation?*
26. *Upon examination of Philippians 4:11-13, how does this explain what Paul learned concerning contentment? Where do you think Christs' strength came upon Paul in his great difficulties?*
27. *How does contentment prove the Christian life?*
28. *Did God spare Paul from life or did God immerse or baptize Paul into all of life, the good, bad and ugly?*
29. *What does abased mean?*
30. *What does abound mean?*
31. *According to 2 Corinthians 12-1-4, describe how Paul abounded?*
32. *In Philippians 4:11-13, what did Paul learn?*
33. *How does Paul arrive to a state of contentment from*

the things he suffered and learned?

34. *What is God saying to you at this moment? Take a few minutes, be still and see what the Holy Spirit has to say to you.*
35. *According to Paul's testimony in Galatians 2:20, what happened to him? What is his reality?*
36. *What are the two principles Paul grasped and we should also?*
37. *According to John 3:5, how do we enter the kingdom of God?*
38. *How does Paul sum this up in 2 Corinthians 5:17?*
39. *Paul's Christ strength came by a deep faith in what God has said, does yours?*
40. *Was this faith easy to attain or did it come by much struggle to him (Read Romans 7)?*
41. *What is the key in activating Christs' strength into our own strength?*
42. *How difficult is it to trust God over trusting yourself?*
43. *According to Hebrews 11:5, without __?___ you cannot please God?*
44. *How pleasing to God are you? This is a deep question and requires much honesty.*
45. *How does James 2:18-20 explain this principle?*
46. *What is the teaching of Romans 1:17?*
47. *What is the teaching of Habakkuk 2:4?*
48. *What is Paul's prayer in Ephesians 3:17? Should this not be our prayer and also the church's?*
49. *What was Peter's dilemma in Matthew 14:23-29?*
50. *How does this incident teach how fast we can move from faith to faithlessness?*
51. *What is a warning you can take away from Peter?*
52. *How does Jesus show His wonderful grace in this water incident with Peter?*
53. *How wonderful is John 6:21 concerning being with faith in Christ in a storm?*

54. *What does Jesus promise us in Matthew 28:20?*
55. *What may we boldly say about this in Hebrews 13:6?*
56. *What is John's stamp of approval on finding Christ's conquering strength in 1 John 5;4-5?*
57. *In Hebrews 11 describe the faith of the saints who lived by faith in the strength of Christ.*
58. *What are the lessons we should learn from these people?*
59. *According to Hebrews 11:30-40, what are the realities of a vibrant life of faith?*
60. *Does your life have a vibrancy to it (you may need to ask the brethren about this)?*
61. *According to Jesus how should we begin our journey of faith in Mark 4:30-32?*
62. *What is God's promise for our strength in Isaiah 41:10 and Isaiah 40:28-31?*
63. *What does Jesus tell us in Matthew 11:28-30, Matthew 28:20, John 14:15-28?*
64. *Are all of these promises a positive of God's desire to be with us and strengthen us?*
65. *How does this encourage you?*
66. *Will this enable you to conquer your problems and giants?*
67. *How does Jesus teach the imparting strength from the Holy Spirit in John 16:14-15?*
68. *What are the educational points of Paul's prayer in Ephesians 3:16-19?*
69. *Now what must you do?*
70. *How did Israel fail according to Paul in Romans 9:31-32?*
71. *What is the warning of Hebrews 3:12?*
72. *Let us Declare today: I can do all things through Christ who strengthens me!*

God Bless and Strengthen You

LESSON TEN: WALKING GOD'S WAY BEING UNWISE OR UNDERSTANDING OF THE WILL OF GOD EPHESIANS 5:17-21

"Therefore do not be unwise, but understand what the will of the Lord is. And do not be drunk with wine, in which is dissipation; but be filled with the Spirit, speaking to one another in psalms and hymns and spiritual songs, singing and making melody in your heart to the Lord, giving thanks always for all things to God the Father in the name of our Lord Jesus Christ, submitting to one another in the fear of God."

Unwise or Understanding of the Will of God

CHAPTER ONE

"Therefore do not be unwise, but understand what the will of the Lord is. And do not be drunk with wine, in which is dissipation; but be filled with the Spirit, speaking to one another in psalms and hymns and spiritual songs, singing and making melody in your heart to the Lord, giving thanks always for all things to God the Father in the name of our Lord Jesus Christ, submitting to one another in the fear of God." Ephesians 5:17-21 NKJV

LESSON ONE - GOD'S WILL

How interesting is Paul's command, ***"Therefore do not be unwise, but understand what the will of the Lord is!"*** Many Christians are scratching their heads with great confusion saying, ***"What is God's will for me?"*** I acknowledge this question as something we all have. In myself, I find it foolish to think so and needful to ask God for His will. Paul did not say, do not ask about God's will for your life, but not to be unwise about it. Indirectly speaking, he was telling us not to be fools concerning the will of God. There are two aspects to the will of the Lord. One side of this will is plain for all to understand, while the other side is not so easy to figure out. Moses explains this concept about the aspects of Gods will beautifully in Deuteronomy 29:29.

"The secret things belong to the Lord our God, but those things which are revealed belong to us and to our children forever, that we may do all the words of this law." (NKJV)

We do not need a written four-volume commentary to understand what Moses means. The revealed things, concerning the will of God, are written in black and white on the pages of the Bible. The secret things are those mysteries in the Bible and those plans in the heart of God not revealed to us but understood and known only by God. For example, we know there will be an end to this world's existence and the second coming of Christ. This will of God belongs to us. However, when, where, and how it will happen belongs to the Father. Do you remember the words of Jesus concerning this?

"But of that day and hour no one knows, not even the angels of heaven, but My Father only," Matthew 24:36 NKJV.

It is wise for us to understand, knowing He is coming again, and we are to live accordingly. Nevertheless, it is unwise, even foolish for us to split the church concerning, the time it will happen. Only the Father knows when He will allow the Son to come back. We just need to keep looking up and living according to the revealed will of His coming again. A question to ask concerning this is, "Are you unwise or understanding of the will of God?"

The First and Foremost Revealed Will of God

The number one revealed will of God for mankind is the salvation of every human being. The salvation which comes through the sacrifice of Jesus Christ crucified for our sins, died for our punishment, and rose from the dead for our justification, for the salvation which washes away our sins by the shed blood of the Lamb, Jesus Christ. John the Baptist cried out concerning this to Israel, ***"John saw Jesus coming toward him, and said, 'Behold! The Lamb of God who takes away the sin of the world!'"*** (John 1:29 NKJV) The writer of the book of Hebrews states, ***"And according to the law almost all things are purified with blood, and without shedding of blood there is no remission,"*** Hebrews 9:22 NKJV. Jesus Christ, the Son of God was sacrificed for us, took our judgement upon Him, so we may be forgiven and saved. This is the number one will of God for all. It is important to understand this first because, ***"The Lord is not willing that any should perish but that all should come to repentance,"*** 2 Peter 3:9 NKJV. We need to be understanding concerning the Gospel. Jesus died for the whole world, and this truth is for all to hear. We are not to be unwise about this. In fact, this was the Lord's last command to the apostles before His ascension.

"Go therefore and make disciples of all the nations, baptizing them in the name of the Father and of the Son and of the Holy Spirit, teaching them to observe all things that I have

commanded you; and lo, I am with you always, even to the end of the age. Amen," Matthew 28:19-20 NKJV.

This is the foremost will of God. Salvation was promised to Adam and Eve (Read Genesis 3). For many centuries, this promise was a mystery, a secret known only to God. However, it is no longer a secret (unless we hide it from everyone). Paul speaks of God making known a secret mystery of His for us to have.

"The mystery which has been hidden from ages and from generations, but now has been revealed to His saints. To them God willed to make known what are the riches of the glory of this mystery among the Gentiles: which is Christ in you, the hope of glory," Colossians 1:26-27 NKJV.

Are you unwise about this or understanding of it? Your answer to this has temporal and eternal implications.

The Behavioral Revealed Will of God

Due to the sensitive nature of this subject, may I say WE, as Christians, seem to be very unwise concerning obedience to many of the commands of God's will for us. Perhaps the problem of obedience is centered in our ignorance of victory God's way. Paul gives us a few secrets to help us in our walk to behave according to the revealed will of God. We can write about these secrets. However, the mystery of it happening for us seems foreign. Before we explore the secrets, let us look at a few revealed behaviors (there are too many for this writing) God desires in us. Paul exhorted the Thessalonians about this. ***"That you would walk worthy of God who calls you into His own kingdom and glory,"*** 1 Thessalonians 2:12 NKJV.

The Diamonds of God's Behavioral Will for Mankind

1. The ultimate behavior required is, Love God with all we are. This is the *First Commandment,* Matthew 22: 37-38.

2. We are to love our neighbor as ourselves. This is the Second Commandment, Matthew 22:39.

"On these two commandments hang all the Law and the Prophets," Matthew 22:40 NKJV.

This love is not a touchy-feely emotion of sensory throbbing. It is a love of willful obedience to God and sacrificial actions towards others, no matter what we are feeling or thinking. Jesus said an incredible thing, ***"You are My friends if you do whatever I command you,"*** John 15:14 NKJV. Paul told us not to be unwise about this. Jesus is not speaking to us as a person who says, do what I say, and not as I do. He does and behaves and loves as He commands us to. ***"If you keep My commandments, you will abide in My love, just as I have kept My Father's commandments and abide in His love,"*** John 15:10 NKJV. Jesus totally loved His Father, God, because He obeyed Him fully. He loved us, His neighbor, as Himself because He sacrificed and denied Himself for us. ***"But God demonstrates His own love toward us, in that while we were still sinners, Christ died for us,"*** Romans 5:8 NKJV.

The Corinthian church was not understanding of the will of God. They were unwise concerning it. Paul was genuinely concerned about their behaviors. He heard many bad reports about them. He wrote to them concerning his fears they were not walking in the diamonds of God's behavioral will for them. Furthermore, remember what Jesus commanded concerning our attitudes and actions. ***"A new commandment I give to you, that you love one another; as I have loved you, that you also love one another. By this all will know that you are My disciples, if you have love for one another,"*** John 13:34-35 NKJV.

The Evidence of Failure in Obeying God's Will

Here is what Paul said to Corinth.

"For I fear lest, when I come, I shall not find you such as I

wish, and that I shall be found by you such as you do not wish; lest there be contentions, jealousies, outbursts of wrath, selfish ambitions, backbitings, whisperings, conceits, tumults; lest, when I come again, my God will humble me among you, and I shall mourn for many who have sinned before and have not repented of the uncleanness, fornication, and lewdness which they have practiced," 2 Corinthians 12:20-21 NKJV.

It really looks bad concerning the behavior at the Corinth Church. There is no obedience, by them, to the diamonds of God's behavioral will.

- They are contentious, where loving is being of one-mind. ***"Fulfill my joy by being like-minded, having the same love, being of one accord of one mind,"*** Philippians 2:2 NKJV.
- They are jealous, which is being covetous of each other, while loving looks for the good of others. ***"Let each of you look out not only for his own interests, but also for the interests of others,"*** Philippians 2:4 NKJV.
- They had anger issues with outbursts of wrath, where loving turns the cheek, has self-control, and is not provoked. ***"But I tell you not to resist an evil person. But whoever slaps you on your right cheek, turn the other to him also,"*** Matthew 5:39. ***"Beloved, do not avenge yourselves, but rather give place to wrath; for it is written, 'Vengeance is Mine, I will repay,' says the Lord,"*** Romans 12:19 NKJV.
- They were selfish and ambitious, while loving puts others first. ***"Yet it shall not be so among you; but whoever desires to become great among you, let him be your servant. And whoever desires to be first among you, let him be your slave— just as the Son of Man did not come to be served, but to serve, and to give His life a ransom for many,"*** Matthew 20:26-28 NKJV.
- They were backbiters, which is defamation, while loving never speaks evil.
- They were whispers, which is slandering, while loving at no time lies about anyone. ***"Do not speak evil of one another,***

brethren. He who speaks evil of a brother and judges his brother, speaks evil of the law and judges the law. But if you judge the law, you are not a doer of the law but a judge," James 4:11 NKJV.

- They were conceited, while loving is being humble. ***"For if anyone thinks himself to be something, when he is nothing, he deceives himself,"*** Galatians 6:3 NKJV.
- They were tumultuous, which is being loud, causing commotions, while love is harmonious and peaceful. ***"Now the fruit of righteousness is sown in peace by those who make peace,"*** James 3:18 NKJV.
- They were sexually promiscuous, unclean, fornicating, lewd persons, while love keeps itself wholesome. ***"For this is the will of God, your sanctification: that you should abstain from sexual immorality; that each of you should know how to possess his own vessel in sanctification and honor, not in passion of lust, like the Gentiles who do not know God,"*** 1 Thessalonians 4:3-5 NKJV.

It is reasonable and logical to deduce a sad fact; the Corinthians were not loving God nor their neighbor as God commands. Remember, love is a willful action not an act from emotion. The love God wants is obedience to His will. I am not talking about Christianity, and salvation built on the works of the law, but the love of God shown in our life and activities.

"For by grace you have been saved through faith, and that not of yourselves; it is the gift of God, not of works, lest anyone should boast. For we are His workmanship, created in Christ Jesus for good works, which God prepared beforehand that we should walk in them," Ephesians 2:8-10 NKJV.

These works are loving God by obeying God. How wise and understanding is the church of today to the will of God. Do you wonder if 2 Corinthians 12:20-21, was written about us too? I find, it is easy to deceive myself thinking, "I am understanding and obedient to the will of God." Nevertheless, an honest self-examination teaches how unwise I am of God's will. Have you ever listened to yourself? Your thoughts and words speak volumes and teach what type of fruit you are producing. It is best to be honest and repentant now before it is too late. ***"Therefore do not be unwise, but understand what the will of the Lord is."***

The Secret Will of God

The revealed will of God is easy to see, no matter how hard it is to accomplish. The secret will of God, seems to be an exasperating problem to solve. Many of us are always crying out to God for the secret plans He has for us. Time goes by; it seems harshly, as we wait for an answer from God, concerning His hidden will for us. I bet, if you are in this struggle with God, Jeremiah 29:11-14, has become a worn-out promise. I wonder if it is causing an evil heart of unbelief to develop in your mind. I can say this with authority because I am in a monumental thirty-year wrestling match with God over it, even to the point of total despair and unbelief. The wrestling has been on the mountains into the valleys in a never-ending stream of ups and downs. More often than can be counted, it seems I am with Joseph, a prisoner in the jails of Egypt. Like Joseph, I look out the prison bars wondering when and if the Lord will open the prison doors and reveal His secret plan for me. Constantly wondering and seeking of this becomes exhausting.

I hear God crying out, ***"For I know the thoughts that I think toward you, says the Lord, thoughts of peace and not of evil, to give you a future and a hope. Then you will call upon Me and go and pray to Me, and I will listen to you. And you will seek Me and find Me when you search for Me with all your heart. I will be found by you, says the Lord, and I will bring you back from your captivity; I will gather you from all the nations and from all the places where I have driven you, says the Lord, and I will bring you to the place from which I cause you to be carried away captive,"*** Jeremiah 29:11-14 NKJV.

I hear myself saying as Joseph said to his fellow prisoner,

Pharaoh's Butler, after he told him, he would be released. ***"But remember me when it is well with you, and please show kindness to me; make mention of me to Pharaoh, and get me out of this house,"*** Genesis 40:14 NKJV. There is Joseph, with no family or parents to help him, and sold into slavery by his brothers. He is without a friend in the world lonely and confused. Wondering if God really had spoken to him in his dreams many years ago. Crying to the Butler, please help me, because the darkness of his imprisonment is deep and disturbing. Joseph is beginning to become what everyone around him thinks, a loser, even though, in secret God calls him victorious.

John the Baptist also had his time of the darkness of imprisonment. John a man who lived the secret plan of God openly, knew it plainly. He testified of this to his critics. ***"He said: 'I am The voice of one crying in the wilderness: Make straight the way of the Lord,' as the prophet Isaiah said,"*** John 1:23 NKJV. John had the revelation of Jesus the Messiah before anyone else. ***"And John bore witness, saying, 'I saw the Spirit descending from heaven like a dove, and He remained upon Him. I did not know Him, but He who sent me to baptize with water said to me, Upon whom you see the Spirit descending, and remaining on Him, this is He who baptizes with the Holy Spirit. And I have seen and testified that this is the Son of God,'"*** John 1:32-34 NKJV. John had a powerful preaching ministry where many came to hear his words. ***"Then he said to the multitudes that came out to be baptized by him, 'Brood of vipers! Who warned you to flee from the wrath to come?'"*** (Luke 3:7 NKJV)

John the Baptist was a man experiencing the kingdom of heaven in a supernatural way. Unlike many of us, he knew God's secret plan for his life. This will of God was revealed to his parents, who raised him up in the way he should go. John had heavenly dealings with God directly. He saw the glory of the Spirit descending on the Messiah. His mission was being fulfilled right before his eyes. He prepared the way for

Jesus to fulfill His purpose in the work. John, being very full of the power of God in his life, confronted the King, Herod the tetrarch about his adulterous affair with Herod's brother Philip's wife, Herodias. John probably felt invincible and did not think anything would happen to him speaking out against Herod. However, Herod put John in jail! ***"For Herod had laid hold of John and bound him, and put him in prison for the sake of Herodias, his brother Philip's wife. Because John had said to him, 'It is not lawful for you to have her,'"*** Matthew 14:3-4 NKJV.

It is at this point we learn John enters the prison of darkness in his soul. This darkness is deep and causes serious doubt about who he is and what he did. I can understand and think he was saying to God, *"God, it is me John, why am I imprisoned?"* He even doubts what he saw concerning Jesus and who He is. ***"And when John had heard in prison about the works of Christ, he sent two of his disciples and said to Him, 'Are You the Coming One, or do we look for another?'"*** (Matthew 11:2-3 NKJV) The man who spoke with power and authority, who rebuked the religious leaders of the day, who baptized multitudes, saw the Holy Spirit baptize the Messiah, is now in darkness in the imprisonment of his soul. So great is his darkness, he sends two of his disciples to question Jesus, wondering if He is who He says He is! Like Joseph, John wants an answer of freedom from his imprisonment. Unlike Joseph, John is not freed but has his head chopped off. The darkness surrounding the secret things of God for our lives is sometimes soul shattering. It is in these moments the hardest action to do is necessary. ***"Trust in the Lord with all your heart, And lean not on your own understanding; In all your ways acknowledge Him, And He shall direct your paths,"*** Proverbs 3:5-6 NKJV.

Unfortunately, many of us falter in applying this verse in the times of the darkness of imprisonment because God is not revealing His secret plan for us but carrying it out in the deepness of the desert experience. One lesson I have learned in this deep darkness is, God still expects me to obey His revealed will during the crisis. I am, no matter what the situation, commanded to love Him, the neighbor, the spouse, the children, even though the rug has been pulled from under my feet. The dungeon of darkness surrounding us with God really proves to us what we are. ***"Therefore do not be unwise, but understand what the will of the Lord is."***

Hope in the Darkness

Truthfully speaking, I go through periods of hopelessness, frustration, and anger in the quietness of God's will, kept secret. Trusting God has a plan for me, sometimes seems laughable. However, it is promised. Sarah felt the same way in the darkness of barrenness, even though she was promised she would give birth to a son. So, exasperated about this, she took matters into her own hands and gave Hagar to Abraham. As the record shows this did not work out well for her. As the years swiftly fly by Sarah finds herself old, barren, childless and ultimately hopeless. Nevertheless, the promise still stands, and God once again meets Abraham to confirm it. It is at this moment; we learn Sarah finds the promise of God laughable.

"And He said, 'I will certainly return to you according to the time of life, and behold, Sarah your wife shall have a son.' (Sarah was listening in the tent door which was behind him.) Now Abraham and Sarah were old, well advanced in age; and Sarah had passed the age of childbearing. Therefore Sarah laughed within herself, saying, 'After I have grown old, shall I have pleasure, my lord being old also?'" (Genesis 18:10-12 NKJV)

Yes, sad to say, sometimes God brings us to a point of decision after many years of quiet and dryness. When confronted with the promises of God in a quiet time of desperation, they almost seem laughable to us. However, God is not laughing, He is serious. Therefore, as we struggle in prayer and waiting for God to reveal His secrets to us, we must be careful. I do not think God is not kind and understanding of our ups and downs. Nevertheless, we must be careful we do not walk away from God in the low point of frustration. He even warns us about this because leaving Him is a very real possibility. ***"Beware, brethren, lest there be in any of you an evil heart of unbelief in departing from the living God,"*** Hebrews 3:12 NKJV.

As we seek hope in the darkness, let us return to Joseph, who was wallowing in self-pity in an Egyptian prison. God gave Joseph two dreams concerning His future for Him in Genesis 37. Through many events, Joseph is wrongly sold into slavery and cast into a filthy prison. He has suffered much and his two dreams of his family bowing down to him seem laughable. However, God has not forgotten the word in a dream He gave to the seventeen-year-old Joseph. Like God's promise to Sarah, Joseph's great grandmother, He moved to fulfill His word. Joseph is alive because God kept His word to Abraham and Sarah, and in old age Isaac was born. Isaac married Rebekah, who gave birth to Jacob. Jacob married Rachel, who gave birth to Joseph. Although Sarah laughed, God kept His promise. Likewise, we read God fulfills the dreams He gave to Joseph. God works through a special dream to Pharaoh, which was greatly troubling. No one could explain it to Him. However, the Butler whom Joseph helped in prison, remembers Joseph before Pharaoh.

Pharaoh Calls Joseph:

"Then Pharaoh sent and called Joseph, and they brought him quickly out of the dungeon; and he shaved, changed his clothing, and came to Pharaoh," Genesis 41:14 NKJV.

Joseph Interprets the Dreams and Gives a Remedy. Pharaoh Elevates Joseph:

"Then Pharaoh said to Joseph, 'Inasmuch as God has shown you

all this, there is no one as discerning and wise as you. You shall be over my house, and all my people shall be ruled according to your word; only in regard to the throne will I be greater than you.' And Pharaoh said to Joseph, 'See, I have set you over all the land of Egypt,'" Genesis 41:39-41 NKJV.

Joseph's Dream Comes True and His Brothers Bow Down Before Him:

"And when Joseph came home, they brought him the present which was in their hand into the house, and bowed down before him to the earth."

"So Judah and his brothers came to Joseph's house, and he was still there; and they fell before him on the ground." (Genesis 43:26,44:14 NKJV)

Sarah and Joseph learned the hard way; God keeps His word and promises. This is our hope in the darkness.

What Must We Do?

Before we answer a question of action in times of deep darkness, we need to acknowledge a truth about ourselves.

***"Hope deferred makes the heart sick,
But when the desire comes, it is a tree of life."***
Proverbs 13:12 NKJV

The first action we must take is to examine ourselves to see if our heart has become spiritually sick in the waiting for God to answer. If we are ill, we need to acknowledge the truth and seek help from God.

Some of the symptoms of being heart sick are:
- Depression
- Spiritual dullness
- Lack of interest in the Bible
- Cold heart towards God and neighbor

- Loss of trust in God's Word
- Wanting the world and its lusts
- A return to carnal behavior
- A yielding to sin
- Lack of interest in Church
- Envy and jealousy towards those who seem blessed
- Extreme self-centeredness.

These are issues we must defeat in the darkness of the prison of waiting. If you have any of these issues and cannot handle them, seek professional help.

Therefore, in seeking the secret will of God wrapped up in His promises, you must remember they belong to Him. If you are seeking them, remember He promised He would reveal it to you. He said, ***"And you will seek Me and find Me, when you search for Me with all your heart. I will be found by you, says the Lord, and I will bring you back from your captivity; I will gather you from all the nations and from all the places where I have driven you, says the Lord, and I will bring you to the place from which I cause you to be carried away captive,"*** Jeremiah 29:13-14 NKJV. The revealing is on His time not ours. Nevertheless, when it seems dark and empty, acknowledge one truth, the Word of God stands forever. Jesus said concerning this, ***"For assuredly, I say to you, till heaven and earth pass away, one jot or one tittle will by no means pass from the law till all is fulfilled,"*** Matthew 5:18 NKJV. The prophet Isaiah and the Apostle Peter spoke of this truth forcefully.

- ***"The grass withers, the flower fades, But the word of our God stands forever,"*** Isaiah 40:8 NKJV.
- ***"But the word of the Lord endures forever." Now this is the word which by the gospel was preached to you,"*** 1 Peter 1:25 NKJV.

Furthermore, God does not lie to us. ***"God is not a man, that He should lie, Nor a son of man, that He should repent. Has He said, and will He not do? Or has He spoken, and will He not make it***

good?" (Numbers 23:19 NKJV)

Concerning the promise giver and doer, we must understand; God is not a fast-food server nor is He the genie in a lantern. God is the giver and performer of the promises, and we are the seekers and receivers of His graciousness. Moreover, God does not give or perform His promises on those who seek them carnally. ***"You ask and do not receive, because you ask amiss, that you may spend it on your pleasures,"*** James 4:3 NKJV. The desire for the promise must not be greater than our desire for God, Himself, remember the first commandment.

It seems Timothy, Paul's son in the faith, had his moments of darkness waiting on the Lord. We learn, he too was imprisoned for his faith. We see this in Hebrews 13:23, ***"Know that our brother Timothy has been set free, with whom I shall see you if he comes shortly."*** He must have had his ups and downs. Therefore, Paul exhorted him how to live in the ups and downs. ***"But you must continue in the things which you have learned and been assured of, knowing from whom you have learned them, and that from childhood you have known the Holy Scriptures, which are able to make you wise for salvation through faith which is in Christ Jesus,"*** 2 Timothy 3:14-15 NKJV.

The book of Hebrews addresses Christians who are in the darkness of prison concerning their walk with the Lord. These believers suffered heavily for their belief in Jesus our Lord and were faltering in their faith. All the exhortations to handle the darkness of prison and the delayed answers to prayers and promises were summarized in Hebrews 10:23.

"Let us hold fast the confession of our hope without wavering, for He who promised is faithful."

Finally realize a simple truth, ***"For all the promises of God in Him are Yes, and in Him Amen, to the glory of God through us,"*** 2 Corinthians 1:20 NKJV. Whether it is here on earth or in heaven, all God's promises will be fulfilled for us. Therefore, brethren, we are commanded, even in the darkness of prison waiting for release, to, ***"Not be unwise, but understand what the will of the Lord is."***

What must we do when all the promises seem no to us?

We must:

- Remember the promises belong to God and the fulfilling of them belong to Him.
- Remember the promises are written forever.
- Remember we are expected to obey the revealed will of God no matter our situation.
- Remember God does not lie.
- Remember we are to hold fast, the confession of our faith.

Brethren, the long dark night of souls wandering can make our hearts sick. The answer will be a tree of life for us. Our walk-in darkness must not become a sickening event but a journey of being wise and understanding of the will of God. I know these are hard truths to hear and perform. Many thousands of our brothers and sisters in Christ have been crushed and fallen away from the faith not being wise nor understanding what the will of the Lord is. The secret things which are Gods became more important than the relationship with God.

Paul's Handling and Example When He and Silas Hit Darkness

"Then the multitude rose up together against them; and the magistrates tore off their clothes and commanded them to be beaten with rods. And when they had laid many stripes on them, they threw them into prison, commanding the jailer to keep them securely. Having received such a charge, he put them into the inner prison and fastened their feet in the stocks. But at midnight Paul and Silas were praying and singing hymns to God, and the prisoners were listening to them. Suddenly there was a great earthquake, so that the foundations of the prison were shaken; and immediately all the doors were opened and everyone's chains were loosed," Acts 16:22-26 NKJV.

How is our testimony? Paul and Silas did not let the darkness of beatings, and imprisonment, turn them away from the love of God. They were wise in understanding the will of the Lord! Are we unwise or understanding the will of the Lord in all situations? Or, in today's language, are we grumbling or praising? If we are to be disciples of Christ, this is a lesson, we must all learn, understanding the will of the Lord for us. May God grant us this understanding.

REFLECTIONS CHAPTER ONE

1. What does Paul mean when he is telling us, *"Do not be unwise, but understand what the will of the Lord is?"*
2. How understanding are you of God's will?
3. Are you wise concerning alcohol or drug consumption?
4. Define dissipation.
5. What does wisdom have to do with drugs and alcohol?
6. How is your understanding of the Holy Spirit?
7. In Ephesians 5:17-21, what is the wisdom of being filled with the Spirit?
8. Do you prove you are filled with the Spirit, by the way, you speak to others, by singing a melody to the Lord, by being thankful to God?
9. How unwise is the behavior of Christians in submitting to each other, in family and church?
10. Are you confused about God's will for you?
11. Did Paul say do not ask about God's will? What did he say?
12. What are the two aspects of God's will?
13. How does Moses explain the two aspects of God's will in Deuteronomy 29:29?
14. What are the revealed things of the will of God? Where are they found? How good are you in obedience to them?
15. Explain some of the revealed will of God, which belongs to us.
16. What is the first and foremost revealed will of God for all?
17. What was the testimony of John the Baptist concerning

this in John 1:29?

18. How does Hebrews 9:22 explain the redeeming work of Christ?
19. What is the Lord not willing to happen according to 2 Peter 3:9?
20. According to Jesus in Matthew 28:19-20, what are His followers to do to try to get people to Christ?
21. What is the revealed mystery of Colossians 1:26-27? How unwise or understanding are you of this revealed mystery?
22. Please answer question one again. Is your understanding of being unwise or understanding different?
23. Concerning the behavioral will of God, why are Christians unwise about Christian behavior?
24. Describe the two Diamonds of God's behavioral will?
25. Be honest, are you understanding of these two commandments?
26. How does your behavior teach if you are wise or unwise in loving God and neighbor?
27. According to Jesus, our Lord, what does He say concerning this revealed behavioral will of God in Matthew 22:40?
28. How unwise or understanding are you of the meaning of Matthew 22:40?
29. How does Jesus describe His friends in John 15:14?
30. Did Jesus in John 15:10 demonstrate His understanding of the behavioral will of God?
31. How did God demonstrate His love to us in Romans 5:8?
32. How understanding or unwise was the Corinthian Church concerning the behavioral will of God?
33. What lesson or lessons can they teach us?
34. List the evidence of the Corinth Church's failure in obeying God's will, according to Paul in 2 Corinthians 12:20-21.
35. List the proper behaviors they should have been understanding of in each sinful behavior.
36. Apply your two lists to yourself and to your congregation, where are you, unwise or understanding the will of the Lord?

37. Please answer question one again. Is your understanding of being unwise or understanding different?
38. Why is the secret will of God exasperating to us?
39. Why would it be exasperating since it does not belong to us?
40. Has the promise of Jeremiah 29:11-14, caused confusion or joy for you? Explain why? Has it strengthened your faith or weakened it?
41. Through the life of Joseph and John the Baptist, explain how God's secret will affect them. What lessons can we gain from them and apply in our walk?
42. What is the prison of darkness in a believer's life?
43. How prepared are you for it? It takes wisdom and understanding to get to the light at the end of the tunnel.
44. How important is Proverbs 3:5-6?
45. How easy or hard is it to obey trusting God and not leaning on our own understanding?
46. What does God expect a person who is in the prison of darkness to do?
47. What does the dungeon of darkness reveal about a person?
48. Please answer question one again. Is your understanding of being unwise or understanding different?
49. How does God's dealing with Abraham and Sarah teach hope in the darkness?
50. What is the warning of Hebrews 3:12 concerning a person in the prison of darkness?
51. How did God work to get the depressed Joseph out of his darkness?
52. How does God prove, in the life of Joseph, He keeps His will and promises to us?
53. What does God teach about hope in Proverbs 13:12?
54. What are the symptoms of a sick heart from hope deferred?
55. Hopefully, you are not in this situation of darkness, if you are in darkness, examine your heart for these symptoms and get right with God.

56. How much hope can we have from Jeremiah 29:13-14?
57. How long does the Word of our God stand? How helpful is the understanding of this concerning the will of the Lord? How long does God have to work His will out in our saved lives?
58. What does Numbers 23:19 say to our hearts in understanding the will of the Lord?
59. How are we not to ask God for aid, according to James 4:3?
60. According to Hebrews 10:23, how did Paul handle all his sufferings?
61. Is this wise advice for us to understand?
62. How are we to understand 2 Corinthians 1:20?
63. What must we do when all the promises seem no to us?
64. Compare your testimony against the testimony of Paul and Silas in the prison of darkness. How understanding are you in the will of God in comparison to Paul and Silas?
65. Please answer question one again. Is your understanding of being unwise or understanding different?

CHAPTER TWO

"Therefore do not be unwise, but understand what the will of the Lord is. And do not be drunk with wine, in which is dissipation; but be filled with the Spirit, speaking to one another in psalms and hymns and spiritual songs, singing and making melody in your heart to the Lord, giving thanks always for all things to God the Father in the name of our Lord Jesus Christ, submitting to one another in the fear of God."

Ephesians 5:17-21 NKJV

Unwise or Understanding

of the

Will of God

LESSON TWO - THE SPIRIT

How incredulous is Paul to the Ephesians, asking them if they are unwise or understanding concerning two Christian actions? The first action concerns understanding the will of God in life. The second action, concerning the will of God, is being filled with the Holy Spirit. Are we unwise or understanding about this? Please allow me to speak truthfully about this. I am quite confused about the subject and command to be filled with the Holy Spirit. Nevertheless, I tell you the truth, it was not for a lack of seeking this. Therefore, this writing is not a how to, but the need to be obedient and filled with the Spirit.

Well, after 40 years of trying to understand Acts 2 and the falling of the Holy Spirit with the speaking of tongues, I had to study and come to a few conclusions. According to the Charismatic side, tongues are the evidence of the Spirit and proof of your salvation. A few questions came into my mind. What are tongues? I said, after reading 1 Corinthians 12, a gift. Did the Apostles talk in tongues when Jesus breathed on them to receive the Holy Spirit in the Upper Room? No, I said, after reading John 20:22. Then what happened on the Day of Pentecost according to Acts 2 (please read)? Well, the Lord said, ***"You will receive power from on high,"*** (Luke 24:49) and Scripture says, ***"With men of other tongues and other lips I will speak to this people!"*** (1 Corinthians 14:21) Okay, what are tongues? Paul said a gift! Wow, power, and gifting came upon the Apostles and disciples who already had the Spirit. The same is true with Peter and Cornelius and the Gentiles, they received the Spirit and gifts were given to them at the same time, not to prove they had the Spirit but as a sign to Peter and the Jews with him. ***"While Peter was still speaking these***

words, the Holy Spirit fell upon all those who heard the word. And those of the circumcision who believed were astonished, as many as came with Peter, because the gift of the Holy Spirit had been poured out on the Gentiles also. For they heard them speak with tongues and magnify God. Then Peter answered, "Can anyone forbid water, that these should not be baptized who have received the Holy Spirit just as we have?" (Acts 10:44-47 NKJV)

The Progression of the Holy Spirit in the New Testament

In the writings of Moses, it is remarkably interesting the first person of the Trinity introduced to us is the Spirit. ***"In the beginning God created the heavens and the earth. The earth was without form, and void; and darkness was on the face of the deep. And the Spirit of God was hovering over the face of the waters,"*** Genesis 1:1-2 NKJV. I wonder why this is so since all things were created by and for the second person of the Trinity. ***"For by Him all things were created that are in heaven and that are on earth, visible and invisible, whether thrones or dominions or principalities or powers. All things were created through Him and for Him. And He is before all things, and in Him all things consist,"*** Colossians 1:16-17 NKJV. Perhaps, it is because of what Jesus says about the Spirit, we are introduced to Him first? ***"It is the Spirit who gives life,"*** John 6:63 NKJV. The third person of the Trinity is the *life* giver. Therefore, the Bible starts its narrative with the Spirit of God hovering over the earth, giving life to the formless and void planet, which was being created by the Father through the Son. Without life, may I say, the creation is useless. Furthermore, when Adam was made, it is interesting how God brought Him into life. ***"And the Lord God formed man of the dust of the ground, and breathed into his nostrils the breath of life; and man became a living being,"*** Genesis 2:7 NKJV.

How interesting does this narrative concern our creation? God forms us from the earth, then he gives life by the hovering Spirit, then God breathes the breath of life into the nostrils and the man has life and is alive. Inert matter becomes a living being by the breath of God. Let us examine John 20:21-22 to understand visually what happened invisibly when man was created. "***So Jesus said to them again, 'Peace to you! As the Father has sent Me, I also send you.' And when He had said this, He breathed on them, and said to them, 'Receive the Holy Spirit.'***" As this happens to the Apostles, the Father through the Son, breathes the Spirit on them to receive, so it was with Adam. Adam received the breath of life and so do the Apostles. Jesus is now risen from the dead and the Apostles believed in Him and are saved. We know, because of sin Adam lost life! He became dead in his trespass and sin. Likewise, so were the Apostles and us, whom the second person of the Trinity died and became salvation for. ***"But God, who is rich in mercy, because of His great love with which He loved us, even when we were dead in trespasses, made us alive together with Christ (by grace you have been saved),"*** Ephesians 2:4-5 NKJV. We need life; therefore, we need the Spirit.

The Scriptural Promise of Jesus to Us

Firstly: ***"The thief does not come except to steal, and to kill, and to destroy. I have come that they may have life, and that they may have it more abundantly,"*** John 10:10 NKJV.

Secondly: Remember, it is the Spirit who gives life! Therefore, Jesus promises Him to us. ***"Nevertheless I tell you the truth. It is to your advantage that I go away; for if I do not go away, the Helper will not come to you; but if I depart, I will send Him to you,"*** John 16:7 NKJV.

Thirdly: Jesus tells us something astonishing about the life giver we are going to have. ***"If you love Me, keep My commandments. And I will pray the Father, and He will give you another Helper, that He may abide with you forever— the Spirit of truth, whom the world cannot receive, because it neither sees Him nor knows Him; <u>but you know Him, for He dwells with</u>***

you and will be in you," John 14:15-17 NKJV (Underlined for emphasis).

What is Jesus saying here?

1. *He is going to give the Holy Spirit to His followers.*
2. *The Holy Spirit will abide or remain with us forever.*
3. *We will know Him.*
4. *His abiding with us will be by dwelling in and being present with us.*
5. *His dwelling place will be in us.*

We must not be unwise at this point but understanding the will of the Lord. God is specific about something wonderful. He not only does the miraculous by giving us His Son as the propitiation for our sins, ***"And He Himself is the propitiation for our sins, and not for ours only but also for the whole world,"*** (1 John 2:2 NKJV) but on top of this He wants us to have His Spirit, the Holy Spirit, living in and with us. When does this happen for us? The Apostles received the Holy Spirit when Jesus breathed on them, John 20:22. When does Jesus breathe on us to give the Holy Spirit to you and Me? The much-maligned verse by Christians, Acts 2:38 tells us when. ***"Then Peter said to them, 'Repent, and let every one of you be baptized in the name of Jesus Christ for the remission of sins; and you shall receive the gift of the Holy Spirit. For the promise is to you and to your children, and to all who are afar off, as many as the Lord our God will call.'"*** Acts 2:41 further tells the first step, ***"Then those who gladly received his word were baptized; and that day about three thousand souls were added to them."*** The key is, because of the remission of sins through Christ, faith and receiving Him through repentance, we receive the gift of the Holy Spirit. Our submission to baptism confirms this. However, you want to interpret this verse, one truth we can agree on, God has given the Holy Spirit to us. Titus 3:4-5, explains this wonderfully. ***"But when the kindness and the love of God our Savior toward man appeared, not by works of righteousness which we have***

done, but according to His mercy He saved us, through the washing of regeneration and renewing of the Holy Spirit, whom He poured out on us abundantly through Jesus Christ our Savior, that having been justified by His grace we should become heirs according to the hope of eternal life." What Adam lost and later what we did not have, God gives Him back to us through the grace of Jesus Christ our Savior.

We have the Holy Spirit. However, the command is to be filled with the Spirit. If we have Him in us, what is the importance of being filled with Him? I believe before we understand why we need to be filled with the Spirit, we need to be taught His ministry and purpose on earth. The Scripture teaches very specifically concerning His work in us on earth. John 16:5-15, gives the definitive description of this work.

"But now I go away to Him who sent Me, and none of you asks Me, 'Where are You going?' But because I have said these things to you, sorrow has filled your heart. Nevertheless I tell you the truth. It is to your advantage that I go away; for if I do not go away, the Helper will not come to you; but if I depart, I will send Him to you. And when He has come, He will convict the world of sin, and of righteousness, and of judgment: of sin, because they do not believe in Me; of righteousness, because I go to My Father and you see Me no more; of judgment, because the ruler of this world is judged. 'I still have many things to say to you, but you cannot bear them now. However, when He, the Spirit of truth, has come, He will guide you into all truth; for He will not speak on His own authority, but whatever He hears He will speak; and He will tell you things to come. He will glorify Me, for He will take of what is Mine and declare it to you. All things that the Father has are Mine. Therefore I said that He will take of Mine and declare it to you.'"

Jesus tells us, in John 16:14, the sum of everything the Holy Spirit will do when He sends Him to us, ***"He will glorify Me."*** The Holy Spirit is not here with us to glorify

Himself (Although, He is worthy of glory) but to glorify Jesus. Everything the Spirit does is with one purpose only, to glorify the Son of God. The Apostle John told us about the character of Jesus in John 1:14. ***"And the Word became flesh and dwelt among us, and we beheld His glory, the glory as of the only begotten of the Father, full of grace and truth."*** John said being with Jesus revealed something to them. This was Jesus' glory. This glory was not a glowing light but the glowing of the pure, unstained, sinless character of the Son of God. John said the glory of Jesus shone through the fullness of grace and truth. This was so powerful it could only bring praise, admiration and honoring from those who knew Jesus. This is the ministry of the Holy Spirit, to center the glory onto the Son of God. For creation, Jesus is the center point of existence, and He must be glorified for this. Why is this so and why does the Spirit work for this? The reason is, ***"That in the dispensation of the fullness of the times He might gather together in one all things in Christ, both which are in heaven and which are on earth—in Him,"*** Ephesians 1:10 NKJV. The purpose of the Father is to unite and gather all in heaven and earth in Christ. Therefore, the Spirit glorifies Jesus, ***"Because God the Father has set His seal on Him,"*** John 6:27 NKJV. Furthermore, the Spirit is answering the prayer of Jesus concerning His glory. ***"And now, O Father, glorify Me together with Yourself, with the glory which I had with You before the world was,"*** John 17:5 NKJV. Therefore, the Holy Spirit is here to glorify Jesus Christ. If we understand the will of God, we would be filled with the Spirit to glorify Jesus Christ. No matter what we do it should be for Christ's fame only. ***"Therefore, whether you eat or drink, or whatever you do, do all to the glory of God,"*** 1 Corinthians 10:31 NKJV.

How The Spirit Glorifies the Son

A good question to consider at this point is, "*How does the Holy Spirit glorify the Lord Jesus?*" He accomplishes this with us. The Lord said in John 16:7, "***Nevertheless I tell you the truth.***

It is to your advantage that I go away; for if I do not go away, the Helper will not come to you; but if I depart, I will send Him to you." The Lord names the Holy Spirit as our Helper! This word, Helper, in the original language is parakletos (Strong's G3875). Some of the English words used to translate this are, intercessor, advocate, consoler, comforter, and helper. This word has the understanding of someone who comes to the aid of another with evidence. The Holy Spirit is, in human terms, the lawyer or advocate who pleads God's case to us and after salvation for us. He helps us in the knowledge and application of the will and work of God in our life. He is not pleading our case; he is pleading the case of Jesus Christ. It is not our righteousness nor our causes He comes to glorify. He comes to advocate for the glory of Jesus Christ! Do you understand what the purpose of God is? Paul said, ***"To them God willed to make known what are the riches of the glory of this mystery among the Gentiles: which is Christ in you, the hope of glory,"*** Colossians 1:27 NKJV. The Holy Spirit is the one who helps, advocates, intercedes, and comforts, on behalf of Christ to us. Christ is ever living to make intercession for us to the Father. The Spirit does this for Christ to us, to make Christ the center of our life for the glory of God.

In trying to be understanding of the will of God, concerning the Holy Spirit, we have proved three facts. The first fact is God's desire to give to us His Spirit. The second fact is God's desire for the Holy Spirit to glorify Jesus Christ. The third fact is God's desire to carry out all the Spirits activity to glorify Jesus through us. Jesus' life was an open book for all to read. For us today, we learn about Jesus through the Gospels and all of Scripture. The Apostle John said about Jesus, ***"And there are also many other things that Jesus did, which if they were written one by one, I suppose that even the world itself could not contain the books that would be written,"*** John 21:25 NKJV. However, it is a little more difficult for us to understand the life of the Spirit working on earth, because He is not here bodily.

He is living His life through believers. Spirit filled believers testify of this. Those believers who are unwise and not filled with the Spirit, muddy the waters on His work on earth. The book of Acts clearly portrays the life of the Spirit in believers through the lives of various people. We see this with Peter, John, James, Stephen, Philip, Barnabas, Silas, Aquila, Priscilla, and Saul, who became Paul. The one bond which held these people and many others together, was their ability to glorify Jesus in life and death. The spotlight was on them, but the reality was the Spirit in them enabling all to carry out His primary goal.

We have proved the main way the Holy Spirit glorifies Jesus is through us! Why is this so? Let us allow Paul to answer this question. ***"Or do you not know that your body is the temple of the Holy Spirit who is in you, whom you have from God, and you are not your own?"*** (1 Corinthians 6:19 NKJV) Therefore, what are we to receive from the Spirit, to better enable us to glorify Jesus Christ?

THE TWENTY-THREEWORKING AREAS

1. He will be our helper, advocate, and comforter concerning the will of God for us.
2. Through our witness and testimony of faith in Christ, He will be the one who convicts the world of sin.
3. Through our changed life, He will convict the world of God's righteousness based on the resurrection of Christ.
4. Through our being forgiven from sin and freedom from Satan, He will convict the world of judgement.
5. He will become our guide of all the truth Jesus wants us to have.
6. He will bring and tell us the prophetic and those secret things of God which He will be allowed to speak. Wonderfully, He will declare to us all the Father and the Son have! (Points 1-6 from John 16:5-15)
7. The Spirit will be our teacher concerning everything. He will teach us about the goodness of God's ways. He will teach us of the perversion of the sinful ways of people in the world. He will explain the Bible to us.
8. He will be a restorer of our memory. Always bringing up those teachings of Jesus for every particular interaction. (Points 7-8 from John 14:26)
9. He will speak for us in times of persecution, enabling us to refute our enemies. (Matthew 10:19).
10. He will enable the work of God to be carried out not in human strength or wisdom but through the

Spirit, Himself. (Zechariah 4:6)

11. He is the one who strengthens us to withstand the wicked one as Jesus did. (Matthew 12:38)
12. He will be the testimony of Jesus. (John 15:26)
13. He will be the life giver to our mortal bodies.
14. He is our helper in our weaknesses in the things of God.
15. He is our prayer intercessor and helper interceding for us according to the will of God.
16. He enables us to defeat the carnal nature.
17. He gives us the witness of being a child of God. (Points 13-17 from Romans 8)
18. He is our seal of assurance for the day of redemption. (Ephesians 4:30)
19. He gives life to all our ministries when done through Him. (2 Corinthians 3:6)
20. He imparts into our character the characteristics of God, known as the fruit of the Spirit. (Galatians 5:22-23)
21. He enables or gifts the body of Christ to supernaturally exist and minister. (1Corinthians 12)
22. When everything around us fails, the anointing of the Holy Spirit will keep us in the truth. (1 John 2:20-27)
23. He gives us courage, soundness of mind, and the love of God to exist by. (Romans 8:15 and 2 Timothy 1:7)

We are not to be unwise but understanding of the ministry of the Holy Spirit in and around us. Therefore, the words of Jesus are of the utmost importance about the Spirit in relation to us, ***"But you know Him, for He dwells with you and will be in you,"*** John 14:17. When we do not cultivate our relationship with the Holy Spirit, He cannot help or advocate for us in anyway. Paul warned us about this saying, ***"And do not grieve the Holy Spirit of God, by whom you were sealed for the day of redemption,"*** Ephesians 4:30 NKJV. Perhaps, because of our stupidity and unbelief we are not experiencing points 1 to 23. We are the ones who are unwise concerning God's will for us through the Spirit. We do not understand when we ignore the command to be filled with the Spirit. A person filled with the Spirit is a person full of God. If you are full of God, you are free from all which is not of God. Therefore, we need to see what our minds are set upon. Worldly minds and hearts have no room for God nor the will of God. ***"For those who live according to the flesh set their minds on the things of the flesh, but those who live according to the Spirit, the things of the Spirit,"*** Romans 8:5 NKJV. The filling of the indwelling Spirit is the entering into a personal relationship with Him.

There is no secret formula to follow, to obey the command to be filled with the Spirit, we simply need to ask the Father for Him, Luke 11:13. We have seen all God's benefits of this Gift, His Spirit to us. The secret for having this to happen in us depends on what you and I desire most. King David told us his heart's desire in these words, ***"One thing I have desired of the Lord, That will I seek: That I may dwell in the house of the Lord All the days of my life, To behold the beauty of the Lord, And to inquire in His temple,"*** Psalm 27:4 NKJV. David was wanting to see and inquire of God in the temple. We are the temple of the Holy Spirit. We do not have to go up to the tabernacle at Shiloh or Jerusalem. God dwells in us, and our hearts desire should be to behold the beauty of the Lord in us and inquire of Him there! If this is not our desire, we will never experience the filling of the Spirit. You may say with the mouth you want to be filled with the Spirit, but the desire of your heart may not be with what you say. ***"Would not God search this out? For He knows the secrets of the heart,"*** Psalm 44:21 NKJV.

The truth be understood, God has done, carried out, provided, (words fail here) and offered of Himself everything which should make Him the desire of our hearts. God's desire is to fill us with His Spirit our desire must be to be filled with Him. Jesus taught two remarkable facts concerning the filling of the Spirit.

1. ***"If you then, being evil, know how to give good gifts to your children, how much more will your heavenly Father give the Holy Spirit to those who ask Him!"*** *(Luke 11:13 NKJV)*
2. ***"Therefore I say unto you, What things soever ye desire, when ye pray, believe that ye receive them, and ye shall have them,"*** *Mark 11:24 KJV.*

The truth is plain to see, God is able and willing to fill us with the Holy Spirit. The problem of not being filled is not with God's side. The Scripture does not teach God commanding Himself to fill people with the Spirit, but commands us to be filled. The problem of not being filled is on our side. The filling of the indwelling Spirit must become our desire. We must stop grieving the indwelling Spirit by desiring, ***"The lust of the flesh, the lust of the eyes, and the pride of life,"*** 1 John 2:16 NKJV. This is our choice to make, God has already chosen to perform it.

A final prayer concerning, ***"Therefore do not be unwise, but understand what the will of the Lord is. And do not be drunk with wine, in which is dissipation; but be filled with the Spirit,"*** Ephesians 5:17-21, from Paul. He prayed for the Ephesians, ***"That the God of our Lord Jesus Christ, the Father of glory, may give to you the spirit of wisdom and revelation in the knowledge of Him,"*** Ephesians 1:17. May He also do this for us. Therefore, do not be unwise, but understanding what the will of the Lord is!

Reflections

1. Reflect on the command to not be unwise but understanding what the will of the Lord is.
2. Why is it unwise to be drunk with wine (or narcotics and drugs)?
3. What is meant by dissipation?
4. How will dissipation from wine (or narcotics and drugs) affect and effect your life with Christ our Lord?
5. How incredulous is Paul toward the Ephesians, concerning being unwise or understanding of the Lord's will?
6. Why is drinking to inebriation a life problem? List all the problems uncontrolled drinking can cause.
7. How will being filled with the Spirit replace the need for worldly desires?
8. What do Charismatics say speaking in tongues is evidence of?
9. According to 1 Corinthians 12, what are tongues?
10. According to John 20:19-23, when and how did the Apostles and disciples receive the Holy Spirit? Did this happen before the Day of Pentecost?
11. What happened on the day of Pentecost to the disciples and Apostles according to Acts 2?
12. In Luke 24:49 what did Jesus tell His apostles?
13. Concerning tongues, how did Paul explain the tongues of Pentecost in 1 Corinthians 14:21?
14. How unwise or understanding of this are you?
15. Can you explain what the already Spirit filled Apostles received on Pentecost?
16. Was the speaking of tongues a proof the Apostles and the

disciples were saved, or were given power and the gift of tongues as a sign to the Jews listening to Peter's sermon?

17. How does the "Pentecost" action to Cornelius and the gentiles in Acts 10:44-47, astonish Peter and those with Him? Why would this be so?

18. According to Genesis 1:1-2, who is the first person of the Trinity introduced to us?

19. Why would this be so if all things were created by and through Jesus, Colossians 1:16-17.

20. Would the words of Jesus, found in John 6:63, explain why the Spirit is introduced to us first? What does the Spirit give?

21. How does God bring the man formed out of the earth to life in Genesis 2:7?

22. How does John 20:21-22 explain Genesis 2:7? What did the Apostles and disciples receive when they were given the Holy Spirit (remember John 6:63)?

23. How does Ephesians 2:4-5 explain this life-giving process? How does this apply to you?

24. Are you unwise or understanding of the life given to you in salvation?

25. According to John 10:10, what does the devil, the thief, come to do? What did Jesus come to do? What is the difference between the Lord and the devil? What are the affects and effects of the devil's work? Compare that to the wonderful work of Jesus in giving us life.

26. What is the promise of Jesus to all in John 16:7?

27. Dissect John 14:15-17. Do you agree with my five points about this verse?

28. What type of understanding should we have concerning the reality of the Spirit given to us?

29. Could this be why Paul said to not be unwise but understanding about being filled with the Holy Spirit?

30. How marvelous is the grace of God to give us His Son as the propitiation for our sins and the Holy Spirit to give us life?

31. When is the propitiation for our sins happen to us and when is the Holy Spirit given to us, according to Acts 2:38?

32. How does Paul explain this in Titus 3:3-4?

33. Why are we commanded to be filled with the Spirit continually, Ephesians 5:17-21, if we already have Him in us?

34. List the specific work, ministry, and purpose of the Holy Spirit according to Jesus in John 16:5-15.

35. How does this apply to us, with the Holy Spirit in us, and being filled with Him continually?

36. What is the character of Jesus according to John 1:14?

37. How will the Holy Spirit glorify Jesus in us according to the character of Jesus?

38. How does grace and truth show the glory of God in the life of Jesus Christ?

39. Why is the ministry of the Holy Spirit to center the glory on the Son of God?

40. What happens in Christ according to Ephesians 1:10?

41. According to John 6:27 what has the Father set on Jesus? What is this seal? How does the Holy Spirit glorify Jesus in us by exalting these truths?

42. What does Paul expect Christians to do always through the Holy Spirit in 1 Corinthians 10:31?

43. Jesus said the Holy Spirit is our Helper in John 16:7, according to Strong's Concordance word G3875, what does this mean?

44. Who does the Holy Spirit plead for, us of Christ?
45. According to Paul in Colossians 1:27, what is the glory in you?
46. Evaluate your relationship with the Spirit, are you trying to use Him selfishly or allowing Him to glorify Christ in you?
47. What are the three facts concerning the will of God for the Holy Spirit?
48. How does the Holy Spirit carry out His ministry on earth since He is Spirit and not flesh?
49. If the gospels teach us of Jesus, how does the book of Acts teach us of the Spirit?
50. How do you answer the question of 1 Corinthians 6:19?
51. What are the twenty-three working areas of the Holy Spirit to glorify Christ in you?
52. Take some time to digest these workings and try to understand the need to continually be filled with the Spirit.
53. Paul commanded us to not be unwise but understanding what the will of the Lord is. How wise or unwise have we been concerning the filling of the Spirit and His works of glorifying Christ on the earth?
54. According to John 14:17, how is your relationship with the Holy Spirit?
55. According to Paul in Ephesians 4:30, what wrong can we do to the Spirit?
56. What are you filled with if you are filled with the Spirit?
57. What is the teaching of Romans 8:5?
58. Where does your mind dwell?
59. Is there a secret formula to follow to be filled with the

Spirit? In Luke 13:9, how does Jesus tell us to be filled with the Spirit?

60. What type of desire must we have according to David in Psalm 27:4, to ask the Father for the Spirit?
61. How remarkable are the teachings of Luke 11:13 and Mark 11:24?
62. Does the Scripture teach us God is commanding Himself to fill people with His Spirit or commanding you and me to be filled with the Spirit?
63. In conclusion, what is your choice?

CHAPTER THREE

"Therefore do not be unwise, but understand what the will of the Lord is. And do not be drunk with wine, in which is dissipation; but be filled with the Spirit, speaking to one another in psalms and hymns and spiritual songs, singing and making melody in your heart to the Lord, giving thanks always for all things to God the Father in the name of our Lord Jesus Christ, submitting to one another in the fear of God."

Ephesians 5:17-21 NKJV

Unwise or Understanding of the Will of God

LESSON THREE - SPEAKING

It has been an interesting travel in Ephesians 5:17-21. Learning about topics which God wants us to be wise and understanding about is particularly important. So far, we have studied two topics to not be unwise about.

1. We are not to be unwise concerning the written will of God. Also, we are to be looking for understanding of the secret things belonging to God.
2. We are not to be unwise concerning the command, be filled with the Holy Spirit.

A third concern of God, for us to not be unwise about but understanding, is the condition of the heart and the way we express what is in our heart out of our mouths. Paul is concerned about three areas of expressing what is in our hearts.

1. The outer expression of words we speak to each other.
2. The inner expression of worshipping God in our hearts.
3. The heart of gratitude of thankfulness for all God has done for us through Jesus Christ.

It may seem silly to behave this way. However, if we allow ourselves to be this way it will prove a truth of God. This is the giving to us of a new heart. ***"I will give you a new heart and put a new spirit within you; I will take the heart of stone out of your flesh and give you a heart of flesh. I will put My Spirit within you and cause you to walk in My statutes, and you will keep My judgments and do them."*** Ezekiel 36:26-27 NKJV. Furthermore,

"This is the covenant that I will make with them after those days, says the Lord: I will put My laws into their hearts, and in their minds I will write them," Hebrews 10:16 NKJV. When we are wise and understanding of the will of the Lord in our speech and attitudes, we show forth outwardly what God has done inwardly. However, many of us still live outwardly in the old nature and our attitudes and speech confirms this. The way we speak is the evidence of what we believe and whom we believe in. I am not foolish to think we cannot be deceitful about this. Jesus warns us of falseness by quoting the prophet Isaiah.

"These people draw near to Me with their mouth,
And honor Me with their lips,
But their heart is far from Me.
And in vain they worship Me,
Teaching as doctrines the commandments of men."

Matthew 15:8-9 NKJV

What are the ways we prove our attitudes and speech are not of the new heart and spirit God has put in us through salvation in Christ? The Lord spoke strongly about this also! ***"For out of the heart proceed evil thoughts, murders, adulteries, fornications, thefts, false witness, blasphemies,"*** Matthew 15:19 NKJV. If this is your inner life you are living in the old heart. Furthermore, He said, ***"A good man out of the good treasure of his heart brings forth good; and an evil man out of the evil treasure of his heart brings forth evil. For out of the abundance of the heart his mouth speaks."*** Luke 6:45 NKJV.

What is the heart? There have been volumes of books written trying to explain what the heart is. If we remember our Bible lesson, God created man and breathed the breath of life into him. The result was the man became a living soul or being. ***"And Jehovah God formed man of the dust of the ground, and breathed into his nostrils the breath of life; and man became a living soul,"*** Genesis 2:7 ASV. The soul is the living being in the image of God. God is a being who has the heart or mind with the faculty to think, dream, create, formulate, and reason, (words fail here) and act upon His decisions. Adam lost the pure heart or mind in the garden of Eden. What was once spiritually pure, in every way, is now the exact opposite. Paul said, ***"For the mind of the flesh is death; but the mind of the Spirit is life and peace: because the mind of the flesh is enmity against God; for it is not subject to the law of God, neither indeed can it be: and they that are in the flesh cannot please God,"*** Romans 8:6-8 ASV. Simply said, the mind or heart of the Spirit is pure, while the sin filled mind is full of hate towards God and purity. How unwise or understanding are we of this?

The importance of being wise in speech and attitude shows us which heart we live in. God had to do away with our old nature, which is corrupt through sin. This was why He promised a new heart. Jesus taught this with the wine skin illustration. ***"Nor do they put new wine into old wineskins, or else the wineskins break, the wine is spilled, and the wineskins are ruined. But they put new wine into new wineskins, and both are preserved,"*** Matthew 9:17 NKJV. God will not bring your sinful old nature to heaven, nor your body. Sin has no place in God's kingdom. We must be created into new wineskins through salvation. Remember, the mind of the flesh is enmity towards God and will not be subject towards Him. The salvaging work of God, on our lost souls, requires new parts for us to float on the waters of God's kingdom. Therefore, a quick check, by us, ought to be executed seeing what heart we are living in or whatever we are putting into our new heart. Let us perform this check through the eyes of Jesus. Jesus would ask us; What is in your heart? What is coming out of your heart? Are good treasures flowing out? Are evil treasures pouring out of your heart?

The Evil Treasures of the Old Heart

- Evil Thoughts ... What are they? Evil is the opposite of good. Therefore, evil thoughts are not good thoughts. Biblically speaking, evil thoughts are those expressions of the mind which exalt wickedness against the knowledge of God. Evil thoughts are personal arguments of wickedness which range from self-loathing to egocentric pride. They include thoughts of rejection of God and self-aggrandizement over our fellow human being, from lust to covetousness. The evil thought occurs from two sources. The first source is from the demonic realm. They are the fiery arrows which cause us to fall into temptation. The second source, where evil thoughts arise, is the carnal sinful nature. The new creation does not behave in such a way. However, our will can override the good and go with the flow of evil thoughts. This is our choice of which heart to live out of.

- Murders ... What are they? The murders out of the old heart are the hatreds towards someone else. The Scripture is clear, ***"Whoever hates his brother is a murderer, and you know that no murderer has eternal life abiding in him,"*** 1 John 3:15 NKJV. It is a sin to hate and a sin to act out our hate. Hate leads to murder, and murder begins in the heart. This is our choice of which heart to live out of.
- Adulteries ... What are they? For us, adultery is unfaithfulness of a spouse in an extra marital affair. From the Biblical perspective, adultery is man's unfaithfulness to God. Adam and Eve were unfaithful in the Garden. We can say they committed the sin of adultery against God. Since the original adultery by Adam and Eve, Jesus taught us this sin is prevalent in our hearts. I believe I can make this point emphatically; the Ten Commandments are God's covenant for faithfulness to Him. The breaking of the

Commandments or one of them is unfaithfulness to God. This is sin and the sin of adultery. ***"For whoever shall keep the whole law, and yet stumble in one point, he is guilty of all,"*** James 2:10 NKJV. The Scripture is replete with marriage as a picture of God's relationship with us. Adultery of a spouse is the image of the unfaithfulness we have toward God. This emanates out of the sinful heart. The new heart is faithfulness towards God. This is our choice of which heart to live out of.

- Fornications ... What are they? Fornications, coming out of the heart, in a sense is idolatry of the sexual act. Fornications begin with the worship of sex in the heart. This idol worship has its expression in God forbidden sexual activity. This activity ranges from adultery to incest, from same-sex activity to bestiality, and any type of sexual act the mind can imagine, which is contrary to God's will. The new heart does not have this capability because God's laws are written in it. However, if one lives in the carnal mind, they can bring fornication into the new heart and dirty themselves. This is our choice of which heart to live out of.

- Thefts ... What are they? Thefts are the stealing of items which do not belong to you. These actions come from a heart of covetousness. No wonder God said, ***"You shall not covet your neighbor's house; you shall not covet your neighbor's wife, nor his male servant, nor his female servant, nor his ox, nor his donkey, nor anything that is your neighbor's,"*** Exodus 20:17 NKJV. Furthermore, He explicitly says, ***"You shall not steal,"*** Exodus 20:15 NKJV. Our new heart is free from this. This is our choice of which heart to live out of.

- False witness ... What are they? Simply put, it is lying about someone, something, or self! God said, ***"You shall not bear false witness against your neighbor,"*** Exodus 20:16 NKJV. The new heart will not do this. The yielding to false witness, is your choice. One of the greatest and destructive sins of born-again people is the gossip of false witness. God wants truth in the heart. His laws are written in the new heart to enable us to discern between good and evil. This is our choice of which heart to live out of.
- Blasphemies ... What are they? Blasphemy is any thought which exalts itself against the knowledge of God. Blasphemy ranges from idolatry to taking the name of the Lord in vain. This action is making God not God and is very disrespectful and downright rebellious towards Him. As Paul said the mind of the flesh is deep seated hatred towards God and this is blasphemy, the expression of our inner hate of God. The old heart is not the heart of thoughts to choose from, the new heart is! This is our choice of which heart to live out of.

Jesus describes the seven foundational sins of the old man's heart. These seven sins are expressed in a myriad of evil actions. For us to understand the difference of the old and new hearts is especially important. By this knowledge we discern how great a work God has done by giving us a new heart. Remember Jesus said we bring out good or evil treasures from a good or evil heart. Paul said we are not to be unwise about this but understanding of it.

What does Paul mean for us to speak to one another in psalms, hymns, and spiritual songs? Does this suggest we cannot talk about the weather, sports, politics, hobbies, work, history, science, or any other communication we say to one another? Our days are filled with relationships, activities, business, church, and a host of other activities involving people, such as, friends, family, church brethren, and business associates. When I greet them, do I burst out with a praise and worship song or recite the twenty third psalm? Obviously, Paul is talking about how Christians should speak to one another. However, this thought may be extrapolated to all interactions of personal communication. The talk out of our mouth must be the speech of truth and love. This speech must be equivalent to psalms, hymns, and spiritual songs. Remember, Jesus said a good man speaks from the good treasure of his heart! Peter explains the wisdom and understanding of Paul's directive this way. ***"If anyone speaks, let him speak as the oracles of God,"*** 1 Peter 4:11 NKJV. Furthermore, ***"For 'He who would love life And see good days, Let him refrain his tongue from evil, And his lips from speaking deceit,'"*** 1 Peter 3:10 NKJV. And Paul gives this foundation of speaking in psalms, hymns, and spiritual songs in Ephesians 4:15, ***"But, speaking the truth in love."*** If psalms, hymns, and spiritual songs are the good treasure in your heart, your speech will reflect this in every conversation. If we think scripturally, we will understand spiritually and truthfully, and speak and act accordingly. There is a great divide between speaking from the carnal mind which is enmity towards God and the mind which has God's laws written in it. How unwise and not understanding we are of this truth. Paul confirms this emphatically, ***"For those who live according to the flesh set their minds on the things of the flesh, but those who live according to the Spirit, the things of the Spirit. For to be carnally minded is death, but to be spiritually minded is life and peace,"*** Romans 8:5-6 NKJV. Therefore, where does our speech originate from? This is our choice of which heart to live out of.

We are all commanded to, ***"Let no corrupt word proceed out of your mouth, but what is good for necessary edification, that it may impart grace to the hearers. And do not grieve the Holy Spirit of God, by whom you were sealed for the day of***

redemption," Ephesians 4:29-30 NKJV. Therefore, from science to philosophy let us speak as the oracles of God. All truth is from God and speaking the truth with love in all disciplines will be a psalm, hymn, or spiritual song to our Lord. Let us not be unwise about this.

The Heart of Worship

The second attitude of heart we are not to be unwise about but understanding of is, a heart of worship towards God. Paul teaches us to sing and make melodies in our heart to God. The old heart is not the place for this! That heart is phony and is just lip service in its worship. Paul tells us, in Galatians 5:20, one of the works of the flesh is idolatry. Idolatry is a religious activity. Idolatry involves practices considered to be spiritual. We do not want to worship God from the old heart. The new heart of singing and making melody to the Lord is a heart which lives one hundred percent for God. The difference in heart worship is important. Listen to what God says about worship from the flesh.

"Your New Moons and your appointed feasts My soul hates; They are a trouble to Me, I am weary of bearing them. When you spread out your hands, I will hide My eyes from you; Even though you make many prayers, I will not hear. Your hands are full of blood."

Isaiah 1:14-15 NKJV

Listen to what God says about worship in the new heart. ***"Now the purpose of the commandment is love from a pure heart, from a good conscience, and from sincere faith,"*** 1 Timothy 1:5 NKJV. The natural way of the carnal mind is hatred towards God in some form or matter. This attitude is impossible to worship God truthfully. The natural way of the new heart is love towards God. This love is pure and enables our spirits to soar with loving praise to our God and Savior, Jesus Christ. Worship and praise to God shifts our focus of being egocentric to Christ-centric. A worship of God from the new heart enables us to rise above ourselves and earthly problems to the courts of heaven where we see God and understand His care for us. Have you ever noticed, in your spiritual journey, when darkness comes upon you, the worship of singing and making melody in your heart ceases?

King Jehoshaphat faced great darkness in his reign. A great multitude was coming against him. The Bible teaches about Jehoshaphat, ***"He was afraid,"*** (Read 2 Chronicles 20). As Jehoshaphat went out with his armies to face the threat, what did he do to defeat fear and egocentric darkness in the situation? ***"And when he had consulted with the people, he appointed those who should sing to the Lord, and who should praise the beauty of holiness, as they went out before the army and were saying: "Praise the Lord, For His mercy endures forever,"*** 2 Chronicles 20:21 NKJV.

The correct answer is Jehoshaphat, and the people gave God praise through singing and making melody in their hearts to the Lord. This act of worship activated faith and trust in God. What affect did the singing and making melody to the Lord have on God? ***"Now when they began to sing and to praise, the Lord set ambushes against the people of Ammon, Moab, and Mount Seir, who had come against Judah; and they were defeated,"*** 2 Chronicles 20:22 NKJV. Our sincere and heartfelt worship of God affects Him to action on our behalf.

The Scripture is clear, God has given us a new heart and we are individually and corporately as the body of Christ His temple. What does the Scripture teach about the presence of God? King David said, ***"But thou art holy, O thou that inhabitest the praises of Israel,"*** Psalm 22:3 ASV. Israel is a picture of God's people. Therefore, we can say, without losing content or context, ***"God inhabits the praises of His People."*** Do we lack the presence of the inhabiting God because we are not singing and making melody in our hearts to Him? How unwise we seem to be about this! Paul was very understanding of this principle. Paul and Silas were whipped and beaten then thrown into the filth of a disgusting prison for their faith. To make matters worse Paul and Silas were chained by their feet in a prison stock. ***"And when they had laid many stripes upon them, they cast them into prison, charging the jailor to keep them safely: who, having received such a charge, cast them into the inner prison, and made their feet fast in the stocks,"*** Acts 16:23-24 ASV. Paul and Silas were really hurting and humanly discouraged. However, these two knew the way to strength to manage their difficult circumstances. ***"But about midnight Paul and Silas were praying and singing hymns unto God, and the prisoners were listening to them,"*** Acts 16:25 ASV. How did this action of Paul and Silas affect God? ***"And suddenly there was a great earthquake, so that the foundations of the prison-house were shaken: and immediately all the doors were opened; and every one's bands were loosed,"*** Acts 16:26 ASV. What was the result? ***"And they went out of the prison, and entered into the house of Lydia: and when they had seen the brethren, they comforted them, and departed,"*** Acts 16:40 ASV. Paul and Silas received deliverance because of hearts which sing and make melody to the Lord.

Jesus told us an important reality. He said, ***"These things I have spoken to you, that in Me you may have peace. In the world you will have tribulation; but be of good cheer, I have overcome the world,"*** John 16:33 NKJV. We will, even as believers in Christ, have tribulations to deal with. Jesus also gave us the key to victory in them. He said, ***"But be of good cheer!"*** Why so? Our good cheer is based on the fact of Christ overcoming, conquering, the world. How is good cheer brought about? Good cheer comes about by singing and making melody in our hearts to the Lord. This activates the overcoming Spirit of Christ in us to manage all situations. Therefore, we should not be unwise about the will of the Lord here but understanding about worshiping Him. This is the understanding of doing all things through Christ who strengthens us, because the joy of the Lord is our strength. The choice is ours.

The Wisdom of Thankfulness

The third attitude of the heart we are not to be unwise, but understanding is, the heart of gratitude! Paul said we are to give thanks always for all things to God! How is this action done? Where can we find the time to sing and make melody and always be thankful? How am I to be thankful during illness ravaging myself or a loved one, or evil striking and hurting me, or when the bills are due, and I do not have the ability to pay them? These are legitimate concerns and problems affecting us which hinder us being thankful to God in everything. Before we run off with an excuse to not be thankful to God, we need to consider Hebrews 12:5.

"For consider Him who endured such hostility from sinners against Himself, lest you become weary and discouraged in your souls."

Have we considered how Jesus never gave an unthankful word to God His Father? Think about all Jesus was facing His entire life, an incredible, horrible death and yet, He was always thankful to God. On the night before His crucifixion, He does a peculiar thing. ***"Then He took the cup, and gave thanks, and gave it to them, saying, "Drink from it, all of you. For this is My blood of the new covenant, which is shed for many for the remission of sins,"*** Matthew 26:27-28 NKJV. Even though the coming crucifixion was a real stress coming on Him and the night in the garden would be horrible (***"And being in agony, He prayed more earnestly. Then His sweat became like great drops of blood falling down to the ground,"*** Luke 22:44 NKJV) Jesus still gives thanks to God for the cup which signifies His coming death and shedding of blood. How mysterious is the mystery of giving thanks to God in everything?

What example does Paul show, in his Spirit filled directive, to always give God thanks for all things? Paul was an innocent prisoner of the Roman government because of false accusations by the Jews in Jerusalem. Paul languished in a

Roman prison for over two years. After examination by Festus, he appealed to Caesar's judgement seat for justice. Festus sent him to Rome and Caesar. Paul being in chains, was placed under guard and shipped out to Rome. ***"And when it was decided that we should sail to Italy, they delivered Paul and some other prisoners to one named Julius, a centurion of the Augustan Regiment,"*** Acts 27:1 NKJV. The voyage began uneventfully, however the ship's fortune was about to turn. ***"But not long after, a tempestuous head wind arose, called Euroclydon,"*** Acts 27:14 NKJV. The storm was fiercely powerful and destructive. Here is an eyewitness account of how the crew felt, ***"Now when neither sun nor stars appeared for many days, and no small tempest beat on us, all hope that we would be saved was finally given up,"*** Acts 27:20 NKJV. However, Paul through this storm, had a promise he received from Jesus two years into his imprisonment, ***"But the following night the Lord stood by him and said, "Be of good cheer, Paul; for as you have testified for Me in Jerusalem, so you must also bear witness at Rome,"*** Acts 23:11 NKJV. Therefore, with this promise in Paul's heart, we can assume, through the storm, Paul was praying and declaring this promise to God. The result of this prayer was amazing. The promise given to Paul, by Jesus, was confirmed by God. ***"For there stood by me this night an angel of the God to whom I belong and whom I serve, saying, 'Do not be afraid, Paul; you must be brought before Caesar; and indeed God has granted you all those who sail with you,'"*** Acts 27:23-24 NKJV. The situation of Paul's reality does not defeat the promises of God. Therefore, we find Paul serving and exhorting all those on the ship to be of good cheer. Here is where we see Paul's heart of gratitude towards God. ***"And as day was about to dawn, Paul implored them all to take food, saying, 'Today is the fourteenth day you have waited and continued without food, and eaten nothing. Therefore I urge you to take nourishment, for this is for your survival, since not a hair will fall from the head of any of you.' And when he had said these things, he took bread and gave thanks to God in the presence of them all; and when he had broken it he began to eat,"*** Acts

27:33-35 NKJV. Yes, we read the text correctly about Paul, "HE TOOK BREAD AND GAVE THANKS TO GOD IN THE PRESENCE OF THEM ALL!" How mysterious is the mystery of giving thanks to God in everything? The result, they were all saved from the shipwreck, and Paul got to Rome.

As we look to become thankful with a heart of gratitude towards God, let us not behave sinfully in our thanksgiving. We are not to be thankful for evil and the consequences of evil. Please remember the wages of sin is death. Therefore, let us not be thankful because we have cancer or poverty or wickedness of any type which has happened to us or natural disasters and lives in a fallen world. These are a result of the original sin and our continuation in this. These are things to be sorrowful or repentant about, not thankful for. These are not what God has in His heart for humanity. Let us follow the examples of our Lord and His apostle, Paul, and being always thankful to God, no matter what is happening to us, just for the simple reason, He is our God! It is time to stop being unwise of this but understanding of the will of God in speaking, worship, and thanksgiving. For it is written, we are to be,

"Speaking to one another in psalms and hymns and spiritual songs, singing and making melody in your heart to the Lord, giving thanks always for all things to God the Father in the name of our Lord Jesus Christ," Ephesians 5:17-21.

Reflections

1. Name, from Ephesians 5:17-21, what we are not to be unwise about.
2. Describe the three areas of the heart Paul is concerned about with our expressions.
3. How do these expressions of the heart prove Ezekiel 36:26-27 and Hebrews 10:16?
4. In the way you express yourself, are you expressing

outwardly what God has done inwardly?

5. What are the ways of expression in Ephesians 5:17-21?
6. Do those you interact with see the new creation or the carnal nature of expression?
7. How does Jesus warn us of duplicity in the faith walk in Matthew 15:8-9?
8. What are the expressions of heart we should not have come out of our mouths according to Matthew 15:19 and Luke 6:45?
9. What is the heart? Where did our hearts become impure and alienated from God?
10. What is the lesson of the wineskins in Matthew 9:17? How can you apply this lesson?
11. Have you ever checked which heart you live out of? If you have the courage and humility to not get offended, find out how others see your expressions.
12. Do you have evil thoughts and expressions?
13. Is there an expression of hate towards anyone in you?
14. Are you a man or woman of adulterous thoughts and expressions?
15. Is your heart filled with fornications?
16. How covetous are your thoughts?
17. Are you known for lying and excessive exaggeration or false witness of someone?
18. The worse of all how are your thoughts toward God?
19. Why are these thinking patterns and behaviors against the will of God?
20. If these behavioral patterns have disappeared from your life, would you consider it proof of being born

again and having a new heart?

21. What is the wisdom of Romans 12:2? How does this prove the will of God?
22. Does Paul mean for us to speak to one another in psalms, hymns, and spiritual songs?
23. Does this mean we cannot talk to one another about "things in the world"?
24. How active is your day and how many relationships do you have to engage in?
25. What manner of speech do you have towards all you engage with?
26. Explain what you think is the way a born-again believer should speak and act towards others.
27. True or False, the speech out of our mouths must be truth and love.
28. How do you apply speech of truth and love with your spouse, family, coworkers, neighbors, friends, and strangers?
29. Do people know you by the fruit of your mouth as someone saved or somewhat hypocritical?
30. What does Peter mean in 1 Peter 4:1, ***"If anyone speaks, let him speak as the oracles of God?"***
31. Why should psalms, hymns, and spiritual songs, be the good treasure of your heart? What type of fruit of the lips would this produce out of your heart?
32. Explain this maxim of mine, "If we think scripturally, we will understand spiritually and truthfully, and speak and act accordingly."
33. What is the difference between a spiritual mind and a carnal mind? For Help read Romans 8:5-6.
34. What is the command Ephesians 4:29-30? When

should we obey this?

35. What is a heart of worship towards God? What does it mean to sing and make melodies in our heart to God? What songs are in your heart?
36. How serious should the church of today take the warning of Isaiah 1:14-15? How serious should you take this warning?
37. How does 1 Timothy 1:5 describe a worship in the new heart?
38. Why is this important?
39. How does worship adjust our focus of attention?
40. What happens to worship if a darkness enters our life?
41. How did Jehoshaphat face darkness in 2 Chronicles 20?
42. How did he overcome his fear? How can this help Christians when fear enters their life? How did God respond to the worship from Israel?
43. According to King David, where is Gods' habitation? (Psalm 22:3)
44. How important is this for the body of Christ, individually and corporately?
45. How did Paul apply his own advice in Acts 16:23-40?
46. How did God respond to this?
47. What happened to Paul and Silas?
48. According to Jesus, He wants us to be of good cheer even in tribulation, why?
49. How does good cheer in our heart activate the overcoming Spirit of Christ in us?
50. How important is it for a disciple of Christ to have a heart of gratitude?

51. In Hebrews 12:5, what are we to consider in our tribulations and trials so we will not lose our gratitude?
52. In the last Passover supper, how does Jesus express gratitude with the agony of the cross before Him?
53. How is this the highest example of gratitude to God?
54. In Acts 27, how does Paul show gratitude in the midst of a raging sea storm?
55. How does Paul imitate Christ here?
56. Does being thankful for everything include our evil or sins?
57. From this lesson are you wise or unwise in understanding the will of God?

CHAPTER FOUR

"Therefore do not be unwise, but understand what the will of the Lord is. And do not be drunk with wine, in which is dissipation; but be filled with the Spirit, speaking to one another in psalms and hymns and spiritual songs, singing and making melody in your heart to the Lord, giving thanks always for all things to God the Father in the name of our Lord Jesus Christ, submitting to one another in the fear of God."

Ephesians 5:17-21 NKJV

Unwise or Understanding of the Will of God

LESSON FOUR - SUBMISSION

Finally, we hit the big nugget which many Christians are very unwise about and not understanding of. It is the idea of submitting to one another we do not like. Paul is specific about this. Do not be unwise but understand what the will of the Lord is in submitting to one another in the fear of God. There is a lot of bucking concerning this. Many do not like to walk in this manner because they are still Christian broncos. I ran into a herd of broncos at my first ministry. I soon found myself bucking a little at the command to submit to one another also. There was much bucking going on at this church. The women were in rebellion against the men (feminism was in full force), men were dodging their responsibilities, and elders were demanding all be under their authority. They would not submit to the minister and I was finding it hard to submit to them. What was the result of all of this? The result was an angry, rebellious and contentious situation. The fear of God was not there, nor was the obedience of submission. The end result of this intense battle led to my resignation and shortly after this, a split (the story is bigger than I can tell). There also was the never-ending hurt and guilt of dealing with this church failure for many years, not only in myself but for many of the congregation.

The truth of being unwise and not understanding the will of the Lord in submission can lead to a lifetime of problems. We see this in marriage. The miss-understanding and stupidity of many concerning submission is centered on the wife submitting to her husband and not vice versa. Few are they who understand the verses which are under Ephesians 5:21, ***"Submitting to one another in the fear of God."*** This is the thesis which is followed by the paragraphs of where the action of submission is to be applied. I had an eye opening on this around 1983 or so. My wife and I were at the laundromat. As we were waiting on the washing and drying cycles, I was meditating on submitting to one another. I was revolving this in my mind when the light went off and the Holy Spirit opened my mind to understand how everyone was to submit to each other in the fear of God. I had never linked Ephesians 5:21 with 5:22 to 6:9 before. However, God linked them up beautifully with submission upon submission.

The Submissions

1. Ephesians 5:22-24 concerns the wife to the husband.
2. Ephesians 5:22-33 concerns the husband to the wife.
3. Ephesians 6:2-3 concerns children to the parents.
4. Ephesians 6:4 concerns the father to the children.
5. Ephesians 6:5-8 concerns slaves (for us today employees) to masters (employer).
6. Ephesians 6:9 concerns masters (employers) to their slaves (employees).

There is one fact we need to understand before we try to figure out what submission means. This fact is found in Galatians 3:28. ***"There is neither Jew nor Greek, there is neither slave nor free, there is neither male nor female; for you are all one in Christ Jesus."*** The word one is an important word in this verse. Paul is stating all nationalities, classes of people, and male or female, in God's eyes, are not considered differences anymore. No longer does God look at people individually after salvation to be judged on their own merits but through Christ and in Christ all become equal. Therefore, all are one and if we are one there is no two or three or four or more levels of classification of peoples. In simple terms, no one is better, more superior, greater or elevated above anyone else. Jesus puts it this way, ***"So the last will be first, and the first last. For many are called, but few chosen,"*** Matthew 20:16 NKJV. The word of the gospel puts it this way, ***"For all have sinned and fall short of the glory of God,"*** (Romans 3:23 NKJV) and ***"Even the righteousness of God, through faith in Jesus Christ, to all and on all who believe. For there is no difference,"*** (Romans 3:22 NKJV). The point concerning us in God's eyes, there is no difference, we all sinned and equally fall short of the glory of God. Furthermore, every human is equally guilty for the death of Christ, God's Son. Finally, no one is saved apart from faith in Christ. ***"For by grace you have been saved through faith, and that not of yourselves; it is the gift of God, not of works, lest anyone should boast,"*** Ephesians 2:8-9 NKJV. In the kingdom of God, God will not allow anyone to boast of their own self-importance. Therefore, we are all equal with one another or all are on the same footing. However, let us never forget how much God loves each of us and how special we are to Him. ***"Just as He chose us in Him before the foundation of the world, that we should be holy and without blame before Him in love, having predestined us to adoption as sons by Jesus Christ to Himself, according to the good pleasure of His will, to the praise of the glory of His grace, by which He made us accepted in the Beloved,"*** Ephesians 1:4-6 NKJV. Nevertheless, we are warned about prideful superiority concerning others, not to think so. ***"For if anyone thinks himself to be something, when he is nothing, he deceives himself,"*** Galatians 6:3 NKJV.

The fact is in Christ all are one and are being built together in Christ for the glory of God. ***"Now, therefore, you are no longer strangers and foreigners, but fellow citizens with the saints and members of the household of God, having been built on the foundation of the apostles and prophets, Jesus Christ Himself being the chief corner stone, in whom the whole building, being fitted together, grows into a holy temple in the Lord, in whom you also are being built together for a dwelling place of God in the Spirit,"*** Ephesians 2:19-22 NKJV. The people of God need to not be unwise about this but understanding of the equality we have with each other in Christ. Therefore, with all this in our understanding, the logical question we need to ask is, why do we need to be told to submit to one another in the fear of the Lord? It is fairly obvious men and women of the church do not like the idea of submission. The problem with this is a lack of having the mind of Christ reigning in us.

"Let this mind be in you which was also in Christ Jesus, who, being in the form of God, did not consider it robbery to be equal with God, but made Himself of no reputation, taking the form of a bondservant, and coming in the likeness of men. And being found in appearance as a man, He humbled Himself and became obedient to the point of death, even the death of the cross," Philippians 2:5-8 NKJV.

The mind of Christ is always to do the will of the Father. ***"For I have come down from heaven, not to do My own will, but the will of Him who sent Me,"*** John 6:38 NKJV. Therefore, the first understanding for us in submitting to one another is the fact, *God has commanded us to submit to one another in the fear of God.* If we do not agree with the command to submit, we are not having the mind of Christ and we are disobedient. Christians need to understand how serious disobedience is in the sight of God. Let us listen to what Samuel said to a non-submissive king Saul.

"So Samuel said: 'Has the Lord as great delight in burnt offerings and sacrifices, As in obeying the voice of the Lord? Behold, to obey is better than sacrifice, And to heed than the fat of rams. For rebellion is as the sin of witchcraft, And stubbornness is as iniquity and idolatry. Because you have rejected the word of the Lord, He also has rejected you from being king,'" 1 Samuel 15:22-23 NKJV.

With these facts in our understanding, is it not time to deny ourselves and submit to one another in the fear of God? Now let us try to figure out and comprehend what true submitting means. Does submitting mean we are to obey an evil king or spouse or boss or parent who would lead us into immorality, cheating stealing or lying? The Apostles Peter and John were in a dilemma with the authorities of their time. They knew Christ's teachings to submit to authority. The account of the taxes was still fresh in their minds. So was Jesus' answer, ***"And He said to them, 'Render therefore to Caesar the things that are Caesar's, and to God the things that are God's,'"*** Matthew 22:21 NKJV. However, standing before the rulers of Israel, they were commanded to stop preaching Jesus Christ as Savior. They knew they had to obey God and submit to authority, yet we learn by their answer and behavior, submission ends when evil is ruling. ***"But Peter and John answered and said to them, 'Whether it is right in the sight of God to listen to you more than to God, you judge,'"*** Acts 4:19 NKJV. Submission always end when it supersedes submission to God and His moral will.

Nevertheless, the command to submit is still ordered for us to obey. Therefore, what exactly is submission? Does submission mean servitude? Will submission take away our Christian liberty? ***"Stand fast therefore in the liberty by which Christ has made us free, and do not be entangled again with a yoke of bondage,"*** Galatians 5:1 NKJV. Will we become entangled with a yoke of bondage if we submit to one another? The word Paul uses, translated to English as submitting is (Strong's G5293) hupotasso. This is a compound verb, Strong's G5295 hupo, a preposition translated as, under, with Strong's G5021 tasso, a verb meaning to arrange in an orderly manner. Without trying to go beyond Greek scholars, I believe we can say the compound hupotasso has the sense of arranging in order under ... something or someone. Perhaps we can bring in 1 Corinthians 14:33 to see why submitting means arranging ourselves in order under one another. ***"For God is not the author of confusion but of peace, as in all the churches of the saints."*** With this in mind, may we boldly say, the submitting to one another is arranging ourselves under each other to keep God's proper order in a chaotic world? Remember we are all equal, in Christ, in God's eyes. However, we are living in a fallen world which we were part of. Therefore, the people of God must behave God's way through submission to win and bring all under His rule.

Paul refers to lack of submission to proper worship behavior as a witness of insanity. ***"Therefore if the whole church comes together in one place, and all speak with tongues, and there come in those who are uninformed or unbelievers, will they not say that you are out of your mind?"*** (1 Corinthians 14:23 NKJV) If the unsaved thinks unbridled worship tells him we are out of our mind, what will our unwise non-submitting ways tell them about us? Well, I believe you have heard what they think about us, hypocrites. Yes, unbelievers can reason and think and understand. You do not have to be a Christian to understand the words of Jesus, ***"Therefore by their fruits you will know them,"*** Matthew 7:20 NKJV. Even sinners can make a just judgement concerning the fruit of people they know and they will know us by our fruit. The best way for Christians to bear good fruit is by being wise and understanding in submitting to one another in the fear of God.

Points of Order

Since submission is placing ourselves under someone or something and being in a proper order, there are four points of order we need to understand concerning the command to submit to one another.

1. Submitting is about interactions of relationships. Paul states in Ephesians 5:22-6:9, three relational areas for proper submitting, they are, spouses to each other, child and parental submitting, and finally employer-employee submissions. In a normal day most of these three relationship interactions occur for everyone one way or the other. How discomforting is an improper relationship of wife and husband which are not

submitted to each other. An overbearing husband and a nagging manipulative wife are not the Christian norm God commands. The fruit of this behavior is witnessed and understood by all except by those doing the evil behavior. The same is true for an abusive parent or a rebellious child. Furthermore, who likes going into a business when the employees are bad mouthing their employer or the employer is a public ass to his employees. This is really magnified if everyone involved are Christians who are not submitting God's way. The end result is the whole community is affected very badly and the witness of Christianity dies there.

2. The act of submitting or getting into proper order under someone or something requires an exertion of the will deliberately. The secret of every human heart is the desire for liberty and freedom. Since we all want to be free, it is a hard subject for us to hear and do, submit to one another. Jesus understood this problem in us. Therefore, He gave us advice on how to overcome our desires to not submit. ***"Then He said to them all, 'If anyone desires to come after Me, let him deny himself, and take up his cross daily, and follow Me. For whoever desires to save his life will lose it, but whoever loses his life for My sake will save it,'"*** Luke 9:23-24 NKJV. It will take a deliberate act of the will to deny ourselves and put to death our personal desires in-order to follow Jesus into His life of submission. As the Lord says concerning finding life, it can only happen when we lose our life for Jesus' sake by submitting to one another in the fear of the Lord. The choice is ours to submit or not, wives to husbands, husbands to wives, child to

parent, parent to child, employee to employer and employer to employee. There is only one problem, God expects us to do this.

3. Submitting to one another is for the express purpose of serving each other when needs arise. If we are serving each other, we all are considering the other as important, and deserving of our service. However, more often than not, most people want to be served and not to serve. There is one axiom when it comes to serving, "*There are too many supervisors or bosses and not enough servers.*" How strangely true is this axiom for some of the people of God. Many have a Caesar complex, thinking they are special. (Remember all are equal or on the same footing in Christ.) Jesus had this problem with His disciples, they wanted to be the head at the Lord's right hand. He scolded them for being unwise and not understanding of what He has been trying to teach them. ***"But Jesus called them to Himself and said, 'You know that the rulers of the Gentiles lord it over them, and those who are great exercise authority over them. Yet it shall not be so among you; but whoever desires to become great among you, let him be your servant. And whoever desires to be first among you, let him be your slave,'"*** Matthew 20:25-27 NKJV. This is explained, by Paul, in an extremely specific manner. ***"Let nothing be done through selfish ambition or conceit, but in lowliness of mind let each esteem others better than himself. Let each of you look out not only for his own interests, but also for the interests of others,"*** Philippians 2:3-4 NKJV. Did you know the Holy Spirit gives gifts to Christians to serve others through humility for the betterment of their interests? The pastor, priest or minister is gifted

to edify the body, not to be placed on a pedestal to be worshipped. Those who speak with tongues are not to be showoffs, but using the gift for a witness of Christ. ***"There are diversities of gifts, but the same Spirit. There are differences of ministries, but the same Lord. And there are diversities of activities, but it is the same God who works all in all. But the manifestation of the Spirit is given to each one for the profit of all,"*** 1 Corinthians 12:4-7 NKJV. The gifts are not for our own individual profit but for the serving of others. How beautiful would the church be if we were wise and understanding of the power of submission God's way?

4. The behavior of submitting, to one another, brings us into conformity to the image of Christ. ***"For whom He foreknew, He also predestined to be conformed to the image of His Son, that He might be the firstborn among many brethren,"*** Romans 8:29 NKJV. The problem with the egocentric church is we try to conform Christ to us and our image of Him. If we remember John 6:38, Jesus came to do the will of the Father who sent Him and also, ***"For even the Son of Man did not come to be served, but to serve, and to give His life a ransom for many,"*** Mark 10:45 NKJV. The wise and understanding know submitting is actually being conformed to Christs' image which reflects obedience to God and serving others.

In our understanding of submitting, through these four points of order, submitting concerns relationships, it is a deliberate act of the will, it is about serving, and conformity to the image of Christ, we have the knowledge of why we should submit. However, what will cause us to actually do it? Well, James the Lord's brother puts it bluntly to us by saying, ***"Therefore submit to God,"*** James 4:7 NKJV. The first order of business for all Christians is to get themselves under God in a proper position. Jesus said to His non-submitting disciples after He had to wash their feet, ***"So when He had washed their feet, taken His garments, and sat down again, He said to them, 'Do you know what I have done to you? You call Me Teacher and Lord, and you say well, for so I am. If I then, your Lord and Teacher, have washed your feet, you also ought to wash one another's feet,'"*** John 13:12-14 NKJV. The twelve were calling Him Lord and Teacher. However, their behavior shows they had not placed themselves under Him in proper position as Lord and themselves as subjects under His authority. The proof is, not one of the twelve submitted themselves to meet the need of washing their fellow disciples' feet, nor the Lord's feet. The Son of God did the washing! Sometime ago, I was an associate pastor when a break in occurred at the church. The head pastor called me in for support. The entrance door window was smashed and broken. As the pastor and I went in, I stooped down to start picking up the broken glass fragments. The head pastor said to me, get up and stop picking up the glass, let someone in the congregation pick it up! I said no, I can do it. He persisted, so I stopped picking up the glass (This still bothers me today). You tell me, did we submit to the congregation or did we expect to be served by the congregation? The problem is, we have not truly made Jesus Lord of our life. If We are submitting to God we will obey Him and submit to each other when the need arises. Remember, we are known by our fruit and our unwillingness to submit to each other produces the fruit for all to see, we call Jesus Lord by mouth and not by deed and the world knows it. Truly, how unwise or understanding are we of this. Our submitting is really a proper attitude which shows itself in action.

Some Precautions Concerning Submitting

The first precaution to consider is, the person or thing you are submitting to turns you into their personal servants. This may be done through guilt or intimidation. These people take your obedient loving heart and use it against you to make you do things beyond their need. Remember, it is your act of will in stepping out to submit to another in their need. This should not happen through the bullying or coercion of those who need it. This will cause anger in you, more than enjoying giving your time to help. There is a place you can use the words, no I cannot do that, without guilt. Another precaution to watch for is those who connive unscrupulously to get your submission. These know how to use the Christian system to their advantage. With cunning craftiness they prey on your heart and before you know it, you are into a submission you should not be into. One other precaution, to mention is to beware of placing your family, spouse, or self in dangerous, or compromising situations. Ungodly soul ties are a real danger for those who obey the command to submit in service to another. How many ministers or the wives of ministers are there who have stumbled into ungodly soul ties and destroyed their lives? The answer is plenty have! This is also true for all Christians. Many problems have arisen because of carnal submission to another. This is not being under one another in a proper order. This is sin unleashed. Remember, if you lose Christ, you have not done a submitting with wisdom. Submitting is an attitude and a wisdom to move when the need is required of you. If you are not cautious about this you will never have a moment for yourself or family or God! Remember Martha, the serving servant of anger!

The Tale of Two

Recently, a couple my wife and I know well told us of their experiences with two people who had a need. This couple placed themselves in proper order under the people whom they willfully chose to help. The first person was one who was almost immobilized and needed help. The couple said, this one never asked for help at any time, nor demanded anything from them. The couple told us they helped this person in various ways for over two years, with the one being helped asking for assistance a limited number of times. They said to us, if this one needed help they would drop what they were doing and come to this one's aid. They always felt joy to do so. Finally, this first person was able to function without their help. Whenever they see this person now it is with gladness of heart.

However, person number two was something which happened to them, unwillingly. Number two, through situations, found a way to get their help. This submitting to a need was more of a guilt trip, but also trying to love the brethren as the Lord commanded. The couple felt a warning from the Spirit to be careful in this caring. Soon number two started to become demanding and overwhelming. Number two would not heed advice for societal programs which could meet number two's needs. He expected the couple and all Christians, known by number two, to be at the beck and call of service in a minute's notice. After getting food to bring to number two, by demand, the man received a ten-minute lecture about the poorness of the couple's service. This lecture ended the couple's submission of helping number two. They also found out from other Christians the extent of number two's web of bringing people into this person's service. They all had dreaded outcomes. Whenever this couple hears from number two, it is with dread in their heart.

As you see, submitting can be a joyous or dreadful experience. The Lord warns us of one more precaution in the submitting to serving. It is found in the story of two sisters He knew. They were Martha and Mary, the sisters of Lazarus, who Jesus raised from the dead. Let us have the Bible tell us of this precaution.

"Now it happened as they went that He entered a certain village; and a certain woman named Martha welcomed Him into her house. And she had a sister called Mary, who also sat at Jesus' feet and heard His word. But Martha was distracted with much serving, and she approached Him and said, 'Lord, do You not care that my sister has left me to serve alone? Therefore tell her to

help me.' And Jesus answered and said to her, 'Martha, Martha, you are worried and troubled about many things. But one thing is needed, and Mary has chosen that good part, which will not be taken away from her,'" Luke 10:38-42 NKJV.

In this story, we learn, any service which does not have Christ preeminent, produces worry and distraction. In the tale of two, the service to person one increased the personal relationship of the couple with Christ. The service to person two put a wedge between the couple and Christ. Therefore, in submitting to one another in the fear of the Lord we must not be unwise but understanding what the will of the Lord is.

Finally, any Christian person who is receiving the submitting of service must understand they are also under the command to submit to those who are serving them. Therefore, their behavior should be thankful for whatever assistance they receive. They should not be demanding nor critical of the way it is done. The failure of Christians in behavior towards one another has in many instances caused heartaches and disillusionments with the faith. Many Christians cannot bear to be around other Christians because of the failure of being unwise and not understanding the will of the Lord in submitting to one another in the fear of God! The problem is, many do not fear God but think God excuses all their bad behavior! Guess what, He does not. This is why Paul told the Ephesians to not be unwise but understanding and God also wants us to be so too! Now is our time to let the mind that was in Christ be in us! Christian are you unwise or understanding of the will of God? If not it is time to change your ways. Please submit to one another in the fear of God!

Reflections

1. Why is the command of submission such a difficult concept for Christians?

2. What does this command mean, ***"Submitting to one another in the fear of God?"***
3. Is this command clear and specific or cloudy and ambiguous?
4. Can being unwise and not understanding the will of the Lord concerning submission cause problems and hurts?
5. How does God expect us to submit in these relationships: Ephesians 5:22-24 wives to husbands, Ephesians 5:22-33 husbands to wives, Ephesians 6:2-3 children to parents, Ephesians 6:4 fathers to children, Ephesians 6:5-8 employees to employers, Ephesians 6:9 employers to employees?
6. What is an important fact Paul teaches in Galatians 3:28, which will make submission easier in the Christian life?
7. What does it mean we are all *ONE in Christ Jesus?*
8. With this oneness in mind why do you think God wants us to submit to one another?
9. Explain Matthew 20:16 concerning this oneness.
10. Explain Romans 3:22 concerning oneness.
11. How do these to concepts work for us in obeying submission?
12. Does self-importance have any place in the Kingdom of God?
13. How will submitting to each other do away with self-importance?
14. How important is God's love for you in enabling you to submit to others?
15. According to Galatians 6:3 how can you deceive yourself?

16. How does submission work in Ephesians 2:19-22?
17. What type of mindset should we have according to Philippians 2:5-8?
18. If you have Christs' mindset, will it make submission a command you could do?
19. In John 6:38 what did Jesus not do and what did He do?
20. If we are disobedient to God, how does 1 Samuel 15:22-23 describe us?
21. What is true submission according to Gods' point of view?
22. How does Acts 4:19 explain the proper order of submission?
23. If we, in Christ, are called to liberty, Galatians 5:1, how does submission arrange things according to the order of God?
24. How is this a witness for God?
25. What will people think of a church which does not practice submission according to 1 Corinthians 14:23?
26. Summarize Point of Order number one.
27. Summarize Point of Order number two.
28. Summarize Point of order number three.
29. Summarize Point of Order number four.
30. How does Jesus Christ teach this in John 13: 1-14?
31. Does He actually expect us to follow His lead?
32. List some precautions you should be aware of before committing to submitting to someone.
33. If submitting will be detrimental to your walk with Christ in a certain situation, would the Lord allow

us to say no to it?

34. How well do you obey God in this command to submit?

God Bless You!

Now Walk God's Way!

LESSON ELEVEN: LIVING SPIRITUALLY FOLLOWING CHRIST'S EXAMPLE

SPIRITUAL BEHAVIORS

As I grow up in the faith, I finally grasp the word spiritual, or the phrase walk in the Spirit, or think spiritually. Christianity has made the understanding of spirituality so esoteric nobody understands it, nor tries to live spiritually anymore. Would you agree with me on this statement, *"Jesus of Nazareth is the most spiritual man who walked the earth?"* Why is this so? The reason Jesus is spiritual is simply said this way, *He lived only to please His Father and to do His Father's will.* He proclaimed it, ***"I do not seek My own will but the will of the Father who sent Me,"*** John 5:30. The Lord always obeyed the will of God His Father. If Jesus did not obey the commands of God or God's will, it would have been accounted as sin toward Him. The religious leaders of His day were openly antagonistic toward Jesus. Jesus asked them a pointed question, ***"Which of you convicts Me of sin?"*** (John 8:46) Those antagonistic leaders could not give evidence of one sin they could accuse Jesus of. Why so? Jesus always did what His Father (God) wanted Him to do. He was obedient to the Word of God. Therefore, He is spiritual.

Reflections

1. What do you think being spiritual means?
2. How did Jesus prove He lived a spiritual life?
3. Can anyone convict Jesus of sin?
4. Does spiritual mean we are obedient to God?
5. Are you spiritual?

THE WAY OF THE SPIRIT OF OBEDIENCE EXEMPLIFIED BY JESUS

In order for us to be spiritual, we must follow the example Jesus gave to us. Jesus is the Son of God and also the Son of Man. He is Immanuel, God with men. He was conceived by the Holy Spirit and born of the Virgin Mary. ***"Now the birth of Jesus Christ was as follows: After His mother Mary was betrothed to Joseph, before they came together, she was found with child of the Holy Spirit,"*** Matthew 1:18. Since Jesus is the God-Man, He is our example of how to be spiritual. We are to walk as He walked in His earthly life, God working in man. ***"He who says he abides in Him ought himself also to walk just as He walked,"*** 1 John 2:6. Jesus walked spiritually because He was born of the Spirit. Jesus had power to obey in Himself because He is God, the second person of the Trinity. However, in human form He had the power of God because He was born of the Holy Spirit. Furthermore, when John baptized Jesus, He received power from on high when the Holy Spirit descended on Him. ***"When all the people were baptized, it came to pass that Jesus also was baptized; and while He prayed, the heaven was opened. And the Holy Spirit descended in bodily form like a dove upon Him, and a voice came from heaven which said, 'You are My beloved Son; in You I am well pleased,'"*** Luke 3:21-22. The Lord having the Holy Spirit on Him is at once led by Him. ***"Then Jesus was led up by the Spirit into the wilderness to be tempted by the devil,"*** Matthew 4:1. Jesus expresses where the source of His authoritative power comes from, the Holy Spirit. ***"But if I cast out demons by the Spirit of God, surely the kingdom of God has come upon you,"*** Matthew 12:28. Finally, we are taught the secret of Jesus' ability to obey the Father even unto death. ***"How much more shall the blood of Christ, who through the eternal Spirit offered Himself without spot to God, cleanse your***

conscience from dead works to serve the living God?" (Hebrews 9:14) Not only did Jesus offer Himself through the Spirit but He rose again or took His life back by the Spirit.

"Therefore My Father loves Me, because I lay down My life that I may take it again. No one takes it from Me, but I lay it down of Myself. I have power to lay it down, and I have power to take it again. This command I have received from My Father," John 10:17-18.

"But if the Spirit of Him who raised Jesus from the dead dwells in you, He who raised Christ from the dead will also give life to your mortal bodies through His Spirit who dwells in you," Romans 8:11.

Paul tries to explain the greatness of Jesus to Timothy, ***"And without controversy great is the mystery of godliness: God was manifested in the flesh, Justified in the Spirit, Seen by angels, Preached among the Gentiles, Believed on in the world, Received up in glory,"*** 1 Timothy 3:16. Therefore, in trying to understand the power of Jesus through the Holy Spirit, we must be careful not to make it a formula, it is a mystery of God. The wonderful revelation from God to us is He wants us to have, ***"The mystery of godliness manifested in the flesh,"*** in us.

Reflections

6. Who gives us the example of being Spiritual?
7. Who is Jesus?
8. Define the name Immanuel.
9. Describe the birth of Jesus Christ.
10. What role did the Holy Spirit have in the conception of Christ?
11. What does this statement mean, Jesus is the God-Man?

12. How does this become our example of being spiritual?
13. What does it mean to be born of the Spirit?
14. According to 1 John 2:6, how are we to walk?
15. Describe the Trinity in Luke 3:21-22.
16. List the ways the Spirit worked in the life of Jesus.
17. How great is the mystery of godliness according to 1 Timothy 3:16? Does God want this mystery to be in us?

THE LESSON OF THE INCARNATION

Let us examine the Scriptural teachings on the Incarnation of Christ from these above verses: Matthew 1:18, 1 John 2:6, Luke 3:21-22, Matthew 12:28, and Hebrews 9:14.

- Jesus, the second person of the Trinity, assumed human form.
- Jesus was conceived by the Holy Spirit.
- Jesus was born of the Virgin Mary.
- Jesus was baptized with the Holy Spirit.
- Jesus was led by the Holy Spirit.
- Jesus ministered through the Holy Spirit.
- Jesus gave Himself to the cross through the Holy Spirit for our salvation.
- Jesus rose from the dead through the Holy Spirit for our justification.

Although Jesus, the Eternal Son of God had life in Himself in His incarnation life, He lived by the life power of the Holy Spirit. ***"He was in the beginning with God. All things were made through Him, and without Him nothing was made that was made. In Him was life, and the life was the light of men,"*** John 1:2-4. Since, we are to look to Jesus for all of our life's needs, we must live like Him, through the Spirit, to experience the Christ life in us. When we do this the Scripture will be fulfilled, ***"Love has been perfected among us in this: that we may have boldness in the day of judgment; because as He is, so are we in this world,"*** 1 John 4:17. If we live as He lived in the Spirit, we will be like Him in this world!

Reflections

18. What is the lesson of the incarnation?
19. How do we experience the Christ life?

THE HUMAN PROBLEM

The Bible teaches we all have a problem.

- ***"For all have sinned and fall short of the glory of God,"*** Romans 3:23.
- ***"But your iniquities have separated you from your God; And your sins have hidden His face from you, So that He will not hear,"*** Isaiah 59:2.

Our joint problem is, we all have sinned and we are separated from the life and nature of God. We have an inherited nature from Adam which was not the original human nature designed by God. This inherited nature came into Adam through his sin. Then through Adam's sin nature to us. This is so because of his rebellious act against the Law of God.

Reflections

20. What does God say in Romans 3:23?
21. What does God say in Isaiah 59:2?
22. What is our joint problem?
23. What has this problem caused in your life?
24. How many scars and regrets do you have because of sin?

THE PROGRESSION OF OUR PROBLEM

- We were created perfect ... ***"So God created man in His own image; in the image of God He created him; male and female He created them,"*** Genesis 1:27.
- God considers us "Good" ... ***"Then God saw everything that He had made, and indeed it was very good,"*** Genesis 1:31.
- God gives man a purpose ... ***"Then God blessed them, and God said to them, 'Be fruitful and multiply; fill the earth and subdue it; have dominion over the fish of the sea, over the birds of the air, and over every living thing that moves on the earth,'"*** Genesis 1:28.
- God legislates one law ... ***"And the Lord God commanded the man, saying, 'Of every tree of the garden you may freely eat; but of the tree of the knowledge of good and evil you shall not eat, for in the day that you eat of it you shall surely die,'"***Genesis 2:16-17.
- The law is broken ... ***"So when the woman saw that the tree was good for food, that it was pleasant to the eyes, and a tree desirable to make one wise, she took of its fruit and ate. She also gave to her husband with her, and he ate,"*** Genesis 3:6.
- After this act, we are genetically changed, we lose immortality, we lose the image of God ... ***"And Adam lived one hundred and thirty years, and begot a son in his own likeness, after his image, and named him Seth,"*** Genesis 5:3.
- The inherited changed nature of Adam from the nature in the likeness of God and His consciousness of goodness to the nature of a consciousness of good and evil leads to horrendous human behavior ... ***"Then the Lord saw that the wickedness of man was great in the earth, and that every intent of the thoughts of his heart was only evil continually,"*** Genesis 6:5.

- The human problem is manifest ... ***"For all have sinned and fall short of the glory of God,"*** Romans 3:23.

Reflections

25. Describe Biblically how we became sinners.
26. How does the activity of humans today prove the Biblical account of sin?

ESTABLISHED FACTS

- Adam and Eve's original sin of disobedience infects and affects all their progeny, including you and me.
- In our consciousness or nature we have the embedded genetic code of the knowledge of good and evil.
- This genetic knowledge of good and evil is not endorsed by God. It is a knowledge which is apart from God.
- This caused our separation from God, because evil breaks the law of God and the knowledge of good is not what God declared for us to have. Therefore, this good we have breaks the law of God.

Our problem is great. Once humans had a mind in the likeness of God. This mind was said to be good by God. We were able to walk with God and work with Him because our mind was set on the things of God. ***"Out of the ground the Lord God formed every beast of the field and every bird of the air, and brought them to Adam to see what he would call them. And whatever Adam called each living creature, that was its name,"*** Genesis 2:19. However, after sinning with the fruit of the knowledge of good and evil, we lost the mind of God. Our minds were changed into a carnal mind. The mind revolving around the self of good and evil. This mind is not seen as *"good"* by God, but from God's view is an enemy to Him. ***"Because the carnal mind is enmity against God; for it is not subject to the law of God, nor indeed can be. So then, those who are in the flesh cannot please God,"*** Romans 8:7-8. We are in great distress because we are in the bondage of sin through the carnal mind. ***"Even so we, when we were children, were in bondage under the elements of the world,"*** Galatians 4:3. We are a world cursed by God because of Adam's sin and our continuation in sin and our inability to please God.

We are in need to get back to the image of God and a mind which is pleasing to God because it does the will of God. God does this for us through Christ. ***"But when the fullness of the time had come, God sent forth His Son, born of a woman, born under the law, to redeem those who were under the law, that we might receive the adoption as sons. And because you are sons, God has sent forth the Spirit of His Son into your hearts, crying out, 'Abba, Father!' Therefore you are no longer a slave but a son, and if a son, then an heir of God through Christ,"*** Galatians 4:4-7. As we can see, we have a serious problem of alienation from God and the mind of God. Jesus Christ is the solution to our problem. Through Him we are restored to God and reborn to God's creation purpose. ***"Therefore, if anyone is in Christ, he is a new creation; old things have passed away; behold, all things have become new,"*** 2 Corinthians 5:17.

Reflections

27. How does Adam and Eve's sin infect and affect us, their offspring?
28. Why is the knowledge of good, from the tree of good and evil, a sinful knowledge?
29. What type of mind did we lose because of sin?
30. What type of mind did we inherit from sin?
31. How does this mind think of God according to Romans 8:7-8?
32. What are we in need of?
33. What do we become in Christ?

FIXING OUR PROBLEM

Let us remember the verse, ***"Because as He is, so are we in this world,"*** 1 John 4:17. The question is, *"How do we become as the Lord Jesus in this life?"* We enter into God's fix by accepting and entering into His gift of salvation. ***"Now all things are of God, who has reconciled us to Himself through Jesus Christ, and has given us the ministry of reconciliation, that is, that God was in Christ reconciling the world to Himself, not imputing their trespasses to them, and has committed to us the word of reconciliation,"*** 2 Corinthians 5:18-19. Therefore, if God has reconciled us to Himself through Christ, being in Christ must enable us to be spiritual as Jesus was spiritual. Also, it must enable us to obey God's will through the Spirit. This happens to us because in our salvation in Christ, God recreates us to be conformed to the image of His Son. ***"For whom He foreknew, He also predestined to be conformed to the image of His Son, that He might be the firstborn among many brethren,"*** Romans 8:29.

How Does this conformed predestined image of Christ in us happen? What does it mean to be conformed? Conform is translated from the Greek word *σύμμορφος (summorphos)* (Strong's G4832) *"jointly formed, i.e. (figuratively) similar:--conformed to, fashioned like unto."* Summorphos is a compound word. It combines a preposition *σύν (sun or soon)* and a noun *μορφή (morphe).*

- *σύν* from Strong's G4862: a primary preposition denoting union; with or together, together with (expresses association with)
- *μορφή* from Strong's G3444: (through the idea of adjustment of parts); shape; figuratively, nature:--form.

We are studying to learn how to be spiritual people.

Those people who obey God. We have learned how Jesus did this through the Holy Spirit. Therefore, according to Strong's definition, to be conformed means we are *jointly formed,* like Jesus with the Spirit. Our lives must have the *union of person* as Jesus did with the Holy Spirit. Therefore, we may say, ***"For whom He foreknew, He also predestined to be jointly formed to the image of His Son!"*** Let us again review the incarnation of Jesus Christ our Lord and Savior.

- Jesus the second person of the Trinity assumed human form.
- Jesus was conceived by the Holy Spirit.
- Jesus was born of the Virgin Mary.
- Jesus was baptized with the Holy Spirit.
- Jesus was led by the Holy Spirit.
- Jesus ministered through the Holy Spirit.
- Jesus gave Himself to the cross through the Holy Spirit for our salvation.
- Jesus rose from the dead through the Holy Spirit for our justification.
- Jesus cast out Demons through the Holy Spirit.

Therefore, if we are going to be conformed to the image of God's Son, we must be as Jesus was in His incarnation, in union with the Holy Spirit.

- We must be born as Jesus was born: ***"Jesus answered and said to him, 'Most assuredly, I say to you, unless one is born again, he cannot see the kingdom of God,'"*** John 3:3.
- We must be conceived by the Spirit as Jesus was: ***"Jesus answered, 'Most assuredly, I say to you, unless one is born of water and the Spirit, he cannot enter the kingdom of God. That which is born of the flesh is flesh, and that which is born of the Spirit is spirit,'"*** John 3:5-6.
- We must be baptized as Jesus was baptized: ***"Then Peter said***

to them, "Repent, and let every one of you be baptized in the name of Jesus Christ for the remission of sins; and you shall receive the gift of the Holy Spirit,'" Acts 2:38.

- We must be continually filled with the Spirit as Jesus was: ***"And do not be drunk with wine, in which is dissipation; but be filled with the Spirit,"*** Ephesians 5:18.
- We must be strengthened by the Spirit as Jesus was: ***"That He would grant you, according to the riches of His glory, to be strengthened with might through His Spirit in the inner man,"*** Ephesians 3:16.
- We must be led by the Spirit as Jesus was: ***"For as many as are led by the Spirit of God, these are sons of God,"*** Romans 8:14.
- We must be taught and learn through the Spirit as Jesus learned: ***"But the anointing which you have received from Him abides in you, and you do not need that anyone teach you; but as the same anointing teaches you concerning all things, and is true, and is not a lie, and just as it has taught you, you will abide in Him,"*** 1 John 2:27.
- We must pray through the Spirit as Jesus did: ***"Likewise the Spirit also helps in our weaknesses. For we do not know what we should pray for as we ought, but the Spirit Himself makes intercession for us with groanings which cannot be uttered. Now He who searches the hearts knows what the mind of the Spirit is, because He makes intercession for the saints according to the will of God,"*** Romans 8:26-27.
- We must minister through the Spirit as Jesus ministered: ***"There are diversities of gifts, but the same Spirit. There are differences of ministries, but the same Lord. And there are diversities of activities, but it is the same God who works all in all. But the manifestation of the Spirit is given to each one for the profit of all,"*** 1 Corinthians 12:4-7.
- We must be guided into all truth in every matter by the Holy Spirit as Jesus was: ***"However, when He, the Spirit of truth, has come, He will guide you into all truth; for He will***

not speak on His own authority, but whatever He hears He will speak; and He will tell you things to come," John 16:13.

- We must have a witness which glorifies Jesus through the Holy Spirit: ***"He will glorify Me, for He will take of what is Mine and declare it to you,"*** John 16:14.

The sum of this, God has fixed our problem. Our sin and separation from God has been repaired, through the sacrifice of His Son. He has made us right in His eyes again and given us the Spirit to walk justly before Him. The example of living in the Spirit was given by Jesus. Jesus was conceived by the Spirit, lived in the Spirit and walked in the Spirit. We who believe in Him are also born of the Spirit. We now are able to live and walk in the Spirit. ***"If we live in the Spirit, let us also walk in the Spirit,"*** Galatians 5:25. In doing this we will be conformed to the image of Christ as spiritual people who obey God. We must be spiritual as Jesus was, a life lived in obedience to the Father through the Spirit from our new birth to our death and finally to our ascension into the presence of God. Our daily motivation should be to establish our reliance on the Holy Spirit and not on our own strength. In ignoring the Holy Spirit we stop God's regenerating work in us. ***"Do not quench the Spirit,"*** is our command, 1 Thessalonians 5:19. Let us always remember our old nature needs to be crucified with Christ daily. It is a nature not endorsed by God, because it is a nature apart from God. If we walk in the old nature we will be subject to the law of sin and death. This separates us from God and quenches His Spirit in us. Nevertheless, if we live ***jointly formed*** with the Spirit, the Spirit regenerating and us yielding to Him we become the obedient image of Christ. ***"For the law of the Spirit of life in Christ Jesus has made me free from the law of sin and death,"*** Romans 8:2.

Paul had an early problem of living spiritually, as Christ did. He confessed, ***"For I know that in me (that is, in my flesh) nothing good dwells; for to will is present with me, but how to***

perform what is good I do not find. For the good that I will to do, I do not do; but the evil I will not to do, that I practice," Romans 7:18-19. He found this problem was occurring because of what was going on in His mind. ***"But I see another law in my members, warring against the law of my mind, and bringing me into captivity to the law of sin which is in my members,"*** Romans 7:23. Although Paul said, in Romans 7:6, ***"But now we have been delivered from the law, having died to what we were held by, so that we should serve in the newness of the Spirit and not in the oldness of the letter."***

Paul understood:

- We have been delivered from the law.
- In our baptism we have died to what we were held by, Adam's nature.
- We are jointly formed in the newness of Spirit.

Paul understood these things just like many of us know them. However, his Romans chapter seven teaches us of his struggle to spirituality, living God's way. Although born again his mind was still subject to the law of sin and death. To solve this problem he needed to get His mind subject to ***the law of the Spirit of life in Christ Jesus.*** Can you feel the agony of Paul's cry to God in Romans 7:24? ***"O wretched man that I am! Who will deliver me from this body of death?"*** This is a real tormenting reality for Christians. Listen to Paul's agony again, ***"For to will is present with me, but how to perform what is good I do not find. For the good that I will to do, I do not do; but the evil I will not to do, that I practice."***

The problems of Paul:

- Paul had the will to be spiritual (obedient).
- Paul, although born again, could not find the way of living spiritually.
- Paul, born again, understood the holiness of goodness and

had the will to do it, but could not.

- Paul found himself doing the evil he knew he should not do in thought, word, and deed.

Reflections

34. How should you apply 1 John 4:17?
35. What does it mean to be reconciled to God?
36. How does Christ reconcile us to God?
37. If we are reconciled to God through Christ, what does this enable us to be?
38. Define conformed to the image of Christ.
39. How does conformity happen to us?
40. List all the ways the Holy Spirit was involved in the incarnation life of Christ.
41. According to these verses, how does the Spirit jointly form us into the image of Christ; John 3:3, John 3:5-6, Acts 2:38, Ephesians 5:18, Ephesians 3:16, Romans 8:14, 1 John 2:27, Romans 8:26-27, 1 Corinthians 12:4-7, John 16:13, and John 16:14?
42. Summarize how God has fixed our problem of sin and separation.
43. How does Jesus exemplify living in the Spirit?
44. What should our daily motivation be with the Holy Spirit?
45. What is the command of 1 Thessalonians 5:19? How can we do this bad thing?
46. How does Romans 8:2 apply for us in not quenching the Spirit?
47. According to Romans 7:18-19, what was the Apostle Paul's early Christian problem?
48. What was happening in the mind of Paul in Romans 7:23?
49. What three facts did Paul understand but could not

enable himself to live that way?

50. To solve this problem, what must he do with his mind in Romans 8:2?
51. Are you in the spiritual torment of Romans 7:18-19?
52. Are you finding hope in this lesson to get victory?

A CASE STUDY

Paul and Barnabas went on their first missionary journey and took John, who is Mark, with them. ***"As they ministered to the Lord and fasted, the Holy Spirit said, 'Now separate to Me Barnabas and Saul for the work to which I have called them.' Then, having fasted and prayed, and laid hands on them, they sent them away. So, being sent out by the Holy Spirit, they went down to Seleucia, and from there they sailed to Cyprus. And when they arrived in Salamis, they preached the word of God in the synagogues of the Jews. They also had John as their assistant,"*** Acts 13:2-5. This missionary journey begins spiritually. The church obeys the voice of the Holy Spirit. The Christian "Three Musketeers" set out together in harmonious joy for the advancement of the kingdom of heaven. The relationships seem intact, however we read, ***"Now when Paul and his party set sail from Paphos, they came to Perga in Pamphylia; and John, departing from them, returned to Jerusalem,"*** Acts 13:13. Something happened to Mark (John). What happened is a matter of speculation among scholars. Perhaps, Mark could not overcome his fear? Maybe, he felt inadequate for the job? Also, Mark might have been homesick for his home and family in Jerusalem. Whatever the reason, the Spirit tells us, John (Mark) departed from Paul and Barnabas. The Scripture is silent about Paul's reaction to Mark's leaving until Acts 15.

Paul probably went into one of his, *"the good I want to do and do not do it, but the evil I do,"* moments. Paul knows the good of love and forgiveness and understanding and mercy. As much as Paul wanted to be loving, forgiving, merciful, and understanding about Mark's desertion, he did the evil and condemned Mark. We do not know the struggle in the heart of Paul over Mark's leaving for Jerusalem, but we do know the bitter root of evil he built up towards Mark. So great was his emotional anger towards Mark, it led to a bitter argument and breaking of Christian unity with Barnabas. Paul was not spiritual concerning Mark, but Barnabas was. Barnabas had a loving Holy Spirit filled attitude toward Mark. Paul succumbing to his lower nature did not. Here are the explosive details and results of this situation. ***"Then after some days Paul said to Barnabas, 'Let us now go back and visit our brethren in every city where we have preached the word of the Lord, and see how they are doing.' Now Barnabas was determined to take with them John called Mark. But Paul insisted that they should not take with them the one who had departed from them in Pamphylia, and had not gone with them to the work. Then the contention became so sharp that they parted from one another. And so Barnabas took Mark and sailed to Cyprus,*** Acts 15:36-39.

Did you read the words, "*The contention became so sharp that they departed from one another?*" What we have here is the first example of how churches split. Paul went one way and Barnabas another. Christian friendship is broken. Paul wrote to the Galatians concerning the works of the flesh (the evil we do not want to do). One of those works is ***"contentions!"*** (See Galatians 5:20) Paul fell into the trap of trying to be a "Christian" in his old nature and the animosity he built up for John-Mark destroyed his friendship with Barnabas.

As Paul was growing in the faith he realized the dark side of his life needed to be defeated. Therefore, he cried out, as said above, ***"Who will deliver me from this body of death?"*** Finally, he received the answer and entered into the jointly formed Holy Spirit filled Christian life. ***"I thank God—through Jesus Christ our Lord! So then, with the mind I myself serve the law of God, but with the flesh the law of sin,"*** Romans 7:25. He explains this victory in Romans 8:1-2,5-6, ***"There is therefore now no condemnation to those who are in Christ Jesus, who do***

not walk according to the flesh, but according to the Spirit. For the law of the Spirit of life in Christ Jesus has made me free from the law of sin and death ... For those who live according to the flesh set their minds on the things of the flesh, but those who live according to the Spirit, the things of the Spirit. For to be carnally minded is death, but to be spiritually minded is life and peace. Furthermore, in Galatians 2:20, ***"I have been crucified with Christ; it is no longer I who live, but Christ lives in me; and the life which I now live in the flesh I live by faith in the Son of God, who loved me and gave Himself for me."***

Paul, now living and yielding or walking in the Spirit was able to make things right between him and Barnabas and Mark. We can surmise this healing with Barnabas in a little blurb in the first letter to the Corinthians. Paul was not with Barnabas when he went to Corinth, they might still have been estranged. However, when he wrote the letter to Corinth it seems they made up. ***"Or is it only Barnabas and I who have no right to refrain from working?*** 1 Corinthians 9:6. What about Paul and Mark. Many believe Paul wrote the letter to the Colossians from Rome in His first imprisonment. In this letter we see John-Mark was with him in Rome. ***"Aristarchus my fellow prisoner greets you, with Mark the cousin of Barnabas (about whom you received instructions: if he comes to you, welcome him), and Jesus who is called Justus. These are my only fellow workers for the kingdom of God who are of the circumcision; they have proved to be a comfort to me,"*** Colossians 4:10-11. Furthermore, in a letter to Timothy he expresses his love for Mark. ***"Only Luke is with me. Get Mark and bring him with you, for he is useful to me for ministry,"*** 2 Timothy 4:11.

What a wonderful work of regeneration by the Holy Spirit in Paul's life. He was conformed to the image of Jesus, loving, kind, repentant, humble and more. By now walking in the Spirit, Paul was able to do the good he wanted! Paul finally became spiritual and was reconciled with Barnabas and Mark. This only happened because Paul found the way to obedience. He understood the new birth and being born of the Spirit. He understood his being jointly formed with the Holy Spirit to walk God's way. He started to yield or walk in faith and trust in all the promises of Jesus concerning the Spirit in him. No wonder he wrote this exhortation to us. ***"Now then, we are ambassadors for Christ, as though God were pleading through us: we implore you on Christ's behalf, be reconciled to God,"*** 2 Corinthians 5:20. When Paul, Barnabas, and Mark had their problem in a certain way this split caused an area of separation from God in their lives. They still walked with God and worked for God and loved God, yet there was a feeling of uneasiness and guilt about what happened to them. Paul wanted reconciliation with God. Therefore, Paul through the fruit of the Spirit reconciled himself with Barnabas and Mark. How wonderful it is when we become spiritual people fully reliant on and filled with the Holy Spirit. We then do those things which are pleasing to God.

Reflections

53. Who told the Antioch Church to send Paul and Barnabas on a missionary journey?
54. Would you consider this a walking in the Spirit of obedience?
55. Who went with Paul and Barnabas?
56. How was the relationship at the start of the journey?
57. What change happened to the relationship at Perga in Pamphylia?
58. What happened before the start of the second journey?
59. How did the Holy Spirit filled Apostle Paul handle the Mark episode?

60. How did Barnabas handle the situation?
61. What happened to the great friendship of Paul and Barnabas over Mark?
62. How does this episode warn Christians, they can succumb to the old nature?
63. Describe the different mindset of Paul in Romans 7:18-19,24 and Romans 8:1-2,5-6.
64. How did this new understanding of life in the Spirit enable Paul to become reconciled to Barnabas and Mark?
65. Paul was teachable and the Holy Spirit worked to bring spirituality into Paul's life. The questions are: How teachable are you? Do you hear the lessons of the Spirit in your life? Are you a Romans 7:18-19,24 Christian or a Romans 8:1-2,5-6 Christian?
66. Has the Spirit taught you anything else in this section? Write the lesson down so you will always have it handy when needed.

THE POINT OF THIS

God was not taken by surprise in the act of sin by Adam and Eve and later our choice for sin. Before all was created God prepared for our failure and future reconciliation and rebirth. This truth is attested by Peter and Paul.

Peter's Testimony

"He indeed was foreordained before the foundation of the world, but was manifest in these last times for you who through Him believe in God, who raised Him from the dead and gave Him glory, so that your faith and hope are in God," 1 Peter 1:20-21.

Paul's Testimony

"Blessed be the God and Father of our Lord Jesus Christ, who has blessed us with every spiritual blessing in the heavenly places in Christ, just as He chose us in Him before the foundation of the world, that we should be holy and without blame before Him in love, having predestined us to adoption as sons by Jesus Christ to Himself, according to the good pleasure of His will, to the praise of the glory of His grace, by which He made us accepted in the Beloved," Ephesians 1:3-6.

Christ, our great High Priest and Shepherd, firstly, in His incarnation, showed the life of the Spirit. Secondly, in His death He destroyed our sin. Finally, in His resurrection and ascension He enables us to enter the victory of His life in the Spirit. This was all preplanned and prepared by the blessed Trinity before the foundation of the world was created.

The Apostle Peter gives us a wonderful insight concerning born again believers and their new life in the Spirit. ***"Grace and peace be multiplied to you in the knowledge of God and of Jesus our Lord, as His divine power has given to us all things that pertain to life and godliness, through the knowledge***

of Him who called us by glory and virtue, by which have been given to us exceedingly great and precious promises, that through these you may be partakers of the divine nature, having escaped the corruption that is in the world through lust," 2 Peter 1:2-4.

Let us understand what Peter is teaching:

- The knowledge of God and Jesus our Lord is the source of grace and peace.
- God's divine power has given to us *ALL* things that pertain to life and godliness.
- This supply of the things that pertain to life and godliness comes through the knowledge of Christ (faith in Christ and His work of atonement, by His glory and virtue).
- There are exceedingly great promises, fulfilled in Christ, which gives to us the privilege to have in us the divine nature.
- In Christ we escape and get the victory over the corruptions of the world because of our carnal lusts.

The foreordained plan of God, before the creation of the world and us, is quite astonishingly brilliant. There was no problem overlooked by God and no problem, that could arise, for which He did not plan. Christ is the fulfillment of those plans and we are the beneficiaries of them.

Reflections

67. Is God taken by surprise about Adam and Eve's sin? What about yours?
68. In 1 Peter 1:20-21, what did God prepare before the foundation of the world?
69. What does this testify concerning the forethought of God concerning creating people?
70. According to Ephesians 1:3-6, when were we chosen

in Christ?

71. For what were we predestined?
72. How are we accepted by God?
73. How can we renew our minds with this knowledge and behave accordingly?
74. How does Christ our High Priest and Shepherd enable us to enter the life of the Spirit?
75. Explain 2 Peter 1:2-4.
76. How will you apply this knowledge?

THE PROMISES WHICH ALLOW US TO PARTAKE OF THE DIVINE NATURE

Old Testament Promises Become New Testament Reality

"I will give you a new heart and put a new spirit within you; I will take the heart of stone out of your flesh and give you a heart of flesh. I will put My Spirit within you and cause you to walk in My statutes, and you will keep My judgments and do them," Ezekiel 36:26-27.

"Then I will give them one heart, and I will put a new spirit within them, and take the stony heart out of their flesh, and give them a heart of flesh, that they may walk in My statutes and keep My judgments and do them; and they shall be My people, and I will be their God," Ezekiel 11:19-20.

"But this is the covenant that I will make with the house of Israel after those days, says the Lord: I will put My law in their minds, and write it on their hearts; and I will be their God, and they shall be My people. No more shall every man teach his neighbor, and every man his brother, saying, 'Know the Lord,' for they all shall know Me, from the least of them to the greatest of them, says the Lord . For I will forgive their iniquity, and their sin I will remember no more," Jeremiah 31:33-34.

"Behold, I will do a new thing, Now it shall spring forth; Shall you not know it? I will even make a road in the wilderness And rivers in the desert. The beast of the field will honor Me, The jackals and the ostriches, Because I give waters in the wilderness And rivers in the desert, To give drink to My people, My chosen. This people I have formed for Myself; They shall declare My praise," Isaiah 43:19-21.

"He has put a new song in my mouth— Praise to our God; Many

will see it and fear, And will trust in the Lord," Psalm 40:3.

These promises are for Israel and Gentiles of all nations. ***"Now the Lord had said to Abram ... And in you all the families of the earth shall be blessed."*** Genesis 12:1-3.

Peter was serious about the promises of the Old Testament enabling us to be partakers of the divine nature. Partakers in the Greek from Strong's G2844: *κοινωνός (koy-no-nos: koinonos) a sharer, i.e. associate:--companion, X fellowship, partaker, partner.*

Points to Partake (or Be a Sharer) of the Divine Nature to be Jointly Formed into Christ's Image

- God will give us a new heart.
- God will put a new spirit within us.
- God will take our heart of stone away and give us a heart of flesh. (A dead heart to a living heart towards God)
- God will put His Spirit in us.
- God, through His Spirit, will enable us to be obedient to Him.
- God will make us His people and He will be our God.
- God will put His laws in our minds and write them on our new hearts.
- God will forgive us our sins and He will have an intimate relationship with us.
- He will put a new song in our mouths to the praise of His glory.

All these prophecies get fulfilled when we come to faith in Christ and are born again of the Spirit. These Old Testament prophecies proclaim a rebirth for mankind to be able to enter into the spiritual life of obedient fellowship with God. The Apostle Paul explains it this way, ***"Therefore, if anyone is in Christ, he is a new creation; old things have passed away; behold, all things have become new,"*** 2 Corinthians 5:17. The Apostle Peter teaches how these promises enable us to walk spiritually, ***"As His divine power has given to us all things that pertain to life and godliness, through the knowledge of Him who called us by glory and virtue,"*** 2 Peter 1:3.

Therefore, considering all the prophetic promises God has fulfilled through Christ, let us come to one conclusion, God through His Spirit will enable us to be spiritual (obedient) in the conformed image of Jesus. We who believe are born of the Spirit. We have been given eternal life through the Spirit. We have the Spirit in us to help and comfort us. We have Christ in us the hope of glory who will never leave us. The next verses explain this beautifully.

Jesus said,
"And I will pray the Father, and He will give you another Helper, that He may abide with you forever, the Spirit of truth, whom the world cannot receive, because it neither sees Him nor knows Him; but you know Him, for He dwells with you and will be in you. I will not leave you orphans; I will come to you," John 14:16-18.
Paul said,
"The mystery which has been hidden from ages and from generations, but now has been revealed to His saints. To them God willed to make known what are the riches of the glory of this mystery among the Gentiles: which is Christ in you, the hope of glory," Colossians 1:26-27.

Jesus said,
"And lo, I am with you always, even to the end of the age," Matthew 28:20.

Reflections

77. List all the promises found in Ezekiel 36:26-27, Ezekiel 11:19-20, Jeremiah 31:33-34, Isaiah 43:19-21, Psalm 40:3.
78. Do you have faith to believe these prophetic promises?
79. Who are they for according to Genesis 12:1-3?
80. How do faith in these promises make us partakers of God's divine nature? How well do you partake of the divine nature?
81. When do these prophecies get fulfilled in us?
82. Where you ever taught how to apply these truths? It is applied by faith.
83. How does 2 Corinthians 5:17 teach the fulfillment of the Old Testament promises written above?
84. What conclusion can we arrive at concerning these prophetic promises?
85. How does John 14:16-18 and Colossians 1:26-27 explain our new creation?

THINK ABOUT THIS

There really is no more need for us to be wandering around in the christian torment of the never-ending cycle of sin and death, of wanting to do good, but always failing, of knowing the truth, but not being able to live in it, of being carnal and not spiritual. The hard reality of trying to break the cycle is, we think we can do it through our own wisdom and power. We must admit mankind has wisdom and power to do incredible things. We can build skyscrapers, airplanes, wage war, unlock mathematical and scientific marvels, explore space, conquer the highest mountains, explore the deepest oceans, and write beautiful words of songs and poetry. Nevertheless, man apart from God cannot be spiritually sound nor morally good. This is as Jesus said, to a rich seeker who came to learn how to be spiritual. ***"Now as He was going out on the road, one came running, knelt before Him, and asked Him, 'Good Teacher, what shall I do that I may inherit eternal life?' So Jesus said to him, 'Why do you call Me good? No one is good but One, that is, God,'"*** Mark 10:17-18. Jesus probed the rich young ruler on his calling Him good. The answer of good, the Lord was asking, was concerning the character and person of God. In paraphrasing the question, *"Do you understand, only God is good, so why do you call Me good? Do you understand, I am God and I am living spiritually through the Spirit? Do you understand My good is the good of God not man?"* Jesus told the young ruler to keep the Ten Commandments to inherit eternal life. ***"You know the commandments: 'Do not commit adultery,' 'Do not murder,' 'Do not steal,' 'Do not bear false witness,' 'Do not defraud,' 'Honor your father and your mother.' 'And he answered and said to Him, 'Teacher, all these things I have kept from my youth,'"*** Mark 10:19-20. The ruler said he kept them from his youth. My what great wisdom and power the ruler had to keep these commands! Nevertheless, Jesus puts him to the test to see if he could keep the first and greatest commandment, ***"And you shall love the Lord your God with all your heart, with all your soul, with all your mind, and with all your strength. This is the first commandment,"*** Mark 12:30. He says to the rich young ruler, ***"One thing you lack: Go your way, sell whatever you have and give to the poor, and you will have treasure in heaven; and come, take up the cross, and follow Me,"*** Mark 10:21. Since Jesus is God, as He pointed out, could the rich ruler do it? This invitation of spirituality went beyond the strength and desire of the young man. The Scripture sadly teaches he had no ability to do this. He could not keep the first commandment. ***"But he was sad at this word, and went away sorrowful, for he had great possessions,"*** Mark 10:22. Jesus explains, those who trust in their power, wisdom, riches, and their own nature of goodness cannot inherit eternal life. ***"Then Jesus looked around and said to His disciples, 'How hard it is for those who have riches to enter the kingdom of God!'"*** (Mark 10:23) However, He explains the hope of salvation to spirituality. ***"And they were greatly astonished, saying among themselves, 'Who then can be saved?' But Jesus looked at them and said, 'With men it is impossible, but not with God; for with God all things are possible,'"*** Mark 10:26-27. The point is summed up in Paul's cry and answer to his cry spoken about above. ***"I thank God—through Jesus Christ our Lord! So then, with the mind I myself serve the law of God, but with the flesh the law of sin,"*** Romans 7:25. The ability to be all God wants us to be does not come from our strength to obey God but through the strength of Christ who fulfilled this Scripture and enables it to be fulfilled in us. ***"Not by might nor by power, but by My Spirit, Says the Lord of hosts,"*** Zechariah 4:6. This is a grace of God. We surrender all and God gives us His life by the Spirit. The Spirit is the third person of the Trinity and God gives Him to you freely through Christ. He is not someone we receive because we earn Him. We also do not earn spirituality. We receive the Holy Spirit by faith, then live spiritually through Him. In this fact, victory over our cry is obtained; ***"O wretched man that I am! Who will deliver me from this body of death?"*** God will, through Christ and by His Spirit.

Reflections

86. Are you wandering around in the christian torment concerning the never-ending cycle of wanting to do good but not doing it?
87. What is our hard reality concerning our ability to stop sinning?
88. What are the many lessons of Mark 10:17-27?
89. How is the point with men it is impossible, but with God all things are possible summed up by Paul in Romans 7:25 concerning his victory in doing God's will?
90. How does Christ fulfill Zechariah 4:6?
91. What does this mean for you?
92. Do you believe you have been given the Holy Spirit?
93. Are you appropriating this wonderful gift of the grace of God or are you living the Christian life in your own strength or through the religious nature of the flesh?
94. Are you ready to live the Spirit filled life through all the temptations and trials which come your way? The jointly conformed life of the believer is there for our working out to victory.

FAITH IS THE VICTORY

The Apostle John has tremendously important insights concerning the victory of God in the jointly formed (conformed) life of the born-again believer. Addition formulas give us the sum of the numbers added together. John gives us the sum of all Jesus taught Nicodemus, in John 3:3-18, in two verses in his first epistle, 1 John 5:4-5. (Please open your Bible and read John 3:3-18 and compare with 1 John 5:4-5.)

"For whatever is born of God overcomes the world. And this is the victory that has overcome the world—our faith. Who is he who overcomes the world, but he who believes that Jesus is the Son of God?" (1 John 5:4-5)

Let Us Put One Plus One Together

- Jesus taught, *We must be born again* ... John applies the teaching as a conquering event, *"For whatever is born of God overcomes the world."* We are to be born of the Spirit so we also may have the power of God to obey God.
- Jesus taught, *We must be born of the Spirit* ... John declares, *To be born of the Spirit is to be born of God!*
- Jesus taught, ***"For God so loved the world that He gave His only begotten Son, that whoever believes in Him should not perish but have everlasting life"*** ... John wrote this teaching is *gained through faith unto the victory of being born again ... The faith which believes Jesus is the Son of God!* ***"Whoever believes that Jesus is the Christ is born of God,"*** 1 John 5:1.

Only the word, ***victory,*** is fitting to describe the glorious born-again Spirit conforming work of faith in Jesus Christ given for the salvation of all who believe in Him! John explains this overcoming or conquering victory in 1 John 5:18.

"We know that whoever is born of God does not sin; but he who has been born of God keeps himself, and the wicked one does not touch him."

John is explaining the wonderful victory of Zechariah 4:6 ***"This is the word of the Lord to Zerubbabel: 'Not by might nor by power, but by My Spirit.'"*** The born-again victory is being born of the Spirit and the power and might to not sin is through the Spirit of God we are born of. This is the victory of faith. This is the victory of God in us. Paul explains this victory of faith in Romans 1:16-17.

"For I am not ashamed of the gospel of Christ, for it is the power of God to salvation for everyone who believes, for the Jew first and also for the Greek. For in it the righteousness of God is revealed from faith to faith; as it is written, 'The just shall live by faith.'"

Furthermore, Paul agrees with John. The victory of the Christian life is through a life lived by faith. As Peter said, through faith in all the exceedingly great and precious promises of God which enables us to be partakers of the Divine nature. ***"For we walk by faith, not by sight,"*** 2 Corinthians 5:7. Paul taught of his great proclivity to always do the things he did not want to do. He kept sinning. He was living by his might, his human power, his feelings of God, what his eyes were seeing in the world and this led to deafening defeat and sin. It was not till he switched from sight and feelings and trusting in his own might to faith in Christ for His strength through the Spirit in him, for the victory that overcomes the world of sin. Therefore, as John said, ***"We know that whoever is born of God does not sin,"*** and Paul now knows through faith the truth of John's statement. Therefore, through faith in Christ, we also can enter into the victory of the might of the Spirit of God as the saints of old did.

Reflections

95. Who is he who overcomes the world?
96. How does the Apostle John explain John 3:3-18 through 1 John 5:4-5, 1 John 5:1, 1 John 5:18?
97. How does Zechariah 4:6 fit into the understanding of John?
98. How does Paul explain the victory of faith Romans 1:16-17?
99. Do Paul and John agree that the victory of the Christian life is a life of continual moment by moment faith?
100. How do we like Paul and John enter into the victory that overcomes the world and sin?

THIS VICTORY IS A GROWING EXPERIENCE

How shall we live?

The truth be told, some Christians have a problem of living victoriously by faith. Many of us fall to the world instead of being victorious over the world. Our sin is a constant irritation, it never seems to let us go free. This problem keeps us in a struggle with the wicked one, when we are to be victors over him. John also said, ***"But he who has been born of God keeps himself, and the wicked one does not touch him."*** Our problem is, we do not know how to keep ourselves in the victory of being born of God. If we understand all which we studied above, God has supplied all we need to be forgiven, reborn into His kingdom, victorious over our sin, and obedient to Him. We need to learn how to keep ourselves in the victory of faith. God has actively done His part for us, we must actively keep ourselves in Him. As Jude exhorted us, ***"Keep yourselves in the love of God, looking for the mercy of our Lord Jesus Christ unto eternal life,"*** Jude 1:21. Only a life of faith will do this because faith is the continual victory which conquers the world!

"But without faith it is impossible to please Him, for he who comes to God must believe that He is, and that He is a rewarder of those who diligently seek Him," Hebrews 11:6.

- It takes faith to believe in God's Son, Jesus Christ ... this pleases God ... the reward is salvation and eternal life.
- It takes faith to receive the gift of God of salvation through His Son, Jesus Christ ... this pleases God ... the reward is new birth of life, being born again.
- It takes faith to believe you are born of the Spirit ... this pleases God ... the reward is spiritual power to obey God.

- It takes faith to be led by the Spirit ... this pleases God ... the reward, (***"For as many as are led by the Spirit of God, these are sons of God,"*** Romans 8:14) is being a child of God.
- It takes faith to yield to the Spirit ... this pleases God ... the reward is being conformed (jointly formed) into the image of God's Son!
- It takes faith, not to trust in what you see or feel leading to doubt, but to live by confident faith trusting in what God says has happened to you ... this pleases God ... the reward is becoming a partaker of the Divine nature.
- It takes faith to walk in the law of the Spirit of life and not walk in the law of sin and death ... this pleases God ... the reward is freedom from sin and death.
- It takes faith to believe you are a new creation ... this pleases God ... the reward, your old self and life are passed away, remembered by God no more.
- It takes faith to live in the Spirit ... this pleases God ... the reward, you get power, love, and a sound mind from God, ***"For God has not given us a spirit of fear, but of power and of love and of a sound mind,"*** 2 Timothy 1:7.

How wonderful it is to please God by being people of faith! There are no ends to His wondrous rewards! In order for us to obtain the victory which God won for us on Calvary's cross, we must have faith, saying and believing, as Jesus said before He died, ***"It is finished!"*** Thereafter, we are to faithfully live accordingly.

"After this, Jesus, knowing that all things were now accomplished, that the Scripture might be fulfilled, said, 'I thirst!' Now a vessel full of sour wine was sitting there; and they filled a sponge with sour wine, put it on hyssop, and put it to His mouth. So when Jesus had received the sour wine, He said, 'It is finished!' And bowing His head, He gave up His spirit," John 19:28-30.

Now, if you remember how He gave up His spirit, He gave it up through the Holy Spirit (Hebrews 9:14). Therefore, the spiritual walk for us is to faithfully live in the Spirit and walk in the Spirit, by faith. If we do this we will be as Jesus is, 1 John 4:17, victorious, obedient children of God in this world.

Reflections

101. Do you understand the victory of faith is a growing experience?

102. Since God has given us all we need for victory, why do we have a problem in keeping what God has committed to us?

103. What does Hebrews 11:6 teach about this?

104. Study all the bullet points under the Hebrews 11:6 in the lesson above, and write your conclusions.

105. How wonderful will it be if you please God?

WARNINGS FOR THE LIFE IN THE SPIRIT

Although, God's perfect redemptive work is complete in us, by faith in Christ, the actual reality of it is not. We are born again of water and the Spirit but like newborn babes we are to grow to the completion of what God has done in us. Peter learned this lesson, even though he was an apostle. ***"As newborn babes, desire the pure milk of the word, that you may grow thereby, if indeed you have tasted that the Lord is gracious,"*** 1 Peter 2:2-3. It takes faith and trust in the Word of God daily to walk in newness of life. Although we are now perfect in the eyes of God the reality of the perfection varies in the life of each Christian. Yes, these are truthful facts:

- We are forgiven, Ephesians 1:7.
- We have crucified the flesh through Christ, Galatians 2:20.
- We are born again new creations, 1 John 5:1.
- We are born of the Spirit, John 3:6.
- We are those who have Christ in us the hope of glory, Colossians 1:27.
- We are the righteousness of God in Christ, 2 Corinthians 5:21.
- We are planted together with Christ in the likeness of His resurrection, Romans 6:5.
- We are children of God, John 1:12.
- We are the temple of the Holy Spirit, 1 Corinthians 6:19-20.

The other truthful facts, we must face, are these; we are individuals with an independent heart, mind and will. The new birth did not make us programmed, mindless robots or computers. We are born again people living in a fallen world. We have a demonic structure which wars against us. Our old nature still hangs out with us, trying to influence us. (Remember Paul's struggles?) There is also the matter of sin always knocking at the door of our mind. God warned the murderous Cain about sin and sin's desire for humans. ***"If you do well, will you not be accepted? And if you do not do well, sin lies at the door. And its desire is for you, but you should rule over it,"*** Genesis 4:7. We are jointly formed and born of the Spirit to be new creations. Nevertheless, our human side of the equation can still answer the knocking of sin and acquiesce to its desire. God told Cain to rule over it, but he could not. God now gives us the means to rule over sin and defeat its desire for us by living and walking in the Spirit. We are people created by God to be able to choose. In this world as new creations we must always make the choice to live and walk in the Spirit. The choice not to is destructive. ***"For to be carnally minded is death, but to be spiritually minded is life and peace,"*** Romans 8:6. Furthermore, Paul states, ***"Likewise you also, reckon yourselves to be dead indeed to sin, but alive to God in Christ Jesus our Lord. Therefore do not let sin reign in your mortal body, that you should obey it in its lusts. And do not present your members as instruments of unrighteousness to sin, but present yourselves to God as being alive from the dead, and your members as instruments of righteousness to God. For sin shall not have dominion over you, for you are not under law but under grace,"*** Romans 6:11-14.

Only people who live by faith, in the Word of God, are able to make the right choice of spirituality! Throughout the history of the church, Christians have had their moments of walking in the Spirit by faith pleasing God and receiving the rewards of God. We also have had our dark moments of choosing to walk in the world by sight, feeling, and our own strength, miserably failing God, grieving the Holy Spirit and receiving the displeasure of God. Some of the darkest moments of carnal Christianity are found in the New

Testament. The churches of Galatia turned from justification by faith in Christ to justification by the works of the law. Paul questioned them about this wrong choice. He brutally asked them why they left from faith in Christ and life in the Spirit to the law!

"O foolish Galatians! Who has bewitched you that you should not obey the truth, before whose eyes Jesus Christ was clearly portrayed among you as crucified? This only I want to learn from you: Did you receive the Spirit by the works of the law, or by the hearing of faith? Are you so foolish? Having begun in the Spirit, are you now being made perfect by the flesh? Have you suffered so many things in vain—if indeed it was in vain? Therefore He who supplies the Spirit to you and works miracles among you, does He do it by the works of the law, or by the hearing of faith?—just as Abraham 'believed God, and it was accounted to him for righteousness.' Therefore know that only those who are of faith are sons of Abraham," Galatians 3:1-7.

We learn three lessons in these verses about the Galatians:

- The Galatians were born again Spirit filled believers.
- They heard a different gospel and rejected justification by faith in Christ for justification by the works of the law.
- It is clear to see Christians not yielding to the Holy Spirit for strength, power, and wisdom, can make a sinful choice! Faith was their original victory, but they were seduced away from the faith which pleases God.

Let these questions of Paul sink into your psyche. ***"Did you receive the Spirit by the works of the law, or by the hearing of faith? Are you so foolish? Having begun in the Spirit, are you now being made perfect by the flesh?"*** Every Christian should answer these important examination questions. Furthermore, having begun in the Spirit, are we faithfully living and walking in Him?

Paul ministered for eighteen months at Corinth. God told him He had many people at Corinth who would come to faith. ***"For I am with you, and no one will attack you to hurt you; for I have many people in this city,"*** Acts 18:10. These Corinthians were born again, Spirit filled believers. Listen to how blessed Paul said they were. ***"I thank my God always concerning you for the grace of God which was given to you by Christ Jesus, that you were enriched in everything by Him in all utterance and all knowledge, even as the testimony of Christ was confirmed in you, so that you come short in no gift, eagerly waiting for the revelation of our Lord Jesus Christ,"*** 1 Corinthians 1:4-7. These Christians were indeed blessed by God. Nevertheless, later on in their Christian walk their behavior was very undesirable. Paul wrote his letter, we call 1 Corinthians, to help that church to correct their behavior and walk spiritually in the Spirit. This letter is far from showing the glories of a people walking spiritually in the Holy Spirit. It is a spanking for their poor choices and worldly sinful ways. They were yielding their minds to the desires of the old sinful nature, instead of the desires of the Holy Spirit! The results were catastrophic for the Church of Corinth. They were a church in carnal chaos, not spiritual bliss.

The first letter to Corinth by Paul spells out their walking according to the law of sin and death and not walking according to the law of the Spirit of life in Christ. In chapter one Verse ten Paul pleads with them to stop having divisions among them. In verse eleven Chloe's household told Paul these divisions came from contentions among them. In this declaration by Chloe's household we learn the Christians at Corinth return to their old nature, the flesh. Contentions is a work of the flesh! Remember in Galatians 5:20, contentions is a star sin? Contentions of carnal understanding of the Spirit's Holy Word causes divisions.

- Division from Strong's G4978: σχίσμα, schisma (Skhis'-

mah) a split or gap ("schism"), literally or figuratively:--division, rent, schism.

- Contention from Strong's G2054: ἔρις, eris (er'-is) of uncertain affinity; a quarrel, i.e. (by implication) wrangling:--contention, debate, strife, variance.

These two words are powerful when understood as one concept of carnal Christian behavior. Someone thinks something carnally, thinks he is spiritually correct, brings it to the church as gospel truth, the spiritually minded see it is false, a quarrel begins with debates, carnality soon reigns overall, causing strife, and contentions, which lead to a division or schism in the body. Paul taught we are to work hard to stay united, ***"Endeavoring to keep the unity of the Spirit in the bond of peace,"*** Ephesians 4:3. The Corinthians were having no unity of the Spirit in the bond of peace. Let us examine the Corinthian situation.

"Now I plead with you, brethren, by the name of our Lord Jesus Christ, that you all speak the same thing, and there be no divisions among you, but you be perfectly joined together in the same mind and in the same judgment. For it has been declared to me concerning you, my brethren, by those of Chloe's that there are contentions among you. Now I say this, that each of you says, 'I am of Paul,' or 'I am of Apollos,' or 'I am of Cephas,' or 'I am of Christ.' Is Christ divided? Was Paul crucified for you? Or were you baptized in the name of Paul?" (1 Corinthians 1:10-13)

Paul wants the unity of the Spirit in the bond of peace to reign supreme at the Corinth church. He pleads for it!

- By the name of the Lord Jesus Christ, they should speak the same thing. This is the speaking of sound scriptural doctrine, not quarreling over them.
- By the name of the Lord Jesus Christ, there would be no divisions among them. In other words no schisms or church splits or clicks from foolish debate and strife.

- By the name of the Lord Jesus Christ, they would be perfectly joined together in the same mind. ***"There is one body and one Spirit, just as you were called in one hope of your calling; one Lord, one faith, one baptism; one God and Father of all, who is above all, and through all, and in you all,"*** Ephesians 4:4-6.
- By the name of the Lord Jesus Christ, they would be perfectly joined together in the same judgement. The judgement given by the Holy Spirit through revelation. ***"But the natural man does not receive the things of the Spirit of God, for they are foolishness to him; nor can he know them because they are spiritually discerned,"*** 1 Corinthians 2:14.

This is the way of the Spirit producing spirituality in us and conforming us to the image of Christ. The proper choice for the Corinthians to do this was to have a faith which trusts the Spirit. They did not and chose the carnal mind to sort things out. They quarreled and debated themselves out of the oneness in Christ through the Spirit into a divided sectarian chaos. "I am of," became their mantra. The mantra of carnal superiority. They were very prideful and very wrong.

The warning of the Bible taught in Galatians and Corinthians is clear. Spirit filled born again believers can become carnal Christians! We most always keep ourselves from falling into this trap of leaving the Spirit filled life and losing the victory that overcomes the world. Legalism and sectarianism has been a church problem even up to today. There was another problem at Corinth which showed the carnal side was winning. The Corinthians were accepting sin as an acceptable practice in Christ. They were claiming this is the spiritual thing to do. This sin was a sexual sin.

"It is actually reported that there is sexual immorality among you, and such sexual immorality as is not even named among the Gentiles—that a man has his father's wife! And you are puffed up, and have not rather mourned, that he who has done this deed

might be taken away from among you," 1 Corinthians 5:1-2.

The church is in a modern version of this perversion and is puffed up about it and not much mourning is happening over it. Sin had knocked at the Galatian and Corinthian churches and they did not yield to the Spirit to walk obediently like Christ. God gave to these Christians the fullness of the redemption in Christ. They did not live by faith and obedience through the Spirit. The result was a walk in the law of sin and death. This is sad when Peter said we have been given, by God's divine power, everything we need for life and godliness, 2 Peter 1:3. Paul said to the church at Corinth, ***"For you are still carnal. For where there are envy, strife, and divisions among you, are you not carnal and behaving like mere men?*** (1 Corinthians 3:3) Paul said to the Galatians, ***"O foolish Galatians! Who has bewitched you that you should not obey the truth, before whose eyes Jesus Christ was clearly portrayed among you as crucified?*** (Galatians 3:1) The warning for us is clear, we can mess up, grieve the Spirit of God, sin, cause trouble, divide our congregations, and behave stupidly, thinking we are spiritual. We must be ever diligent to be filled with the Spirit! It only takes a wrong thought or temptation to yield to, therefore, causing us to walk carnally.

"You therefore, beloved, since you know this beforehand, beware lest you also fall from your own steadfastness, being led away with the error of the wicked; but grow in the grace and knowledge of our Lord and Savior Jesus Christ. To Him be the glory both now and forever. Amen, " 2 Peter 3:17-18.

Reflections

106. Although, God's perfect redemptive work is complete in us, what does 1 Peter 2:2-3, exhort us to do with the completed work of God?

107. What are the truthful facts we need to face in our growth to victorious living?

108. It is clear in the history of the church, Christian's have answered the knock of sin. Do you *sometimes* open the door and sin?

109. What happens if we do not make the choice to live and walk in the Spirit, but answer the knock of sin and do it?

110. Describe the fall of the Galatian church, by people who were Spirit filled.

111. How did Paul address this?

112. How can this happen to us?

113. Describe the fall of the Corinthian church, by people who were Spirit filled.

114. How did Paul address each problem?

115. How can this happen to us?

116. Why do we need to understand the warnings of Galatians and Corinthians? Can spiritually minded christians become carnally minded sinners and not even understand it happened?

117. Why should the Church of today heed 2 Peter 3:17-18?

THE TALE OF TWO FRUITS

The tale of the first fruit begins at creation.

"The Lord God planted a garden eastward in Eden, and there He put the man whom He had formed ... And the Lord God commanded the man, saying, 'Of every tree of the garden you may freely eat; but of the tree of the knowledge of good and evil you shall not eat, for in the day that you eat of it you shall surely die,'" Genesis 2:8,16-17.

The creative mind of God made man in His image and proclaimed all He created was good. It is an interesting question to ponder, if there was no such thing as death in the Garden of Eden, why was food needed? Nevertheless, God created a garden with gastronomic delights. Considering the myriad amounts of edible fruits, vegetables, and herbs we see today, the delights in the Garden must have been overwhelming to Adam and Eve's senses. However, out of the many delicacies allowed to eat for food, there is one fruit which God said was prohibited to eat, the fruit from the tree of the knowledge of good and evil. We learned about this, in the section, *The Progression of Our Problem,* the consequences of Adam and Eve's eating of the fruit.

It is plain to the understanding the fruit of the forbidden tree had some type of chemical or genetic coding, when ingested, assimilated into the body and genetic code of Adam and Eve changing them physically, mentally, and spiritually. It is something God had forbidden us to have. This small but enormous act of disobedience changed human beings forever. Theological discussions abound on the why of this tree and its fruit. The simplest understanding maybe, there needed to be a "*do not eat*" to Adam to prove his fidelity to his God and friend. One thing is certain, this fruit was forbidden and eating it has caused countless evils in the hearts of men and women.

The tail of the second fruit begins after the death and resurrection of Jesus.

The tale of the second fruit begins after the crucifixion of Christ, God's remedy for the sin of Adam. This fruit is offered by God and is not forbidden for us to eat. The fruit comes to us by being born of the Spirit. This fruit belongs to God, the Holy Spirit, and God wants us to take of this fruit and have it assimilate into us physically, mentally, and spiritually! Every born-again believer receives the gift of the Holy Spirit and His fruit at the time of conversion. The fruit of good and evil gave us thoughts and intents of evil continuously. These became part of us. Likewise, now the fruit of the Spirit wants to become part of us, so we will be by nature what God desires. ***"But the fruit of the Spirit is love, joy, peace, longsuffering, kindness, goodness, faithfulness, gentleness, self-control,"*** Galatians 5:22-23. This is the conformed or jointly formed image of Christ in us.

The bad fruit gives us the physical changes to die, the mental changes to think evil, the spiritual changes which separates us from God. The good fruit gives us physical changes to eternal life, mental changes transforming our minds to goodness, and the spiritual changes which unites us to God in Christ. On the cross He took back the fruit of good and evil. In His resurrection and ascension He gives us the fruit of His Spirit. He became sin for us and in Him we become the righteousness of God. This is the great exchange and a wondrous fruit to be able to eat.

The fruit of the Spirit is the spiritual person we become in Christ. This enables us to be obedient to God as a natural way of life. We do not try to make our old nature be love, joy, peace, longsuffering, kindness, goodness, faithfulness, gentleness, and self-control. We are conformed in our new creation to become in our being, love, joy, peace, longsuffering, kindness, goodness, faithfulness, gentleness, and self-control. The fruit in us is of the Holy Spirit! It is not something we do but become! One fruit grew on a branch and we were forbidden to eat. Now we are the branch and the fruit is to bud and be us. This is the fruit of the nectar from Christ the vine, the Holy Spirit and His fruit. Jesus taught this in His powerful message on vineyard growth.

"Abide in Me, and I in you. As the branch cannot bear fruit of itself, unless it abides in the vine, neither can you, unless you abide in Me. I am the vine, you are the branches. He who abides in Me, and I in him, bears much fruit; for without Me you can do nothing," John 15:4-5.

Only the life of faith produces all of what Jesus said. A faithless life is a withered life. Remember, faith is the victory that overcomes the world? It takes faith to believe in Jesus Christ for salvation and it takes faith to abide in Jesus Christ to bear His fruit. It takes faith to believe we are born of the Spirit and it takes faith to be filled with the Spirit moment by moment. It takes faith and trust to allow the fruit of the Spirit to conform us into the image of Christ.

Many of us are still stuck in the cycle, I want to do good but do not and I do not want to do bad but I do. It is our failure. We are trying to force our sin nature to obey God. The fruit of Good and evil, unfortunately, is our choice of fruits. This fruit is in our old man's being. The victory comes to us when we become what God works in us, the fruit of the Spirit, a new recreated being. We can leave the fruit of the knowledge of good and evil in Christ and partake of the fruit of the Spirit from Christ. Therefore, becoming spiritually conformed into the image of Jesus. The victory comes down to a simple, yet profound question Paul asked King Agrippa. ***"King Agrippa, do you believe the prophets? I know that you do believe,"*** Acts 26:27. Although, Paul was confident Agrippa believed in the

Old Testament prophets, Agrippa did not have the faith which overcomes the world. ***"Then Agrippa said to Paul, 'You almost persuade me to become a Christian,'"*** Acts 26:28. This may be our problem to constant spiritual frustration, we may believe the prophets and apostles, but are not fully persuaded with the faith that overcomes the world.

We have been given exceedingly great and precious promises. We are born again Christians. We have the Holy Spirit. Christ is in us. We are new creations with new hearts and God's laws written on them. Nevertheless, the King Agrippa syndrome of not being persuaded of these Scriptural facts, permeates the lives of many believers. The problem for many is the overcoming faith is not applied in the times of trials, darkness, diseases, financial difficulties, or our own behavior leading to defeat. The not persuaded attitude shines forth. The Spirit filled and Spirit led life is not lived. What does God think about this? He does not think highly of faithless behavior. He said through Isaiah how to have overcoming faith and strength and the verdict given on those Israelites who had the Agrippa syndrome.

"For thus says the Lord God,
the Holy One of Israel:
'In returning and rest you shall be saved;
In quietness and confidence shall be your strength.'
But you would not,"
Isaiah 30:15.

Faith gives us a way to return and find rest and bring us the quiet and confident spirit to overcoming victory. Let us not hear this condemnation said to us, ***"You would not!"*** We need to return to a faith which believes God and overcomes the world. Start living and walking in the Spirit today faithfully.

Reflections

118. What are the two fruits of Scriptural importance?
119. Where does the tale of the first fruit begin?
120. What was the prohibition concerning this fruit?
121. What are the ramifications to all humans because of this fruit?
122. How has this fruit brought spiritual death in your life?
123. Where does the tail of the second fruit begin?
124. Is there a do not eat prohibition on this fruit?
125. What are the wonders to gain from this fruit of the Spirit for all?
126. Compared to the forbidden fruit, what are the amazing changes the fruit of the Spirit can produce in us?
127. How is it possible to feed on this fruit according to Jesus in John 15:4-5?
128. How does the King Agrippa syndrome keep us from enjoying the fruit of the Spirit?
129. What is the lesson and warning of Isaiah 30:15? Does your walk show faith or an almost persuaded faith?

THE HOLY SPIRIT

"And I will pray the Father, and He will give you another Helper, that He may abide with you forever—the Spirit of truth, whom the world cannot receive, because it neither sees Him nor knows Him; but you know Him, for He dwells with you and will be in you."

John 14:16-17

The Lord Jesus confirms the Old Testament truth spoken by Moses, (***"Hear, O Israel: The Lord our God, the Lord is one!"***) when He was questioned by a scribe about commandments. ***"Jesus answered him, 'The first of all the commandments is: Hear, O Israel, the Lord our God, the Lord is one.'"*** (Mark 12:29 and Deuteronomy 6:4) The Lord God is one! There is no other God but the God of Israel who expresses Himself through the mystery and wonder of Father, Son, and Holy Spirit, the Trinity. The depth of this is seen at the baptism of Jesus, the only begotten Son of God.

"When all the people were baptized, it came to pass that Jesus also was baptized; and while He prayed, the heaven was opened. And the Holy Spirit descended in bodily form like a dove upon Him, and a voice came from heaven which said, 'You are My beloved Son; in You I am well pleased,'" Luke 3:21-22.

The Son of God is acknowledged with praise from the Father in heaven and hugged by the Holy Spirit coming down from the Father in Heaven. In this event we see God, in three persons, being one! The Father who is God, loving the Son, who is God, being hugged by the Holy Spirit, who is God. These are not three Gods but one God. The Apostle John explains this magnificently in his first epistle. ***"For there are three that bear witness in heaven: the Father, the Word, and the Holy Spirit; and***

these three are one, 1 John 5:7. Athanasius, a church father, taught this truth in his creed, defending the faith from heresy against the Trinity. *"Thus the Father is God; the Son is God; the Holy Spirit is God: And yet there are not three gods, but one God."*

Jesus taught this truth and agreed with ***"The Lord is One"*** truth in an argument with the Jews. He declared emphatically, ***"I and My Father are one,"*** John 10:30. The Jews understood what He meant about being one with the Father and they picked up stones to kill Him. Jesus asked them why they wanted to do this. ***"The Jews answered Him, saying, 'For a good work we do not stone You, but for blasphemy, and because You, being a Man, make Yourself God,'"*** John 10:33. Furthermore, Jesus taught He was sent to us by the Father in John 10:36 and in His commission to the Apostles in John 20:21. ***"So Jesus said to them again, 'Peace to you! As the Father has sent Me, I also send you.'"*** The Lord taught the Holy Spirit will also come to us from the Father in the name of Jesus, ***"But the Helper, the Holy Spirit, whom the Father will send in My name,"*** John 14:26. The conclusion of this is, if Jesus sent from the Father is God, then the Holy Spirit sent from the Father is God. Paul declares this wonder in Galatians 4:6, ***God has sent forth the Spirit of His Son into your hearts, crying out, 'Abba, Father!'"*** The wonder of the blessed Trinity, God the Father, God the Son, God the Holy Spirit is now revealed to us. Let us have victorious faith because, ***"He who is joined to the Lord is one spirit with Him,"*** 1 Corinthians 6:17.

Therefore, if we are born of the Spirit, as Jesus taught Nicodemus in John 3:3-8, we are born of God, as John explains in John 1:10-13. If we are born of God, the Holy Spirit in us will only do through us what the will of God is. He will only work to teach us the Word of God and how to apply the Word, by His might, in obedience to the will of God. ***"All Scripture is given by inspiration of God, and is profitable for doctrine, for reproof, for correction, for instruction in righteousness, that the***

man of God may be complete, thoroughly equipped for every good work," 2 Timothy 3:16-17. Peter explains how this happened, ***"For prophecy never came by the will of man, but holy men of God spoke as they were moved by the Holy Spirit,"*** 2 Peter 1:21. Since Scripture is God breathed, do you think the Holy Spirit in you would behave in contradiction to the inspired Word of God? The Spirit will only behave in us according to the Word of God. ***"For God is not the author of confusion but of peace, as in all the churches of the saints,"*** 1 Corinthians 14:33. Furthermore, ***"For the kingdom of God is not eating and drinking, but righteousness and peace and joy in the Holy Spirit,"*** Romans 14:17. This is truly being spiritual and radiating the image of Christ out of us.

God wants us to be spiritually in tune with Him. This happens when we have faith in all His promises and trust in Jesus as our Savior. In the beginning we were created in the image of God. Adam lost the image through sin. We his offspring are in the image of Adam. However, born again believers are now new creations and are being conformed into the image of Christ. We have been given more than Adam lost. We are born of the Spirit, have Christ in us, and are children of God. Faith in these truths is the victory that overcomes the world. This faith enables us to walk in the law of the Spirit of life in Christ and enables us to be partakers of the divine nature, the Trinity! ***"For through Him we both have access by one Spirit to the Father,"*** Ephesians 2:18. It is time for Faith to arise in the hearts of Christians everywhere. God has given us every spiritual blessing in the heavenly places in Christ, see Ephesians 1:3. Let us have the faith which is victorious as our testimony. We do not want the testimony of ancient Israel.

"But Israel, pursuing the law of righteousness, has not attained to the law of righteousness. Why? Because they did not seek it by faith, but as it were, by the works of the law. For they stumbled at that stumbling stone," Romans 9:31-32.

Let us pursue God by faith, living and walking in the Spirit, understanding this is a growing process to the completion of perfection in heaven. Paul exhorts us to this. ***"Brethren, I do not count myself to have apprehended; but one thing I do, forgetting those things which are behind and reaching forward to those things which are ahead,"*** Philippians 3:13. We are to have eyes that look to Jesus and ears which hear the Spirit, and minds that are set on the things above. The cross behind us, the resurrected life in us, and the ascended life before us. Let us never forget Romans 14:23, ***"For whatever is not from faith is sin."*** Christians, living spiritually is not an impossibility because it is possible for we have Christ in us and in Him all things are possible!

Reflections

130. What does Jesus explain in John 14:16-17?
131. According to Deuteronomy 6:4 and Mark 12:29, what is taught?
132. How does the Lord God, who is one, express Himself?
133. How is this expression of God taught in Luke 3:21-22?
134. How does 1 John 5:7 teach the oneness of God?
135. With this understanding we know the Father is God, the Son is God, the Holy Spirit is God. Nevertheless, One God not three. Jesus taught we should know the Holy Spirit, God. How is your relationship with Him?
136. How will the understanding of this lesson, Living Spiritually, enable you to walk the victory of faith in the Spirit?

Remember, God wants us to be filled with the Spirit and to become conformed into the image of Christ, a people who are spiritually sound.

Let Us Pray

Father, Grow thy fruit in me! Oh Lord for it is not something I do but become! May all see Christ in me as ***love, joy, peace, longsuffering, kindness, goodness, faithfulness, gentleness, self-control.*** May I ever live in and understand this truth, ***"We have this treasure in earthen vessels, that the excellence of the power may be of God and not of us,"*** 2 Corinthians 4:7. Father, in Jesus' name fill us with thy Holy Spirit and grant us a life that is fully pleasing to you. Amen!

LESSON TWELVE: THE FALLING AWAY A CHRISTIAN WARNING TO REMAIN FAITHFUL TO CHRIST

THE FALLING AWAY

We Are Prophetically Warned About Falling Away

"Now the Spirit expressly says that in latter times some will depart from the faith, giving heed to deceiving spirits and doctrines of demons, speaking lies in hypocrisy, having their own conscience seared with a hot iron, forbidding to marry, and commanding to abstain from foods which God created to be received with thanksgiving by those who believe and know the truth. For every creature of God is good, and nothing is to be refused if it is received with thanksgiving; for it is sanctified by the word of God and prayer."
1 Timothy 4:1-5

There is much to be said about the perilous times our generation is in. The Holy Spirit said, ***"But know this, that in the last days perilous times will come,"*** 2 Timothy 3:1. Society is moving towards a depth of depravity the history of the world has not seen since the days of Noah. However, Holy Spirit expressly says to Paul a matter of deep concern in the perilous times; *Christians will depart from the faith.* The love of the world and its allurements will be a driving force turning people away from the Savior they once loved. We see this in Demas, a former companion of Paul. Paul sadly states, ***"For Demas has forsaken me, having loved this present world, and has departed for Thessalonica,"*** 2 Timothy 4:10.

It is a shocking reality and a source of great disagreement between Christians, that Christians can walk away from the faith. Many believe once saved always saved. This is true if we continue in the faith and endure to the end. Jesus taught us this truth. ***"But he who endures to the end shall be saved,*** Matthew 24:13. Nevertheless, ***"The Spirit***

expressly says that in latter times some will depart from the faith!" (1Timothy 4:1)

Reflections

1. What does the Holy Spirit warn Christians about in 1 Timothy 4:1-5?
2. Why is this something Christians of today should be concerned about?
3. Which coworker of Paul fell away and what lesson can you learn from him?

Before we examine the reasons why Christians will depart from the faith; let us look at the Scriptural assurances of eternal salvation and the warnings to admonish us not to depart from Christ.

THE GREAT ASSURANCES

Let us examine a few wonderful verses teaching once saved always saved.

"And as Moses lifted up the serpent in the wilderness, even so must the Son of Man be lifted up, that whoever believes in Him should not perish but have eternal life. For God so loved the world that He gave His only begotten Son, that whoever believes in Him should not perish but have everlasting life," John 3:14-16.

"My sheep hear My voice, and I know them, and they follow Me. And I give them eternal life, and they shall never perish; neither shall anyone snatch them out of My hand. My Father, who has given them to Me, is greater than all; and no one is able to snatch them out of My Father's hand. I and My Father are one," John 10:27-30.

"For I am persuaded that neither death nor life, nor angels nor principalities nor powers, nor things present nor things to come, nor height nor depth, nor any other created thing, shall be able to separate us from the love of God which is in Christ Jesus our Lord," Romans 8:38-39.

"In Him you also trusted, after you heard the word of truth, the gospel of your salvation; in whom also, having believed, you were sealed with the Holy Spirit of promise, who is the guarantee of our inheritance until the redemption of the purchased possession, to the praise of His glory," Ephesians 1:13-14.

What wonderful verses affording a guarantee of salvation forever! By believing in Jesus the Son of God, God saves us! These verses teach great profound truths we can confidently trust and live by.

The Wonderful Truths

- ***We shall never perish*** — from Strong's G622, "ἀπόλλῡμῐ (apollumi) ***to destroy fully*** (reflexively, to perish, or lose), literally or figuratively: --destroy, die, lose, mar, perish." Oh, how wonderful; we will not be fully destroyed because of forgiveness of sins in Christ!
- ***We shall have eternal life*** — from Strong's G166, "αἰώνιος (aionios) ***perpetual*** (also used of past time, or past and future as well): --eternal, forever, everlasting." Oh, how wonderful; in Christ, instead of the destruction of death we have perpetual everlasting life!
- ***No one can snatch us out of the hand of Christ and the Father!*** Snatch — from Strong's G726, "ἁρπάζω (harpazo) ***to seize*** (in various applications): --catch (away, up), pluck, pull, take (by force)." Oh, how wonderful; no one can remove us from the protective hands of Christ and the Father! We are safe!
- ***No created being or force can separate us from God's love to us in Christ!*** Separate — from Strong's G5563, "χωρίζω (chorizo) ***to place room between***, i.e., part; reflexively, to go away: --depart, put asunder, separate." Oh, how wonderful; there will never be a separation or darkness of space between God and us again!
- ***We are sealed by the Holy Spirit!*** Sealed from Strong's G4972, "σφραγίζω (sphragizo) ***to stamp (with a signet or private mark)*** for security or preservation (literally or figuratively); by implication, to keep secret, to attest: --(set a, set to) seal up, stop." Oh, how wonderful; we are stamped with the living signet of authority the Holy Spirit! He is our security against all evil of destruction!
- ***The Holy Spirit is our guarantee of the inheritance of eternal life!*** Guarantee from Strong's G728, "ἀῤῥαβών (arrhabon) ***a pledge***, i.e., part of the purchase-money or property given in advance as security for the rest: --earnest." Oh, how wonderful; we have the advanced guarantee of God, through the Holy Spirit sealing us as a pledge of security to gain

heaven.

We have just examined a few Scriptures teaching us of the assurance of our salvation. We must walk in these assurances with victorious faith; by which we can rejoice saying, "*Once saved always saved.*"

Reflections

1. What is the assurance of John 3:14-16? Do you believe? If you say yes, will you perish?
2. In John 10:27-30 who does Jesus know? What does He give those He knows? What does He promise about perishing? How safe are His sheep in His hand? Where did the sheep come from? How safe are the sheep in the Father's hand? Explain what Jesus means in these verses and apply the meaning to yourself.
3. What is the promise of Romans 8:38-39? How persuaded are you?
4. For people who trust in Christ, what happens to them by the Holy Spirit? What does this guarantee? Does your faith rest in this guarantee?
5. How compelling is once saved always saved according to these verses? How can you apply this to your Christian walk?

THE GREAT WARNINGS

Now let us look at the other side of the Scripture verses of assurances which give us warnings about losing our salvation.

"Beware, brethren, lest there be in any of you an evil heart of unbelief in departing from the living God," Hebrews 3:12.

"For if, after they have escaped the pollutions of the world through the knowledge of the Lord and Savior Jesus Christ, they are again entangled in them and overcome, the latter end is worse for them than the beginning. For it would have been better for them not to have known the way of righteousness, than having known it, to turn from the holy commandment delivered to them. But it has happened to them according to the true proverb: 'A dog returns to his own vomit,' and, 'a sow, having washed, to her wallowing in the mire,'" 2 Peter 2:20-22.

"If indeed you continue in the faith, grounded and steadfast, and are not moved away from the hope of the gospel which you heard, which was preached to every creature under heaven, of which I, Paul, became a minister," Colossians 1:23.

"For it is impossible for those who were once enlightened, and have tasted the heavenly gift, and have become partakers of the Holy Spirit, and have tasted the good word of God and the powers of the age to come, if they fall away, to renew them again to repentance, since they crucify again for themselves the Son of God, and put Him to an open shame," Hebrews 6:4-6. (All underlined sections are for emphasis.)

We just examined a few Scriptures giving us dire warnings of the possibility of losing our salvation! These are warnings we must listen to and strongly pay attention to.

- ***We can lose our salvation, if we stop believing (evil heart of unbelief) and leave the faith.***
- ***We can lose our salvation, if we go back to our former behavior and become lost in sin.***
- ***We can lose our salvation, if we get moved away from the hope of the gospel and fall away.***

What a juxtaposition we have concerning our salvation. On the one hand, we have the great assurance of eternal security. On the other hand, we have the great warning of losing our assurance of salvation. Let us heed the Apostle Paul's exhortation, ***"Let us hold fast the confession of our hope without wavering, for He who promised is faithful,"*** Hebrews 10:23. Let us walk in faith and always have the assurance of once saved always saved!

Nevertheless, if we think we cannot fall away and lose our salvation, we need to be mindful of the warnings which teach us we can lose it. We need to understand the warnings about falling away so it does not happen to us; considering we are living in the latter times. ***"Now the Spirit expressly says that in latter times some will depart from the faith,"*** 1 Timothy 4:1. The quantity of believers who fall away are tied up in the word some. This number will only be known when it happens. Let us examine what the Spirit is saying about some. Some defined: Strong's G5100, "τις (tis): an enclitic indefinite pronoun; ***some or any person or object:***--a (kind of), any (man, thing, thing at all), certain (thing), divers, he (every) man, one (X thing), ought, + partly, some (man, -body, - thing, -what), (+ that no-)thing, what(-soever), X wherewith, whom(-soever), whose(-soever)." It is clear to see by this indefinite pronoun, Paul is saying that anyone can, or many believers will depart from the faith in these latter times. Let us make sure we are not a fulfillment of this prophetic warning.

Reflections

1. What is the frightening warning of Hebrews 3:12?
2. What is the frightening warning of 2 Peter 2:20-22?
3. What are we not to be moved away from in Colossians 1:23?
4. What is the frightening warning of Hebrews 6:4-6?
5. Do these Scriptures teach a Christian can lose their salvation?
6. How should a Christian apply the two Scriptural teachings of, "*Once saved, always saved*" and "*Christians can lose their salvation?*"
7. Who are the "*some*" in latter times? How can you make sure you are not one of the some who will fall away?

WHAT WILL CAUSE THE FALLING AWAY

Let us return and look at 1 Timothy 4:1-5.

"Now the Spirit expressly says that in latter times some will depart from the faith, giving heed to deceiving spirits and doctrines of demons, speaking lies in hypocrisy, having their own conscience seared with a hot iron, forbidding to marry, and commanding to abstain from foods which God created to be received with thanksgiving by those who believe and know the truth. For every creature of God is good, and nothing is to be refused if it is received with thanksgiving; for it is sanctified by the word of God and prayer," 1 Timothy 4:1-5.

These are the points Paul made in this section of his letter to Timothy.

- Christians will turn away from listening to the Holy Spirit and His doctrines to paying attention to deceiving spirits and their demonic doctrines.
- Instead of being rooted and grounded in the truth, the fallen ex-Christian will mouth lies of their demonic beliefs exposing their hypocrisy.
- The once self-examining Christian who made corrections in their behavior, will no longer accept advice or criticism. They will have a hard heart and a conscience closed to God. As Peter wrote, these people will be worse-off than before they were saved.
- The fallen Christian will become an enemy of Christ!

Paul further clarified the reasons people will fall away to Timothy:

"For the time will come when they will not endure sound doctrine,

but according to their own desires, because they have itching ears, they will heap up for themselves teachers; and they will turn their ears away from the truth, and be turned aside to fables," 2 Timothy 4:3-4.

Who are the *"they"* Paul is warning Timothy about? They are professing Christians. These Christians have lost their desire for Biblical truths, laws, and doctrines. They lost their ability to endure sound Biblical teachings. Their Christian faith is based on their own desires of self-righteousness. The itching ears are for listening to those who will support their desires for affirmation and to be able to hear those who agree with them to attack those holding fast to the gospel. How can we understand this? This incident may explain it. A few years ago, in a church I was attending, the same-sex marriage debate was raging. One Sunday, the Bishop of the diocese, had the congregations read his letter defending marriage as God's design for one man and one woman joined together. Well, this letter caused a great deal of anger among the *"professing Christians."* People stomped with loud footsteps in disgust leaving the building. A prominent church leader and warden who was disgusted with the defense of marriage by the bishop came over to my wife and me. He thought we did not agree with the bishop's letter. When he started his complaining, I spoke quickly and said, *"I agree with the bishop!"* I quoted to him Paul's writings concerning this issue and he said to my face, *"Who is Paul! He has no authority! He made himself an apostle!"* This is the *"they,"* who Paul warned would turn from the truth and be turned to antichrist fables. The warning is clear, beware of leaving the truths of Scripture for doctrines of demons. These fables can cause anyone to *fall away!*

Reflections

1. In 1 Timothy 4:1-5 what did the Holy Spirit expressly say would happen to Christians in the latter times (maybe in our days)?

2. What will these Christians listen to which causes them to reject Christ?
3. What type of changes happen to these fallen Christians?
4. How is the forbidding of eating traditional foods becoming a sign of the latter times?
5. As a Christian do you adhere to the modern food cult?
6. What does Paul teach about eating meat and in some way, drinking milk?
7. Looking at 2 Timothy 4:3-4, what will some latter time Christians be like?
8. How should 1 Timothy 4:1-5 and 2 Timothy 4:3-4 instruct you in the latter times we live in?

GOD SPEAKS

"Now the Spirit expressly says that in latter times some will depart from the faith," 1 Timothy 4:1.

The Lord speaks clearly concerning the falling away of Christians. Let us be honest, it is Christians He is talking about. 1 Corinthians 12:3 emphatically teaches only people who have been given the Holy Spirit can call Jesus Lord. ***"Therefore I make known to you that no one speaking by the Spirit of God calls Jesus accursed, and no one can say that Jesus is Lord except by the Holy Spirit."*** The Lord Jesus, in the Sermon on the Mount, is alluding to the judgment day explained by Paul to the Corinthians. He wrote, ***"For we must all appear before the judgment seat of Christ, that each one may receive the things done in the body, according to what he has done, whether good or bad,"*** 2 Corinthians 5:10. Listen to what Jesus teaches about that fearful day concerning the Lord professing Christians who fall away.

"Not everyone who says to Me, 'Lord, Lord,' shall enter the kingdom of heaven, but he who does the will of My Father in heaven. Many will say to Me in that day, 'Lord, Lord, have we not prophesied in Your name, cast out demons in Your name, and done many wonders in Your name?' And then I will declare to them, 'I never knew you; depart from Me, you who practice lawlessness!'" Matthew 7:21-23.

Let us remember where and when the Lord spoke these words. ***"And seeing the multitudes, He went up on a mountain, and when He was seated His disciples came to Him. Then He opened His mouth and taught them, saying:"*** — the Sermon on the Mount, Matthew 5:1-2. Is this historical moment a future picture of the multitudes appearing before the judgment seat of Christ? Jesus is proclaiming a terrifying warning concerning His future judgment on people who proclaim Him Lord but are not His.

When the multitudes of people, who call Jesus Lord, are pressing to enter the gates of heaven, Jesus is going to tell certain ones to go away. He will say to them ***"I never knew you!"*** Those who are told they are not entering heaven will shout out with a cry of protest to the supposedly wrong judgment of Jesus. Listen to their bulletin point list of why they think they should get into heaven.

Jesus, We Belong in Heaven

- We call you Lord, Lord.
- We preached and prophesied in your name, Lord.
- We warred against the demons and cast them out of people in your name, Lord.
- We performed many wonders in your name, Lord. (Wonders: From "Strong's G1412 δύναμις, dunamis - (worker of) miracles.") Have we not healed in your name? Have we not raised vast amounts of money in your name? Have we not fed the hungry and clothed the poor in your Name?

To the human ear, these proclamations sound plausible to obtain entrance into heaven. We did good works! Nevertheless, from God's viewpoint, these Lord, Lord professing people did not do the good works in Christ but apart from Christ. ***"For we are His workmanship, created in Christ Jesus for good works, which God prepared beforehand that we should walk in them,"*** Ephesians 2:10. Paul told Timothy we need the proper faith and good conscience which is rooted in Christ that leads to works in Him. ***"This charge I commit to you, son Timothy, according to the prophecies previously made concerning you, that by them you may wage the good warfare, having faith and a good conscience."*** Paul also tells Timothy about two Lord, Lord professing Christians who may hear

Jesus say to them, ***"I never knew you!"*** These two are an example of the great falling away in latter (our) times. ***"Having faith and a good conscience, which some having rejected, concerning the faith have suffered shipwreck, of whom are Hymenaeus and Alexander!"*** The question facing us is Paul's handling of Hymenaeus and Alexander a picture of Jesus and His handling of those who fall away in the day of judgment? ***"Whom I delivered to Satan that they may learn not to blaspheme."*** How incredible is the action of Paul toward Hymenaeus and Alexander? Paul delivered them to Satan so they may learn not to blaspheme. (See 1 Timothy 1:18-20.) In comparison to this action of Paul, Jesus sends the blasphemer to the lake of fire! The sad part about this is when someone falls away a self-deception is on them. They still think they are saved but are not. Nevertheless, the Scripture says emphatically in the latter times some will fall away.

Reflections

1. How clear is the Lord's teaching about some Christians falling away?
2. What does Paul teach in 1 Corinthians 12:3?
3. What does this teach concerning those who say, Lord, Lord to Jesus on the judgment day taught In Matthew 7:21-23?
4. In Matthew 7:21-23, what did these people do in the name of Jesus?
5. Why are their proclamations of works not impressive to Jesus?
6. Where do the works in Ephesians 2:10 come from which we are to perform?
7. What type of attitude are we to have in working for God in 1 Timothy 1:18-20?
8. Describe the sad story of Hymenaeus and Alexander.
9. What is the lesson we should learn from them?

THE LORD RESPONDS

Jesus sitting on the judgment seat allows us to make a case to enter heaven. However, He is the final judge on who gets in. Jesus responds with His answers to those fallen away Christians. He says *you did good works,* ***"Nevertheless I have this against you, that you have left your first love, giving heed to deceiving spirits and doctrines of demons, speaking lies in hypocrisy,*** (Revelation 2:4, 1 Timothy 4:1-2). Then He will give them His reasons why they will not get in.

You made a mockery of My creative power!
You made a mockery of My sacrificial death and shedding of My blood for your sins!
You made Me a condoner of sin!
You made a mockery of my created image man and woman!
You made a mockery of the marriage bed!
You made a mockery of deceit on little boys and girls!
You made a mockery concerning skin colors!
You made a mockery of Me by having other gods before you!
You made a mockery of Me, teaching I am not the only way to heaven!
You called the profane holy (evil good) and the Holy profane (good evil)!

Then He declares, ***"Depart from Me, you who practice lawlessness!"*** Again, the fallen say, ***"but Lord, Lord!"*** Again, Jesus responds to them, *"You have your bullet points on why you think you should get into heaven; here are mine and why you are not getting into heaven."*

- ***"But I have a few things against you, because you have there those who hold the doctrine of Balaam, who taught Balak to put a stumbling block before the children of Israel, to eat things***

sacrificed to idols, and to commit sexual immorality. Thus you also have those who hold the doctrine of the Nicolaitans, which thing I hate," Revelation 2:14-15.

- ***"Nevertheless I have a few things against you, because you allow that woman Jezebel, who calls herself a prophetess, to teach and seduce My servants to commit sexual immorality and eat things sacrificed to idols,"*** Revelation 2:20.
- ***"I know your works, that you have a name that you are alive, but you are dead,"*** Revelation 3:1.
- ***"I know your works, that you are neither cold nor hot. I could wish you were cold or hot. So then, because you are lukewarm, and neither cold nor hot, I will vomit you out of My mouth,"*** Revelation 3:15-16.

At this point the discussion is closed and the verdict from the judgment seat rings out. ***"Depart from Me, you who practice lawlessness!"***

Let us heed the prophetic warning by Paul for a third time! ***"Now the Spirit expressly says that in latter times some will depart from the faith, giving heed to deceiving spirits and doctrines of demons, speaking lies in hypocrisy, having their own conscience seared with a hot iron, forbidding to marry, and commanding to abstain from foods which God created to be received with thanksgiving by those who believe and know the truth. For every creature of God is good, and nothing is to be refused if it is received with thanksgiving; for it is sanctified by the word of God and prayer,"*** 1 Timothy 4:1-5.

If you want to be assured of being once saved, always saved, then follow the Holy Spirit's guidelines.

- Do not depart from the faith in Christ.
- Do not listen to deceiving spirits.
- Do not accept the doctrines of demons.
- Do not become a liar denying Christ.

- Do not let your conscience die and be seared shut towards God.
- Do not mess with God's laws of marriage.
- Do not be idolatrous about food.
- Do not call evil good and good evil.
- Do not call the profane holy or the holy profane.

If you want to fall away and lose your eternal security, then ignore the warnings of God. If you do this you will hear Jesus, say, "***Depart from Me, you who practice lawlessness!***"

Reflections

1. How does Jesus respond to the "Lord, Lord crowd?
2. List what He has against the churches in Revelation 2:14-15, Revelation 2:20, Revelation 3:1, and Revelation 3:15-16.
3. According to Paul in 1 Timothy 4:1-5 what will cause us to fall away? What should we do to not fall away?
4. How can you apply this information to keep from falling away?

ONE FINAL WARNING

If you are a person, on the edge of the cliff, thinking of leaving Christ; please listen to a final warning written in Hebrews 10:26-36. The passage is a little long but highly instructive and worthy of much thought and meditation.

"For if we sin willfully after we have received the knowledge of the truth, there no longer remains a sacrifice for sins, but a certain fearful expectation of judgment, and fiery indignation which will devour the adversaries. Anyone who has rejected Moses 'law dies without mercy on the testimony of two or three witnesses. Of how much worse punishment, do you suppose, will he be thought worthy who has trampled the Son of God underfoot, counted the blood of the covenant by which he was sanctified a common thing, and insulted the Spirit of grace? For we know Him who said, 'Vengeance is Mine, I will repay,' says the Lord. And again, 'The Lord will judge His people.' It is a fearful thing to fall into the hands of the living God. But recall the former days in which, after you were illuminated, you endured a great struggle with sufferings: partly while you were made a spectacle both by reproaches and tribulations, and partly while you became companions of those who were so treated; for you had compassion on me in my chains, and joyfully accepted the plundering of your goods, knowing that you have a better and an enduring possession for yourselves in heaven. Therefore do not cast away your confidence, which has great reward. For you have need of endurance, so that after you have done the will of God, you may receive the promise."

The Points of Hebrews 10:26-36

- Willful sin is still a possibility in the life of a believer.
- There is a willful sin which quenches the sacrifice of Christ.

The greatest example of willful sin occurred after God, by mighty miracles, delivered Israel out of Egypt. The gratitude of Israel was quickly displayed in the willful choice to make a god of gold. ***"Now when the people saw that Moses delayed coming down from the mountain, the people gathered together to Aaron, and said to him, "Come, make us gods that shall go before us; for as for this Moses, the man who brought us up out of the land of Egypt, we do not know what has become of him ... And he received the gold from their hand, and he fashioned it with an engraving tool, and made a molded calf. Then they said, 'This is your god, O Israel, that brought you out of the land of Egypt!'"*** Exodus 32 :1-4

- When we sin willfully (premeditated disobedience to God's will) we become an adversary of God. God will judge us harshly. A fiery indignation is awaiting us. This may be alluding to the fires of hell. Furthermore, there no longer remains a sacrifice for sins, salvation is lost.
- A saved person rejecting Christ is a person who tramples the Son of God underfoot. They discount the blood of the covenant (Christ's blood) as nothing special, just ordinary blood. This is an insult to the Holy Spirit's grace. Let us remember what the Lord taught; ***"Therefore I say to you, every sin and blasphemy will be forgiven men, but the blasphemy against the Spirit will not be forgiven men. Anyone who speaks a word against the Son of Man, it will be forgiven him; but whoever speaks against the Holy Spirit, it will not be forgiven him, either in this age or in the age to come,"*** Matthew 12:31-32.
- If we walk away from the sacrifice of God's Son, after we have received it for forgiveness of sins, we face a fearful vengeance from God. The God, who is love, will now be to us a fearfully, terrifying God of vengeance. A God who will repay us for a slap of rejecting hate in turning away from Christ. ***"For our God is a consuming fire,"*** Hebrews 12:29.
- Hear the cry to remember the early days of your Christian

walk and love for Christ, where you suffered and loved for Him and others; so, we do not fall away. To the Hebrews Paul wrote, ***"But recall the former days in which, after you were illuminated."***

A. You endured a great struggle with sufferings.
B. You were made a spectacle both by reproaches and tribulations.
C. You became companions of those who were so treated.
D. For you had compassion for me in my chains, and joyfully accepted the plundering of your goods, knowing that you have a better and an enduring possession for yourselves in heaven. To the Galatians Paul clarified this concerning their falling away. ***"Are you so foolish? Having begun in the Spirit, are you now being made perfect by the flesh? Have you suffered so many things in vain—if indeed it was in vain?"*** (Galatians 3:3-4.)

Falling away is a very foolish thing for a believer to do! There is much written about salvation. The joy of being saved and always saved is the greatest of all comforts. Nevertheless, because of the difficulties of being a Christian, the loss of saving faith is a fearful possibility. We are in the latter times where some will fall away. Therefore, we need to hear Paul's plea, ***"Do not cast away your confidence, which has great reward."***

Reflections

1. In Hebrews 10:26, what is the consequence of willful sinning?
2. In Hebrews 10:27, what is the fearful expectation for those who fall away?
3. In Hebrews 10:28, what happened to those who rejected the Law of Moses?
4. In Hebrews 10:29, what will happen to those who insult

the Spirit of grace?

5. What is the warning of Hebrews 10:30?
6. What is the fearful thing of Hebrews 10:31?
7. According to Hebrews 10:32 to 36, how can remembering our early salvation days keep us from falling away?
8. Describe the willful sin of Aaron and Israel in Exodus 32:1-4.
9. What are the lessons Christians should learn from this?
10. What is the warning of Jesus in Matthew 12:31-32 and what lesson should Christians learn from this?
11. How can you apply these lessons in your life?

THE FINAL DESTINY OF THE SAVED AND THE FALLEN AWAY AND DISBELIEVERS.

Before we discuss the destiny of the saved and the fallen from grace; we need to understand a Biblical fact concerning our life in this world. The great fact for us to realize is, *there is no future in our earthly existence*. It is plain for all of us to see, we will die. It does not matter; death comes to the poor and rich. Death is not a respecter of persons. King Solomon put it this way, ***"This is an evil in all that is done under the sun: that one thing happens to all. Truly the hearts of the sons of men are full of evil; madness is in their hearts while they live, and after that they go to the dead,"*** Ecclesiastes 9:3 NKJV. Whether you like it or not, death is always knocking at your door. When you are laid to rest you are gone and all you have remains behind. There is no future for your life on earth nor with your fortunes.

A second reason for us to consider, *there is no future in our earthly existence*. This revolves around the prophetic writing by the Apostle Peter. ***"But the day of the Lord will come as a thief in the night, in which the heavens will pass away with a great noise, and the elements will melt with fervent heat; both the earth and the works that are in it will be burned up,"*** 2 Peter 3:10. We have no future or hope for existence on this earth because we all will die and in the end the universe and earth and all the works we have built will be melted away, burned up, and destroyed. Did you notice this will happen in the day of the Lord? Therefore, we can understand from this, we will all appear before the judgment seat of Christ for eternal life or a life in perdition.

The Place for The Fallen and Disbelievers

As Christians, we know our future is heavenly and eternally secure living in the presence of God. Even-so, Christians know those who are not of the faith, nor rooted in Christ and His sacrificial death, or fall away from the faith go to perdition. Therefore, what is the destiny or future for those who fall away from the faith and return to sin. Where do these people go after the Lord Jesus Christ declares to them, "***Depart from Me, you who practice lawlessness***?" Since the universe and earth exist no more where do they depart to? Do they end-up with the disbelieving? The answer is yes, they end-up with the disbelieving.

The Apostle John gives a vivid futuristic picture of the lost and those who have fallen away from the faith in Christ where their end is. Let us peek into the living picture of the events at the Judgment Seat of Christ and see what happens.

"Then I saw a great white throne and Him who sat on it, from whose face the earth and the heaven fled away. And there was found no place for them. And I saw the dead, small and great, standing before God, and books were opened. And another book was opened, which is the Book of Life. And the dead were judged according to their works, by the things which were written in the books. The sea gave up the dead who were in it, and Death and Hades delivered up the dead who were in them. And they were judged, each one according to his works. Then Death and Hades were cast into the lake of fire. This is the second death. And anyone not found written in the Book of Life was cast into the lake of fire," Revelation 20:11-15.

What do we see here?

- Along with John, we see Jesus Christ, LORD and KING sitting on His throne ready to pronounce His judgments.

- Along with John, we see our universe and earth gone. As Peter said, melted away and dissolved into nothing.
- Along with John, we see a multitude of people standing before God, Jesus our Lord.
- Along with John, we see the accounting books of all people opened alongside the Book of Life.
- Along with John, we see the breadth, and length, and depth, and height of God's all-encompassing judgments concerning what was written in the books in comparison to the Book of Life.
- Along with John, we see the dead (those who rejected Christ in their life) standing before the one they rejected. We see the dead coming out from the sea, the graves, and Hades itself! We see each book of the dead, small and great, being opened with their life's work being revealed.
- Along with John, we see the LORD judging each one according to their works.
- Along with John, we see the final prison for those not written in the Book of Life but judged by Christ according to their own books. This prison is the Lake of Fire and brimstone.
- Along with John, we hear the verdict of the Judge on the dead and their works. ***"But the cowardly, unbelieving, abominable, murderers, sexually immoral, sorcerers, idolaters, and all liars shall have their part in the lake which burns with fire and brimstone, which is the second death."*** Revelation 21:8.
- Along with John, we hear those fearful words, ***"Depart from Me, you who practice lawlessness!"*** (Matthew 7:23)
- Along with John, we see where those fallen away ex-Christians and the dead go. ***"And anyone not found written in the Book of Life was cast into the lake of fire,"*** Revelation 20:15.
- Along with John, we see the end of Satan and the harshness of the Lake of Fire for all who listened to the devil. ***"The devil, who deceived them, was cast into the lake of fire and brimstone where the beast and the false prophet are. And they will be tormented day and night forever and ever,"*** Revelation 20:10.

The final destiny of the unsaved and fallen away is tremendously horrible. It is the wrath of God expressed in a terminology our finite mind can understand, *"The Lake which burns with fire and brimstone!"* My theory on the lake of fire is terrifying. We know and have faith God created all that is seen and unseen. However, was the lake of fire and brimstone even created? Since all things were created in harmony and purity, there was no need for a place of punishment. My hypothesis is the lake of fire is the actual wrath of God burning inside Him because of the rebellion and sin of the fallen angels and mankind. Remember, ***"Our God is a consuming fire."*** Paul writes about what God does with His wrath; ***"Because of these things the wrath of God is coming upon the sons of disobedience,"*** Colossians 3:6. What comes upon those who are thrown into the lake of fire is the living burning fire of wrath from God's being. This is the very being of God's eternal fire which brings the torment of God upon the judged. This torment is the hurt God received when He was sinned against. Think of the hurt, anger, and wrath you get when you are wronged. What about those intense feelings of vengeance you may want? What would it do to the person who wronged you if you were able to satisfy your animosity toward him or her? Please think how intense the almighty wrath of a consuming God who is fire will be if you reject Christ and are thrown into His living fiery wrath. This is the destiny of the unsaved and fallen away. Why would anyone want to end there? This lake of fire is an inferno like no other, it is a living fire. Once you are thrown into this fire you are there forever. There is no escape, nor can death help you. The only escape from this is faith in Christ with a life lived for Him. Please do not be one of those Christians who fall away in the ***latter times***. The consequences of falling away are too harsh to understand.

The Place for The Saved

The Scriptures are filled with prophetic windows which allow us to see events of the future. We have peeked into the prophetic judgment of those who are outside of Christ. Let us now examine what will happen to those who are saved and faithful in Christ.

"When the Son of Man comes in His glory, and all the holy angels with Him, then He will sit on the throne of His glory. All the nations will be gathered before Him, and He will separate them one from another, as a shepherd divides sheep from the goats. And He will set the sheep on His right hand, but the goats on the left. Then the King will say to those on His right hand, 'Come, you blessed of My Father, inherit the kingdom prepared for you from the foundation of the world,'" Matthew 25:31-34.

What are we seeing here along with what we have seen in Revelation 20:11-15.

- We are shown the second coming of Christ full of His glory.
- We see all the holy angels are with Him.
- We now see the Lord Jesus being seated on His glorious throne, which is the judgment seat of Christ.
- We see every human of every nation which existed on earth brought before the judgment seat of Christ, both the saved and unsaved.
- We see the Good Shepard judging the lost, separating them according to their works, then saying, ***'Depart from Me, you who practice lawlessness!"*** (Matthew 7:23)
- We see Jesus separating the saved (sheep), those whose names are written in the book of life.
- We see and hear the King say the most wonderful words any human could ever want to hear. ***"Come, you blessed of My Father, inherit the kingdom prepared for you from the foundation of the world!"*** (Matthew 25:34.)

Let us now look into the future and see what the saved

will inherit. Isaiah foresaw the kingdom God prepared for the saved to inherit.

"For behold, I create new heavens and a new earth; And the former shall not be remembered or come to mind. But be glad and rejoice forever in what I create; For behold, I create Jerusalem as a rejoicing, And her people a joy. I will rejoice in Jerusalem, And joy in My people; The voice of weeping shall no longer be heard in her, Nor the voice of crying," Isaiah 65:17-19.

The Apostle John saw Isaiah's vision of the kingdom take place in his sight.

"Now I saw a new heaven and a new earth, for the first heaven and the first earth had passed away. Also there was no more sea. Then I, John, saw the holy city, New Jerusalem, coming down out of heaven from God, prepared as a bride adorned for her husband. And I heard a loud voice from heaven saying, 'Behold, the tabernacle of God is with men, and He will dwell with them, and they shall be His people. God Himself will be with them and be their God. And God will wipe away every tear from their eyes; there shall be no more death, nor sorrow, nor crying. There shall be no more pain, for the former things have passed away.' Then He who sat on the throne said, 'Behold, I make all things new.' And He said to me, 'Write, for these words are true and faithful,'" Revelation 21:1-5.

The blessed of the Father are the ones who believed and held the faith in the Son of God to the end. They will enter a brand-new creation.

- They will inherit a new heaven and earth. (The lost inherit eternal wrath.)
- They move into a new Jerusalem. (The lost move into a lake of fire and brimstone.)
- The tabernacle of God is placed among the saved. (The lost are eternally separated from God.)

- God will be physically and visibly dwelling with them. They will be His people forevermore. (The lost will dwell in the wrath of God.)
- God will wipe away all their tears. All the sorrows, hurts, and scars we have will be taken away and remembered no more.
- They will never again face death.
- They will never again experience sorrow.
- They will never cry again.
- They will never feel pain anymore. (The lost will never be free of their tears, living in death and pain forever.)

What a wonderful future for the saved. The Apostle Paul talks about our eternal reward with mystifying words.

"But as it is written:
'Eye has not seen, nor ear heard,
Nor have entered into the heart of man
The things which God has prepared for those who love Him.'"
1 Corinthians 2:9

When the awesome day of the Lord happens, the saved will stand before the judgment seat of Christ. They will hear these awesome words from the mouth of Jesus, ***"Come, you blessed of My Father, inherit the kingdom prepared for you from the foundation of the world,"*** Matthew 25:34. After these words the saved enter New Jerusalem. When they see and hear what God has prepared for those who love Him, when every tear is wiped away, what a magnificent shout of jubilation will come out of the saved praising the Father, Son, and Holy Spirit!

Reflections

1. Why is there no future on earth for humans?
2. What does Solomon say about our future in Ecclesiastes 9:3?
3. What does Peter teach about our future in 2 Peter 3:10?
4. What does Peter mean about the day of the Lord?

5. Explain the Judgment seat of Revelation 20:11-15. Who appears before this seat? How are they judged?
6. Where do those who are not written in the Book of Life go being found guilty at the judgment seat?
7. Where do those go who are written in the Book of Life and pass the judgment seat exonerated?
8. Compare the lake of fire to the New Jerusalem. Which do you prefer?
9. How important is it to be saved and endure to the end?

A LATTER TIME SPIRITUAL PRACTICE

Nevertheless, ***"The Spirit expressly says that in latter times some will depart from the faith,"*** 1 Timothy 4:1. Before any of us consider falling away from Christ, let us remember where the lost go and what the saved inherit. If our hearts are losing their fervor of love for God, let us think twice about it. We need to understand the punishment of God is very fearful to receive and the reward of God is too marvelous to lose. Therefore, knowing we are somewhere in the ***latter times*** and seeing many *Christians are* departing from the faith, giving heed to the *doctrines of demons,* how can we keep ourselves in the love of God? (***"Keep yourselves in the love of God,"*** Jude verse twenty-one.) How shall we keep ourselves in the love of God when everything seems dark and dreary and all we hear in our minds are the fiery darts of Satan's lies? What can we do to keep ourselves from becoming a prophetic casualty in the latter times?

The answer to the question of keeping ourselves from falling away may be found in one word in Hebrews 12:3.

"For <u>consider</u> Him who endured such hostility from sinners against Himself, lest you become weary and discouraged in your souls." (Underlined for emphasis.)

The word to focus on is the imperative verbal action, ***consider***. Consider from "Strong's G357: ἀναλογίζομαι, analogizomai, to estimate, i.e. (figuratively) contemplate: --consider." The Apostle Paul is commanding the Hebrew Christians to consider, to contemplate, to look thoughtfully for a long time at and analyze what Christ endured against Himself to save them. Do you remember what Jesus said to His disciples on the Mount of Olives at the time of His arrest but did not do? The disciples started to resist the arresting of Jesus, but the

Lord did not allow them to do it. ***"But Jesus said to him, 'Put your sword in its place, for all who take the sword will perish by the sword. Or do you think that I cannot now pray to My Father, and He will provide Me with more than twelve legions of angels? How then could the Scriptures be fulfilled, that it must happen thus?'"*** (Matthew 26:52-54.) Jesus could have *fallen away* from taking our punishment of death on the cross, but He did not. The Lord teaches us He considered why He became a man by saying, ***"How then could the Scriptures be fulfilled, that it must happen thus?"*** If Jesus prays for twelve legions of angels to deliver Him from the hands of men, He will fall away from God's purpose of saving us through Him. Praise to Jesus, He overcame any urge to not go to the cross. His love for the Father and us caused Him to stay the course.

Therefore, we all should obey the command to consider Jesus, who considered us, and stay the course to inherit eternal life. Scripturally defining *consider*, we can say, to consider means to take into account what God has done and given to restore our relationship with Him. In today's vernacular, we would say, *"Think about it!"* To think about something is to contemplate, to look thoughtfully for a long time at it, and analyze what you are considering in order to come to a conclusion. When Hebrews 12:3 tells us to consider; it is telling us to come to a healthy conclusion to remain steadfast in the faith. Since we are in the latter times and perilous times are upon us, we must all practice the willful and mental act of considering. We do not want to fall away.

Scriptures to Consider

"For God so loved the world that He gave His only begotten Son, that whoever believes in Him should not perish but have everlasting life," John 3:16.

What are we to consider about John 3:16? Many of us repeat this verse routinely but do not really hear what it is saying.

- In the first contemplation of John 3:16 we need to consider the love God has for the world of people. He <u>so</u> loved the world. So, from Strong's G3779, "οὖτο(ς), hoo'-to- adverb: in this way (referring to what precedes or follows): --after that, after (in) this manner, as, even (so), for all that, like(-wise), no more, on this fashion(-wise), so (in like manner), thus, what." In God so loved, we have so, (*outws,* hootos) being an adverb to love. So, *in this manner,* or *thus,* God loved the world.
- In the second contemplation of John 3:16 we need to consider the way God expresses His love to us. How does God so love us? The answer, ***"He gave His only begotten Son!"*** God gave His only begotten Son to save us. Isaiah prophesied about this, ***"For unto us a Child is born, Unto us a Son is given,"*** Isaiah 9:6. God freely gave His Son for the world. He gave Jesus for us, so we could be saved!
- In the third contemplation of John 3:16 we need to comprehend how did God give His Son for us? He gave Him this way, ***"For He made Him who knew no sin to be sin for us, that we might become the righteousness of God in Him,"*** 2 Corinthians 5:21. The result of this action, ***"Then they crucified Him,"*** Matthew 27:35.
- In the fourth contemplation of John 3:16 we need to consider how the giving of Jesus by God saved us from perishing and grants eternal life.

As we contemplate John 3:16, consider the love of the Father for the Son and the love of the Son for the Father that each are willing to give of themselves in sacrificial love to save us. If you are falling, grab hold of John 3:16 to turn yourself around.

A second verse to consider is Hebrews 12:3. This is the verse which commanded us to consider the life of Christ. Let us look at it more fully to understand how examining what Jesus suffered can keep us from falling away.

"For consider Him who endured such hostility from sinners

against Himself, lest you become weary and discouraged in your souls," Hebrews 12:3.

- In the first contemplation of Hebrews 12:3, consider how much of a sinner you were. Analyze how much of this sinning behavior Jesus endured for you.
- In the second contemplation of Hebrews 12:3, consider how Jesus endured having our sins upon Him. ***"And being in agony, He prayed more earnestly. Then His sweat became like great drops of blood falling down to the ground,"*** Luke 22:44.
- In the third contemplation of Hebrews 12:3, consider the hostility heaped upon Jesus and His sufferings.

Luke 22:48, Jesus is betrayed by His disciple Judas.
Luke 22:54, Jesus is arrested.
Luke 22:63, Jesus is mocked and beaten by the men who held Him in custody.
Mark 14:65, Jesus is spit upon.
Luke 22:64, Jesus is blindfolded, and His captors slap His face.
Luke 23:10-11, Jesus endures vehemently false accusations against Himself before Herod. Herod treats Jesus with mocking contempt.
Mark 15:9-13, Jesus is rejected by the crowds, demanding His crucifixion.
Matthew 27:26, Jesus is scourged by Pilate and sentenced to death.
Mark 15:16-20, Jesus gets a crown of thorns smashed on His head and is mocked by the Romans.
John 19:17, Jesus is forced to carry His cross. ***"And He, bearing His cross, went out to a place called the Place of a Skull, which is called in Hebrew, Golgotha,"*** John 19:17-37, Luke 23:32-48, Mark 15:21-37, Matthew 27:32-50. Jesus, exhausted, is stripped of His clothes, nailed and crucified on the cross, mocked, dies and gets a spear thrust in His side.

- In the fourth contemplation of Hebrews 12:3, consider how Jesus suffers the promised death to Adam, ***"But of the tree of the knowledge of good and evil you shall not eat, for in the day that you eat of it you shall surely die,"*** Genesis 2:17. <u>The death of ultimate separation from God!</u>

"Now from the sixth hour until the ninth hour there was darkness over all the land. And about the ninth hour Jesus cried out with a loud voice, saying, 'Eli, Eli, lama sabachthani?' that is, 'My God, My God, why have You forsaken Me?'" (Matthew 27:45-46)

The Lord Jesus suffered the death of separation from God, so we do not have to. If you are falling away from the faith, grab hold of Hebrews 12:3 and consider the Saviors love for you. Truthfully, start reading the Word again, fight the dejection you think you have in your prayers to God, and start thinking Scripturally again. Please cry out to God to keep you from falling, He can do this. Also, contemplate Jude verse twenty-four.

"Now to Him who is able to keep you from stumbling,
And to present you faultless
Before the presence of His glory with exceeding joy,"

If you are falling think of the above verses to stop the fall. If you are not falling think of these verses to strengthen yourself.

Reflections

1. What is the spiritual practice commanded in Hebrews 12:3?
2. How does Strong's G357 define consider?
3. How will considering the suffering Christ keep us from becoming weary and discouraged in our souls?
4. What great action did Jesus not undertake in Matthew 26:52-54?
5. How should this consideration keep us on the straight

and narrow?

6. Write down your considerations of John 3:16.
7. Write down your considerations of Hebrews 12:3.
8. How can you apply these considerations in your discipleship to keep from falling away in these latter times?

TWO LIVES

Nevertheless, ***"The Spirit expressly says that in latter times some will depart from the faith,"*** 1 Timothy 4:1. We, who may be or are the people of the latter times, need to heed Paul's prophetic utterance warning believers of departing from the faith. One more spiritual practice may help in keeping us strong in the Lord through the judgment seat of Christ. Let us analyze our two lives. The first life is the life we had before faith in Christ. The life of living in sin. Let us not be like Israel thinking life in Egypt was better than the saved life into which we have entered. ***"Now the mixed multitude who were among them yielded to intense craving; so the children of Israel also wept again and said: 'Who will give us meat to eat? We remember the fish which we ate freely in Egypt, the cucumbers, the melons, the leeks, the onions, and the garlic; but now our whole being is dried up; there is nothing at all except this manna before our eyes!'"*** (Numbers 11:4-6.) These people, complaining about their deliverance from Egypt, forgot the reason they wanted deliverance from Egypt! ***"So the Egyptians made the children of Israel serve with rigor. And they made their lives bitter with hard bondage—in mortar, in brick, and in all manner of service in the field. All their service in which they made them serve was with rigor,"*** Exodus 1:13-14.

Let us not make the mistake of thinking our prior life of sin was a more pleasurable and rewarding existence. Israel thought leeks, onions, and garlic more rewarding than the provision of God. These foods were eaten in bitter bondage. While the manna God provided along the way was to be the food of freedom. ***"And the house of Israel called its name Manna. And it was like white coriander seed, and the taste of it was like wafers made with honey,"*** Exodus 16:31. Nevertheless, the Israelites despised the manna and continually complained about God's deliverance. They were always wanting to go back to Egypt. These ancient Israelites teach us lessons about the danger of falling away and losing the reward through enduring faith. What was the end of those backward-looking people? ***"For the children of Israel walked forty years in the wilderness, till all the people who were men of war, who came out of Egypt, were consumed, because they did not obey the voice of the Lord—to whom the Lord swore that He would not show them the land which the Lord had sworn to their fathers that He would give us, 'a land flowing with milk and honey,'"*** Joshua 5:6. Let us beware of falling away thinking sinning is better than holiness in Christ by remembering the punishment of the Israelites. Also remember the warning for anyone who falls away from faith in Christ as expressed in Hebrews 6:4-6. It will be impossible to be renewed to repentance. Therefore, be fearful not to give up Christ. The lake of fire awaits those who fall away. The memory of our prior life gives an illusion of contentment. Therefore, no Christian should want to return to their Egypt.

The second life we should analyze is the new life we have in Christ, the born-again life. We can understand how wonderful the new life is, when we realize how much freedom we have from the bitter bondage of sin. Yes, we stumble and sin but the promises of forgiveness and cleansing always renew us. ***"If we confess our sins, He is faithful and just to forgive us our sins and to cleanse us from all unrighteousness,"*** 1 John 1:9. Our journey from deliverance out of our Egypt to learning how to worship God in Spirit and truth, can be filled with as many problems as the Israelites faced. Nevertheless, if we keep the faith we will enter the promised land, the New Jerusalem! A contemplation on how we behaved before Christ and how we are behaving with Christ now, will refresh the heart and keep one moving along to the finish line of our life. Why be tempted to go back for leeks, onions, and garlic, knowing we were in the death sentence verdict of God, when we have the manna which leads to life, Christ the bread of heaven. ***"And Jesus said to them, 'I am the bread of life. He who comes to Me shall never hunger, and he who believes in Me shall never thirst,'"*** John 6:35.

Let us look at a point of wisdom about the saved which can bring great understanding to our walk. Although, we are all individually saved through Jesus Christ becoming one body in Him, the walk of the individual member in the body of Christ will not be the same for everyone. Your walk in Christ will be different from my walk in Christ! Yes, we are the body of Christ and are dependent upon each member. However, your life, work, family, and circumstances are unique to you. Nevertheless, we should all live our walk-through Christ, obeying His commandments to love one another, exhorting each other to stay the course. ***"But now God has set the members, each one of them, in the body just as He pleased. And if they were all one member, where would the body be? But now indeed there are many members, yet one body,"*** 1 Corinthians 12:18-20. Do you remember what the Lord said to Peter who was worrying about John's walk? ***"Peter, seeing him, said to Jesus, 'But Lord, what about this man?' Jesus said to him, 'If I will that he remain till I come, what is that to you? You follow Me,'"*** John 21:21-22. No matter who is around you or what church you are in, the command is to keep your eyes on Jesus and follow Him.

The message for us, who stand in once saved always saved, is to make sure we follow Jesus all the days of our life. Jesus said, ***"And you will be hated by all for My name's sake. But he who endures to the end shall be saved,"*** Mark 13:13. The warnings of Scripture are true. Let us remember the warning in 1 Timothy 4:1, ***"In latter times some will depart from the faith,"*** and endure to the end. Also, obey Paul's command to help your fellow Christian to make it. ***"But exhort one another daily, while it is called 'Today,' lest any of you be hardened through the deceitfulness of sin. For we have become partakers of Christ if we hold the beginning of our confidence steadfast to the***

end," Hebrews 3:13-14. It is good to remember the beginning of our life in Christ.

Reflections

1. Why is it good to reflect on your life before Christ and your life after Christ?
2. What lesson or lessons can we learn from the ancient Israelites who wanted to go back to Egypt?
3. What sustenance is better for you, leeks, onions, and garlic or the manna from Heaven?
4. What happened to the leek, onion, and garlic crowd according to Joshua 5:6? How is this pertinent for us today in the latter times?
5. How should the members of the body of Christ help each other according to Hebrews 3:13-14? How can you do this?
6. Write your "two lives" testimony down for personal review. Use this testimony to keep from falling away!

PAUL'S TESTIMONY

The Apostle Paul exemplifies the born-again life of enduring to the end. He understood this statement by Jesus, ***"In the world you will have tribulation; but be of good cheer, I have overcome the world,"*** John 16:33. Paul did not have a foolish understanding of Christianity. Therefore, he was able to endure to the end. He told Timothy, ***"I have fought the good fight, I have finished the race, I have kept the faith,"*** 2 Timothy 4:7. He was not living for earthly rewards but for the heavenly inheritance. ***"Finally, there is laid up for me the crown of righteousness, which the Lord, the righteous Judge, will give to me on that Day, and not to me only but also to all who have loved His appearing,"*** 2 Timothy 4:8. Paul crossed his finish line victoriously. Let us follow his example and finish our race victoriously.

An examination of Paul's testimony can help us understand what Paul endured on earth to make it to the heavenly reward. He did not fall away in his time even under extreme brutality toward him.

"Are they Hebrews? So am I. Are they Israelites? So am I. Are they the seed of Abraham? So am I. Are they ministers of Christ? —I speak as a fool—I am more: in labors more abundant, in stripes above measure, in prisons more frequently, in deaths often. From the Jews five times I received forty stripes minus one. Three times I was beaten with rods; once I was stoned; three times I was shipwrecked; a night and a day I have been in the deep; in journeys often, in perils of waters, in perils of robbers, in perils of my own countrymen, in perils of the Gentiles, in perils in the city, in perils in the wilderness, in perils in the sea, in perils among false brethren; in weariness and toil, in sleeplessness often, in hunger and thirst, in fastings often, in

cold and nakedness— besides the other things, what comes upon me daily: my deep concern for all the churches. Who is weak, and I am not weak? Who is made to stumble, and I do not burn with indignation?" (2 Corinthians 11:22-29) Finally, history teaches, Paul was beheaded for the faith.

Let Us Examine Paul's Testimony

- Did the burden of excessive labors for Christ cause Paul to fall away? No!
- Did Paul being imprisoned many times cause him to fall away? No!
- Did five separate whippings totaling 195 lashes cause Paul to fall away? No!
- Did getting beaten by rods on three separate occasions cause Paul to fall away? No!
- Did Paul being dragged out of the city of Lystra by an angry mob throwing rocks at him knocking him out and down to the point of death cause him to fall away? No!
- Did Paul being in three shipwrecks cause him to fall away? No!
- Did Paul drifting around in the depths of the sea for a night and day cause him to fall away? No!
- Did Paul facing eight perils (serious dangers) from flooding, facing robbers on the journeys, angry Jewish leaders who wanted him dead, unbelieving gentiles who eventually chopped his head off, evil people in strange cities, fear in the wilderness, storms in the sea, and dealing with false brethren, cause Paul to fall away? No!
- Did physical exhaustion, hard work, many sleepless nights, being hungry and thirsty, fasting often in prayer, being cold and poorly clothed, cause Paul to fall away? No!
- Did daily cares, worries, stresses, problems of others, and personal desires, cause Paul to fall away? No!

The Apostle Paul teaches remaining faithful and

holding on to Christ is the most important truth to stand for, no matter the cost. In his days, Christianity was a pariah movement filled with dangers for those who put their faith in Christ. Paul's testimony proves this. The dangers of the early church were very real, and, in a sense, they are prophetic for us in the latter times. The tribulations of these saints and the warnings they received to keep strong and not fall away are very prescient for us in the latter times. This Biblical study is written to assure us once we are saved, we are saved! Nevertheless, be **warned**, although you are saved do not fall away! The reasons are clear to hold fast, because in these latter times Christianity is once again becoming a pariah movement around the world. Let us look again at the prophetic warning of 2 Timothy 3:1-5.

"But know this, that in the last days perilous times will come: For men will be lovers of themselves, lovers of money, boasters, proud, blasphemers, disobedient to parents, unthankful, unholy, unloving, unforgiving, slanderers, without self-control, brutal, despisers of good, traitors, headstrong, haughty, lovers of pleasure rather than lovers of God, having a form of godliness but denying its power. And from such people turn away!"

In the latter times we are going to face great evils from malicious people. Therefore, because of perilous times, in the last times, the prophetic warning is clear, ***"The Spirit expressly says that in latter times some will depart from the faith,"*** 1 Timothy 4:1. Let us prepare and make our decision now to hold fast to Christ before the perils of the latter times fully descend upon us. Let us not be those who fall away. Let us be those who are fully persuaded like Paul. He declared it and let us declare it with him. ***"For I am persuaded that neither death nor life, nor angels nor principalities nor powers, nor things present nor things to come, nor height nor depth, nor any other created thing, shall be able to separate us from the love of God which is in Christ Jesus our Lord."*** Romans 8:38-39.

Reflections

1. How did Paul understand Christian truths?
2. How should we understand those same truths?
3. What does Paul's autobiographical account in 2 Corinthians 11:22-29 teach us concerning our life in the latter times?
4. Are you making 2 Timothy 4:7-8 your own personal testimony or has problems in the Christian life caused you to fall away!
5. Give a summary of what you have learned in this lesson and how you are going to apply it as a disciple of Christ.

God Bless You!

A Prayer

Dearest Father, In Jesus name, please fill me with the Holy Spirit giving me the life of your Son that I may endure to the end. Please count me worthy to escape the wrath of the latter times and to appear before the judgment seat of Christ with exceeding joy. You are able to keep me from stumbling; therefore, I trust you to save me in Christ to the uttermost! Thank You! Amen!

A Decree

I choose to follow Jesus! I will not turn back!

Memorize, consider, and claim Psalm 23.

Psalm 23

The Lord is my shepherd;
I shall not want.
He makes me to lie down in green pastures;
He leads me beside the still waters.

He restores my soul;
He leads me in the paths of righteousness
For His name's sake.
Yea, though I walk through the valley of the shadow of death,
I will fear no evil;
For You are with me;
Your rod and Your staff, they comfort me.
You prepare a table before me in the presence of my enemies;
You anoint my head with oil;
My cup runs over.
Surely goodness and mercy shall follow me
All the days of my life;
And I will dwell in the house of the Lord
Forever.

KNOW YOUR FAITH

Do Not Fall Away

The Apostles' Creed

I believe in God the Father almighty,
Creator of heaven and earth.
I believe in Jesus Christ, God's only Son,
our Lord, Who was conceived by the Holy Spirit,
born of the Virgin Mary,
suffered under Pontius Pilate,
was crucified, died, and was buried.
He descended to the dead;
on the third day He rose again;
He ascended into heaven,
He is seated at the right hand of the Father,
and He shall come to judge the living and the dead.
I believe in the Holy Spirit,
the holy catholic Church,
the communion of saints,
the forgiveness of sins,
the resurrection of the body
and life everlasting.
Amen

ABOUT THE AUTHOR

Guy Calandra

About The Author Guy Calandra Guy Peter Calandra is well-traveled on the narrow way. Growing up Catholic, he had little knowledge of the personal relationship one can have with Christ. He was becoming a pharmacist when he had a call from God to find Him. Therefore, he started his journey to God by leaving all things Christian and searching through the many religions of the world. He went from transcendental meditation to eastern religions and various new age "things"! However, he only found God when he finally realized Jesus Christ was the Savior. He and his wife then left all to follow Jesus, from Bible college, to pastoring churches, with failures and successes. More times than not, they felt like Job. Nevertheless, they were in the school of God. He hopes the lessons he learned will protect you from error and make your walk with Christ deeper.

BOOKS BY THIS AUTHOR

Calandra Topical Bible Commentary: Volume One - Christ And His Church

It is with a great compulsion, burning in my heart, which constrains me to write a topical Biblical commentary. In my old age and travels along the straight and narrow path, I have found strange, confusing, contradictory, and blasphemous beliefs and teachings in Christianity. These beliefs and teachings have spawned a new religion I labeled, Churchianity. This religion uses Christ as a shield for its own purposes and worldly carnal systems. Churchianity, incorporates and approves all the world religions to God, and the tenets of progressive liberalism blessing of sin and denying the Gospel and Bible they say they live by. It was like entering my old unsaved life again and the beliefs I had to leave in the ash heap. What a world of confusion the world of church has become. We have taken something beautiful, and as it is with everything, humans touch, corrupted it. This is my humble attempt to bring Christ and holiness back to the "world of church" by exalting Christ and pointing out the errors of our ways. Furthermore, someone has to say it loud and clearly and someone needs to hear it.

The Inside Word

Are you a God seeker? In all your seeking, have you found the true God? Where have you looked for Him? Perhaps you have looked in meditation, nature, Eastern religions, yoga, self-awareness, mysticism, or some type of spiritual system? Maybe you are realizing, in all of this, you haven't found God! Therefore, you may feel confused, disheartened, and on the verge of giving up? I was at that point once, after trying all of the above mentioned I actually said, "I'll try the Bible again and if I don't find God, there is no God!" Yet, I did find God and Immanuel was born inside my heart! Immanuel, God with man, via Jesus Christ. Wouldn't you like to experience this, your own Immanuel? An experience that could shake you to the core of your inside being. The Inside Word was written so you too can have Immanuel.

Made in United States
North Haven, CT
25 September 2025

73149657R00241